Praise for *HR from the Outside In*

This book explains the most important piece of the puzzle: how to determine what the right people need to know and do to run an HR function that truly enables business outcomes. In a time of economic volatility with increased focus on functional effectiveness, the authors have provided real insights into how HR should focus its attention to impact organizational performance.

—Hugo Bague, Group Executive, People & Organization, Rio Tinto

HR from the Outside In is for the HR student to the seasoned HR Director, the business—it is comprehensive and makes a stimulating read.

—Doug Baillie, Unilever CHRO—a seasoned business leader turned CHRO

With *HR from the Outside In*, Dave Ulrich and colleagues have produced another touchstone contribution to the HR field and to organization management more broadly. Leaders within and beyond the HR field should read this book for a unique long-term perspective on where HR competencies have brought us and where they must take us in the future."

—John Boudreau, Professor at the Marshall School of Business, University of Southern California

Pragmatic and to the point. It is inspiring to read how Ulrich, Younger, and Brockbank continue to raise the bar for the HR function. *HR from the Outside In* provides an inspirational framework, rethinking how the HR function has to deliver value in the eyes of our customers. More so, they do it with solid research and intellectual power, rooted in a deep understanding of tomorrow's business reality."

—Karsten Breum, Vice President, Head of Human Resources, DAMCO

Having contributed 20 years as a business leader before starting as the Head of HR nine years ago, I have to admit that this book speaks to my heart. I compliment Dave and his team for the deep insights and the crucial relevance of the content."

—Juergen Brokatzky-Geiger, Head of Human Resources, Novartis International AG

HR from the Outside In is the best guide available for understanding what human resource executives should be doing and how to do it.

—*Peter Cappelli, George W. Taylor Professor of Management, Director, Center for Human Resources, Wharton School, and Professor of Education*

A compelling and breakthrough thought leadership perspective that vividly catapults the human resources profession into the realities of business economics. Every business leader will benefit from the richness of this book. The authors have done an excellent job of challenging human resource professionals to become fluent in the language of business.

—*Karen Carey, Senior Vice President of Human Resources, Atlantis*

Human resource leaders today have a huge responsibility. They're being asked to build talent, rethink outdated organizational practices, and create fresh approaches to engage the changing workforce and reshape the capabilities of their own organizations—all in response to intensifying business demands. The "outside in" approach to understanding the capabilities HR needs today is refreshing and pragmatic—a "must read" for every HR professional.

—*Tammy Erickson, Workforce expert, author, and founder of Tammy Erickson Associates*

This book is spot on, easy to read, and very practical. The core message is that HR is about creating business value. This is the only way to create a successful organization."

—*Dr. Christian Finckh, Chief Human Resources Officer, Allianz SE*

Once again Dave Ulrich and his associates have provided a thought-provoking, in-depth examination of the human resources profession. The research is unmatched and the conclusions are something that every HR professional must understand and make part of their modus operandi. Well done."

—*Jac Fitz-enz*

HR functions will create real business value by taking an outside in approach. The book *HR from The Outside In* makes a compelling case. An indispensable code of practice.

—*Peter Goerke, Group HR Director, Prudential Plc.*

In an age when the role of the human resource function has become ever more central to business success, *HR from the Outside In* is a crucial blueprint of what it takes to succeed. Based on the deep expertise, wisdom, and knowledge of the authors, it describes the roles and competencies of the future-proofed HR expert and what it takes to get there. Packed with research insights, tools, and case studies, the book is a must have for every HR professional.

—Lynda Gratton, Professor of Management Practice,
London Business School

HR from the Outside In builds on solid and practical research, which is the basis for the HR competencies that we at Pfizer have adopted for our global HR workforce.

—Chuck Hill, CHRO, Pfizer

RBL has been an invaluable partner to Applied HR during our transformation journey. From the very beginning. Dave and the team have consistently challenged our paradigms and tested our thinking, which has helped us to push the traditional boundaries of what we thought was possible. I have always valued the strategic thinking coupled with down-to-earth, practical advice. *HR from the Outside In* illustrates that the journey is not over and guides the profession on how it can strengthen its contribution to delivering superior results by the business. I'm delighted to see the emphasis on driving continuous improvement as defined by the customer as this is what will help us achieve a quantum leap forward in how we deliver value to our customers, employees, and investors.

—Mary Humiston, SVP, Global Human Resources Applied Materials

A comprehensive and practical "tool-kit" for any HR practitioner based on applied research that provides empirical data on the areas of focus to achieve business success. Solutions are not just based on looking at past trends, but on what the future of HR looks like and how to prepare for it and be ready to be best you can be."

—Peck Kem Low, Divisional Director, National Human Resources Division,
Ministry of Manpower, Singapore

The definitive work on HR competencies, provides useful ideas and tools that can help HR professionals develop their career and make their organization effective.

—*Edward E. Lawler III, author of* Effective Human
Resource Management: A Global Analysis

The litmus test for any business book is: Does it shed new light, and does it provide a basis for action? *HR from the Outside In* does both, highlighting fundamental shifts in what effective HR is all about, and outlining practical ways in which both individuals and functions can move to meet these new opportunities. If you want to be relevant in our changing world, read this book and put it to work!"

—*Jim Lawler, Chief Human Resource Officer, TASC*

Most professions have existed for centuries. However, pilots and HR professionals are 20th-century professions. When I get on an airplane and see the pilot, I have a high level of confidence that he or she will fly the aircraft to my destination effectively and safely. Then, if I sit next to someone who claims to be a human resource management professional, how do I know how competent they are? *HR from the Outside In* is another major contributor to the authors' 25-year systematic study of HR competencies as the HR profession continues to evolve. HR professionals need to study the findings of this research to ensure not only their own personal development, but also how they can contribute to organizational success.

—*Mike Losey, President, MikeLosey.com*

"You can't argue with the data! *HR from the Outside In* is one of the most comprehensive studies ever completed on our function, and it clearly defines the "new model" for Human Resources. This book is a must read for every contemporary HR leader . . . a definitive and practical guide to learning the key competencies for success."

—*John Lynch, Senior Vice President, HR, General Electric*

HR from the Outside In is packed with facts and evidence—and prescriptive advice—for HR professionals contemplating their future role and impact: It is about being a business leader first and an HR professional second—and being willing to change everything about a company except its values.

—*Randy MacDonald, Senior Vice President, Human Resources, IBM Corporation*

HR from the Outside In is a must read for any HR executive who hopes to add real value to their organization. The authors guide the reader to better understand how specific competencies drive individual effectiveness and have business impact. This research-based competency model is particularly compelling to me because it is not based solely on input from HR professionals, but is informed as well by the perspective of non-HR executives and stakeholders.

—*Sue Meisinger, columnist on HR Leadership and former CEO of SHRM*

Insightful and thought provoking. This book is a culmination of years of research behind the HR profession and new insights that challenge us to focus on "the business of the business" and to look from the "outside-in" to create real value for our company.

—*Marcia Mendes-d'Abreu, OTPP*

While much has been written about the HR profession, the work done by Dave Ulrich and his group by far has had the greatest impact. Consistent with Dave's previous books, *HR from the Outside In* provides the why, what, and how to deliver value in a world that has changed dramatically over the past few years. The future of HR depends on how well this new information is put into practice. Thank you, Dave, for your tireless passion for the HR profession and for providing information that ensures HR professionals around the world have the tools they need to be effective business leaders.

—*Janet N. Parker, SPHR, GPHR, EVP, Corporate Human Resources, Regions Financial Corporation*

A must read for HR leaders who want to broaden their capabilities as strategic thought leaders and business partners as well as for HR professionals who wonder why they are not seen as business partners by their colleagues.

—*Rino Piazzolla, Executive Vice President HR, AXA Equitable*

Powerful, relevant, and timely! Defines "new HR" for the emerging times in a pragmatic way. What should we be seeking from HR? What does HR need to be and do? What really will make the difference to the business and how? Great questions to which solid research-based answers and global insights are the jewels that bedeck this necklace of wisdom. This book is a must for leaders, organizations, and HR folks who seek to create competitive advantage of a sustainable nature.

—Satish Pradhan, Chief, Group Human Resources,
Tata Sons Limited

For more than 20 years, David Ulrich has set the direction for HR: evolving the community from an operational mindset to becoming a strategic business partner. This book, *HR from the Outside In*, takes us in yet a new direction and has caused a fundamental shift in my thinking that grounded me in the reality that my strategy and agenda, currently internally focused, could break new ground by incorporating the voices of our external customers in everything "we do." The principles, concepts, and competencies presented in the book take our practice to a new and even more strategic level, providing HR leaders with new insights to bring to business leaders and thereby enabling a company's competitive advantage and sustainable growth.

—Jian (Gina) Qiao, SVP HR, Lenovo

One single concept changed the entire HR world two decades ago: the "HR business partner." It was just a good and intelligent idea, but it soon became the beginning of a new era in people management. Through consistent cycles of research, studies, and practical application around the world, Dave Ulrich and his team have managed to produce and update the most comprehensive set of HR competencies ever. The latest news is that becoming "HR credible activists" is vital but not enough to succeed. To learn why, we must go deep into this enticing, essential book. With the new "outside in" approach, Dave— as a modern-times Copernicus—helps us turn the HR world inside out.

—Horacio Quiros, President, World Federation of
People Management Associations

This book is yet another shift for HR professionals from these authors. Its helpfulness is that it reframes the HR role through the lens of the customer, enabling an understanding of how HR can create enduring business value for all stakeholders. The book moves our profession on because it clearly articulates the roles and the competences required to add value, both through individual effectiveness and business success. It provokes us to recognize that we need to be effective at using business strategy as a key context through which we, as HR, come up with our actions and solutions. You should read this book because it is a great reminder that we, as HR professionals, need to be effective operators in the marketplace as well as in the workplace!

—Aileen Richards, Vice President, People and Organization,
Mars Incorporated

Now that HR is in the C-Suite, it is imperative that HR teams perform as business executives to effectively use the seat at the table we fought so hard for. This book gives HR a new lens through which to view our important roles as we further evolve. After reading this book, you will be convinced that HR is "the Business"!

—Libby Sartain, former CHRO and board member,
ManpowerGroup and Peet's Coffee and Tea

The table stakes for HR are rising fast, and it is time for HR to fully deliver on its promises. The need for HR support for business goals in a knowledge economy has never been greater. If HR cannot respond to the unique opportunities for impact, leaders will turn elsewhere. To have impact requires that HR professionals master new ways of thinking and acting. The research and insights reported in this book capture the skills required for HR professionals to fully contribute to business results. HR professionals need to step up now or be left in the dust forevermore. This work offers the most comprehensive roadmap for HR professionals to make a difference.

—Matt Schuyler, Chief HR Officer, Hilton Worldwide

Dave and his colleagues produce impressive work. What I like about their latest approach is that they wrap their HR competency model with an all-encompassing focus on the business. Here, they use 360-degree survey data to demonstrate that HR cannot simply focus on its own efficiency and quality, but must also actively identify and develop competencies that contribute directly to the success of the business."

—Jill Smart, Chief Human Resources Officer, Accenture

I have always believed that successful human resources people are those who have a specialization in HR but are actually broader in their background experience—e.g., have worked in other disciplines and other functional areas. That way they bring a broader knowledge base and experience to their HR work. The importance of this should not be underestimated. *HR from the Outside In* clearly explains how to manage with a business focus by looking at the HR function from a different perspective—i.e., through the lens of external influences and other stakeholders. I therefore consider this book as a great resource for those HR practitioners looking to change their perspective, or looking for new ways to add commercial value to a business."

—Conrad Venter, Global Head of Human Resources, Deutsche Bank

Once again, Dave Ulrich and his coauthors are not merely aware of the signs of the times but have also demonstrated their status as thought leaders in the HR arena. Unlike the bulk of theoretical HR literature that already exists, their book is a refreshing, crisp and to the point practical guide that would be of use to any HR professional!

—Nicolas von Rosty, Corporate Vice President
Executive Development, Siemens AG

HR from the Outside In is a must read for all HR professionals. Grounded in research, case studies, and their experience, the authors provide insights and tools that HR professionals everywhere can use to increase their effectiveness in driving business value and making a difference in organizational performance.

—Carole Watkins, Chief Human Resources Officer,
Cardinal Health, Inc.

Talent has moved to the top of CEOs' agendas as they become increasingly aware of the criticality of their firm's human capital to organizational success. They look to the HR function to deliver that talent, but the question is do HR functions possess the functional talent to deliver on the CEO's agenda? *HR from the Outside In* provides a state of the art look at the HR talent necessary to drive business success as well as how functions can develop that talent."

—*Patrick M. Wright, William J. Conaty, GE Professor of Strategic HR, School of ILR, Cornell University*

The Human Resource Competency Study is definitely among the most authoritative research in human resource management. Led by HR gurus and supported by global data in six rounds of study, this book offers the latest insights and practical advices for human resource professionals around the world who aspire to upgrade their professionalism, impact, and contribution in their jobs."

—*Arthur Yeung, Philips Chair Professor of HRM at CEIBS and ex-CHO of Acer Group*

HR from the Outside In provides an intriguing look at the next horizon for HR and our role in providing insights and innovative practices, and building capabilities that ensure and enhance business success. By being "plugged in" to the external market, understanding stakeholder needs and macro-trends and creating aligned solutions through powerful partnerships, HR is in a unique position to both influence and drive the organizational change agenda. This book makes a compelling case for change and provides a sound roadmap for raising the game in HR."

—*Judy A. Zagorski, Senior Vice President, Human Resources, BASF Corporation*

HR
FROM THE
OUTSIDE
IN

Six Competencies for the Future of Human Resources

Dave Ulrich

Jon Younger

Wayne Brockbank

Mike Ulrich

New York   Chicago   San Francisco   Lisbon   London
Madrid   Mexico City   Milan   New Delhi   San Juan
Seoul   Singapore   Sydney   Toronto

2 3 4 5 6 7 8 9 0   DOC/DOC   1 8 7 6 5 4 3 2

ISBN: 978-0-07-180266-6
MHID: 0-07-180266-5

e-ISBN: 978-0-07-179112-0
e-MHID: 0-07-179112-4

This publication is designed to provide accurate and authoritative information in regard to the subject matter covered. It is sold with the understanding that neither the author nor the publisher is engaged in rendering legal, accounting, or other professional service. If legal advice or other expert assistance is required, the services of a competent professional person should be sought.

—From a Declaration of Principles Jointly Adopted by
a Committee of the American Bar Association and
a Committee of Publishers and Associations

McGraw-Hill books are available at special quantity discounts to use as premiums and sales promotions, or for use in corporate training programs. To contact a representative, please e-mail us at bulksales@mcgraw-hill.com.

This book is printed on acid-free paper.

CONTENTS

INTRODUCTION

Why did we write this book? Collectively, we have amassed over a hundred years of observing, cajoling, admiring, encouraging, and challenging the human resources (HR) profession. In that time, we have shared the frustrations of HR leaders when opportunities have not been fully recognized or leveraged, and we have shared delight when HR professionals and leaders tell stories of how the potential for delivering real value was recognized and captured. In good times and bad, we have concluded that HR issues lie at the heart of sustainable organizational success. Research confirms what we intuitively know: aligned, innovative, and integrated HR practices make a dramatic difference in individual and organizational performance.

Since 1987, we have systematically studied the competencies that HR professionals use to contribute to their own effectiveness and to business success. In tracing and shaping the HR profession, we hope that we articulate and enhance HR's ability to deliver on its potential and promises. This book summarizes the sixth round of our 25-year research project, but it goes beyond the data to propose what's next for the HR profession. It is one of two volumes that describes the current findings. In the second book, also published by McGraw-Hill, we describe the detailed results of our HR competency research for each region of the world.

Whom This Book Is For

In this book, we draw on theory, research, and practice to help HR professionals and HR departments answer three questions:

1. What should HR professionals be, know, and do to be seen as personally effective?
2. What should HR professionals be, know, and do to improve business success?
3. What should HR departments focus on to improve business performance?

Individual HR professionals must learn and master skills and abilities to make sure that they are prepared for the future. When they demonstrate the right competencies, they are seen as both personally effective and true partners in driving business success. HR departments must also have the right vision and governance to deliver business success.

This book is for HR professionals and leaders everywhere—a population conservatively estimated at above one million and growing. If consultants operating in the human capital space are added to this number, it increases substantially. Within this broad professional pool, we offer information tailored to the needs of many groups, such as:

- Chief HR officers responsible for leading their departments will learn how to make targeted investments in both HR people and organizational structures to improve personal effectiveness and business success.
- HR professionals primarily responsible for the quality and performance of HR professionals will learn how to set performance expectations and appropriately invest in development.
- HR generalists who work with line managers as leadership coaches, team facilitators, and organization architects will learn how to become valued contributors by mastering and applying the tools we propose.
- HR specialists with deep technical expertise will learn how to make sure that their technical expertise is used and useful.
- Students or others who anticipate a career in HR will learn about what they have to be, know, and do as they enter the field.
- Line managers who are ultimately responsible for fully leveraging talent, culture, and leadership practices within a company will learn what they should expect from their HR professionals. They will have global standards against which to judge their experiences with HR.
- Advisors to the profession will learn what it takes to be an effective HR professional or to build an effective HR department. These insights should inform the advice they give.

• Researchers in the HR field will see how to not only collect global and longitudinal data on HR but apply those data to improving HR.

Outline of the Book

This book answers the three questions above about what HR professionals and departments need to know and do. It begins with a review of our research and then shares implications of the research for HR professionals and HR departments. This is followed by implications for developing HR professionals and HR departments.

Chapter 1 offers the context for HR. We define the history of HR work in waves and describe the next wave, what we have termed "outside-in HR." We propose that as HR professionals and departments recognize and respond to external trends and subsequent paradoxes, they will create value by connecting internal actions with outside expectations.

Chapter 2 traces the evolution of the concept of competencies for HR professionals based on our 25 years of research. The chapter shares the methodology that distinguishes our research from any other approach to identifying the competencies that HR professionals need to have to influence their perceived performance effectiveness and the success of their businesses.

Chapters 3 through 8 offer specific insights into the six domains of HR competency that currently define HR professional effectiveness and help them drive business success. For each of the six competency domains, we review our research findings, report case studies of those who currently demonstrate these competencies, and offer tools to assess and improve each competency.

Chapter 3 reports on being a strategic positioner, the competency domain that describes how effective HR professionals turn insight on external demands and expectations into innovative and aligned HR practices that drive organizational capability development.

Chapter 4 reviews the credible activist who builds trust with people through business results and strong, supportive relationships.

Chapter 5 discusses the role of the capability builder, who defines, audits, and invests in the organization's capacity to do what it needs to do in its current environment.

Chapter 6 covers the tools for initiating and sustaining change as a change champion.

Chapter 7 lays out ways that the effective HR innovator and integrator converts HR initiatives into impactful, aligned, and sustainable processes.

Chapter 8 examines the competency of technology proponent, a new insight focusing on how strong HR professionals use information and new ways of compiling it to address both administrative and strategic requirements.

In Chapter 9, we discuss ways to become a more effective HR professional and to support the development of HR professionalism, based on work with hundreds of organizations and thousands of HR professionals.

Chapter 10 reports our findings on creating and managing an effective HR department. These findings highlight where HR leaders should focus their scarce resources and attention to make sure that their HR department delivers business value.

Finally, in Chapter 11, we offer an overview of the implications of our findings for the HR field both now and in future.

Whom We Have to Thank

This specific work is built on two and a half decades of research and experience, so we have many people to thank. Colleagues at the University of Michigan or associated with UM executive HR programs have been sponsors and thought partners in this round of research, in particular, Melanie Barnett, Graham Mercer, M. S. Naraygan, C. K. Prahalad, and the hundreds of participants in our HR executive programs.

We have had wonderful global partners in this study, including:

- Australia (AHRI): Anne-Marie Dolan, Dana Grgas, and Peter Wilson.
- China (51Job): Rick Yan, Wang Tao, Kathleen Chien, and Cylen Liu.

- India (NRHD): Dhananjay Singh, Jasmine Sayeed, Mohit Gandhi, N. S. Rajan, and Pankaj Bansal.
- Latin America (IAE): Alejandro Sioli and Michel Hermans.
- Middle East (ASHRM): Fouzi Bubshait and Andrew Cox.
- Northern Europe (HR Norge): Even Bolstad, Håvard Bertzen and Professor Christine Cleemann, Copenhagen Business School. We also thank Martin Farrelly and Fergus Barry of Ireland for their help.
- Turkey (SCP): Pelin Urgancilar.
- Africa (IPM): Elijah Litheko and Ruth Kwalanda.
- North America: Patty Woolcock, Fred Foulkes, Ken Shelton, Richard Vosburgh, Tom Nicholson, Kary Taylor, Dan Stotz, and Heather Evans.

We have also relied on outstanding insights from Ron Bendersky, Connie James, Dave Forman, Dani Johnson, Dale Lake, Kurt Sandholtz, Alejandro Sioli, David Yakonich, Arthur Yeung, and Aaron Younger.

Our ideas about HR are shaped by thought partners who continue to teach us far more than we teach them, including John Boudreau, Frank Cespedes, Ralph Christensen, Bob Eichinger, Tammy Erickson, Jac Fitz-enz, Fred Foulkes, Marshall Goldsmith, Lynda Gratton, Gary Hamel, Gordon Hewitt, Mark Huselid, Steve Kerr, Ed Lawler, Mike Losey, David Maister, Paul McKinnon, Sue Meisinger, Jeff Pfeffer, Bonner Ritchie, Libby Sartain, Ed Schein, Bob Sutton, Charlie Tharp, Paul Thompson, Pat Wright, and Ian Ziskin.

And all the friends, colleagues, and partners we've mentioned thus far are outnumbered many times over by the many excellent HR professionals and leaders we've worked with—at all levels and in all three sectors—who are reinventing the field and with whom we've learned the insights we share here. We value you all too much to risk missing any of you!

We are indebted to Hilary Powers for her extraordinary assistance in copy editing and Knox Huston, our editor at McGraw-Hill, for his help in bringing this book to fruition.

We are also grateful to our many associates at The RBL Group, from whom we continuously learn and grow as consultants, writers, and educators. Norm

Smallwood, in particular, is a devoted, fun, and insightful partner. We have also received invaluable help from RBL Group colleagues Kaylene Allsop, Justin Britton, Erin Burns, Joe Grochowski, Sally Jensen, Jayne Pauga, and Elisa Visick.

Finally, we are grateful to our families who support and encourage us to continue our work, and most especially to our spouses: Wendy, Carolyn, Nancy, and Melanie.

CHAPTER 1

NEXT GENERATION HR

1

"Tell us about your business."

That's how we like to start when we sit down to work with senior HR professionals. We find that it is a good litmus test for assessing the current state of HR in a company.

Most replies start with discussing the latest challenges or innovations in HR practices (hiring people, training leaders, building incentive compensation, doing HR analytics, and so forth), relating to business leaders (having a voice at the table, getting buy-in), or managing the increased personal demands of the HR job (allocating time, staying upbeat in the face of overwhelming demands). That is, HR professionals almost invariably define *business* as "*HR* business" and are inclined to talk about their current initiatives in leadership training, recruiting, engagement, or rewards—the areas where they focus their attention on the job.

These efforts are important, but they are not *the business*. They are in support of the business.

The real business is external: the context and setting in which the business operates, the expectations of key stakeholders (customers, investors, communities, partners, employees, and so forth), and the strategies that give a company a unique competitive advantage. If HR professionals are truly to contribute to business performance, then their mindset must center on the goals of the business. They must take that outside reality and bring it into everything they do, practicing their craft with an eye to the business as a whole and not just their own department.

Focusing on the business of the business enables HR professionals to add meaningful and sustainable value. When they start and ground their work with the business, HR professionals think and behave from the outside in.

Working from the outside in shifts the emphasis in a number of subtle but important ways:

- *Placement and promotion from the outside in:* Customer expectations set the standards for bringing new hires into the organization and for promoting people into higher ranks. The new maxim is: Rather than be the employer of choice, we want to be the employer of choice of *employees our customers want to work with.*
- *Training from the outside in:* When experts teach, delegates learn; when line managers teach, delegates act; when external stakeholders teach, delegates *act on the right things.* So customers, suppliers, investors, and regulators are invited to help design the content of training to make sure that what is taught meets external expectations. They also participate in training sessions as delegates who are co-learning with organization employees, and they present materials either as a live case study or as visiting faculty.
- *Rewards from the outside in:* Customers help determine which employees are rewarded for their efforts. For example, an airline we often travel with allocates a portion of its bonus pool to its most frequent fliers, inviting them to distribute bonus coupons worth varying degrees of value to deserving employees. By essentially allowing customers to control 2 percent of the airline's bonus pool, company leaders remind employees that the outside matters.
- *Performance management from the outside in:* Rather than setting standards by HR doctrine, the department gives key customers the opportunity to assess its performance review standards and tell the company if those standards are consistent with their expectations. When external stakeholders participate in assessing performance review standards, leadership 360-degree reviews may be shifted to 720-degree reviews that include customers and other external stakeholders.
- *Leadership from the outside in:* HR helps the company focus on developing a leadership brand, where external customer expectations translate to internal leadership behaviors. We found that a large portion of the top companies for leadership involved customers in defining competencies for their leaders.

- *Communication from the outside in:* HR makes sure that messages presented to employees are also shared with customers and investors, and vice versa.
- *Culture from the outside in:* We like to define culture as the identity of the organization in the mind of key customers, made real to every employee every day. This is a far cry from the inside-out approach that focuses on how a company thinks and acts, as embedded in norms, values, expectations, and behaviors.

Our message of HR from the outside in is simple to say but not easy to do. Outside-in HR is based on the premise that the business of HR is the business. This logic goes beyond the current state of the HR profession, where the focus is on connecting strategy to HR.

We have been active participants in helping HR professionals turn strategy into results. We now believe that rather than a mirror in which HR practices are reflected, business strategy should be regarded as a window through which HR professionals observe, interpret, and translate external conditions and stakeholder expectations into internal actions.

So in this book, as in our conversations, we reply to, "Tell us about the business" with a quick synopsis of business conditions followed by implications for HR.

A word to the wise: If you are not creating, making, or selling our products, you had better have a good reason for being here.

—*Senior executive of PepsiCo's Frito-Lay unit*

The Business of Business

The bar has been raised for HR; HR must create and deliver value in real business terms.

If people are asked to name a business, most could quickly name a famous company (such as Google) or a local establishment (such as a restaurant). But naming and understanding a business are different things. The appreciation of how a business operates requires a three-tiered approach. First, understand the context in which the business functions, including general societal pressures that encourage or discourage it (such as the increased interest in and access to knowledge enabled by rapid technology change that drives Google's phenomenal growth). Second, understand the specific stakeholders who shape and sustain the business, including customers, investors, regulators, competitors, partners, and employees. Third, understand the business strategy to uniquely position the business to serve stakeholders, respond to general conditions, and build a unique competitive advantage.

Business Context

Everyone experiences the changing context or general drivers of business, sometimes without being consciously aware of those changes. The abstract concept of globally connected economies becomes fiercely concrete when Greece, for example, has an economic crisis, and the distress reverberates around the world, increasing the cost of fuel in London, Sydney, and New York. The "Arab Spring of 2011,"[1] where citizens began redefining political institutions, indicates a concern with the status quo and a reform mentality. The 30 million people online at Skype at any given moment, the 900 million monthly users of Facebook, or the 3 billion searches a day on Google show that technology now enables ubiquitous information and global relationships.

Omnipresent information outside a company changes behavior inside a company. After a disappointing experience at a well-respected restaurant, for instance, we wrote a negative review and posted it on one of the many blog sites. Within hours, the owner and manager of the restaurant contacted us to apologize and invite us to revisit the restaurant so we could update our public review.

When informed HR professionals tell us about their business, they often have a relatively long list of general trends that affect them. Unfortunately, such lists may be skewed by personal experience, overemphasizing some points and missing others. We have found it helpful to organize and prioritize these contextual trends into six categories:

1. *Society:* Personal lifestyles are changing with respect to families, urbanization, ethics, religion, and expectations of well-being.
2. *Technology:* New devices and concepts enable access and transparency not only through information but also in relationships, and they can destroy whole industries while bringing new ones to life.
3. *Economics:* Economic cycles shape consumer and government confidence; freer flow of capital across economic boundaries leads to more granular, or precise, thinking about investments and risk taking and gives rise to some industries.
4. *Politics:* Regulatory shifts change the expectations of government in corporate and personal lives; political unrest often signals a loss of confidence in government institutions.
5. *Environment:* The earth's resources that provide energy for growth are limited and need to be managed responsibly; in addition, social responsibility shapes how people behave.
6. *Demographics:* Changing birthrates, education, and income levels affect employee and consumer behavior.

Each of these trends is magnified as it interacts with the others on the global stage. For example, China's one-child policy led to more males than females in the population. Decades later, as these males move into their twenties, many without prospects for marriage, they are primed for political and social unrest. So the Chinese government invests in and invites Western companies to do business in China to maintain full employment and distract these otherwise volatile citizens. This leads to an imbalance of trade and political implications in Western countries.

Effective HR professionals are aware of and sensitive to these external conditions, which determine how their organizations position themselves for the future. When HR professionals have a way to organize and address external business conditions, their fear of an uncertain future turns to confidence because they can define, anticipate, and manage their responses to them.

Business Stakeholders

Within the general business context, organizations have specific stakeholders. Written or implicit contracts with these stakeholders establish expectations of what the organization gives to and gets from each stakeholder. Mapping key stakeholders and their expectations turns general business conditions into specific expectations that the business can choose to respond to.

In Figure 1.1 we identify six types of stakeholders common to most businesses and the expectations that an organization will contract for.

Spelled out in more detail, these expectations can be summarized as follows:

- Customers expect products or services that meet or exceed their expectations, and they in return provide stable revenue as measured in customer share.

Figure 1.1   *Key stakeholders and the value they expect*

Market Value
- Financial performance
- Intangibles
- Risk

Reputational Value
- Social responsibility
- Regulatory oversight
- Cultural awareness

Customer Share
- Target customers
- Customer intimacy

Collaborative Value
- Partnerships
- Outsourcing

Employee Value Through Productivity
- Competence
- Commitment
- Contribution

Strategic Value
- Shaping strategy
- Creating organization traction

Investors — Communities & Regulators — Customers — Stakeholder Value — Partners — Employees — Line Managers

- Investors expect present and future financial performance in return for investment capital, which shows up in market value.
- Communities, including regulators, expect socially responsible and law-abiding companies that treat the earth and their employees with respect in return for a favorable reputation.
- Partners collaborate along the supply chain to find ways to leverage scarce resources for overall success for the company and its partners.
- Line managers expect to be able to both set and deliver on strategic goals.
- Employees expect fair treatment and working conditions in return for their contribution to their company.

A stakeholder map (similar to Figure 1.1, but spelled out in terms specific to the organization) enables an HR professional to translate general and generic business conditions into expectations for specific targets. It also helps the HR professional recognize the interplay among and between the various stakeholders. As a result of specific stakeholder expectations, the HR professional can allocate resources to deliver measurable value to each stakeholder.

Effective HR professionals tell us about their business by articulating specific stakeholder expectations, anticipating the value of working with each stakeholder, and assessing stakeholder progress. For example, we like to ask HR professionals to name the company's top five customers, investors, or partners and then explain why these stakeholders choose to deal with their company. Too often HR professionals shy away from such questions because they see their business exclusively as traditional, administrative, and transactional HR work.

Business Strategies

Strategy characterizes how leaders make choices designed to enable a company to succeed in a changing business context with specific stakeholders. Some strategic choices define an organization's aspirations and lay out where the organization is headed and its unique identity (mission, vision, values). Other strategic choices focus on specific stakeholders. This may mean targeting some customers more than others and developing channels to gain customer or market share. Strategic choices for investors may also segment investor types (such as value as opposed to growth) and manage investor relations.

Strategic choices give businesses unique sources of competitive differentiation. Traditionally, strategic differentiators may include operational efficiency, product leadership, and customer intimacy.[2] More recently, strategic choices define unique ways that companies meet customer expectations. In recent years, competitive differentiation choices have come to include:

- *Managing risk:* The ability to identify and manage compliance, strategic, operational, and financial risks.[3]
- *Global positioning:* The ability to enter emerging markets beyond the relatively well-established BRIC countries (Brazil, Russia, India, and China), a group that Goldman Sachs identifies as N11, including Turkey, Indonesia, Vietnam, the Philippines, Nigeria, Iran, Mexico, and Egypt.
- *Leveraging information:* The ability to use information as a way to anticipate customer expectations and to do predictive analytics to figure out how to prioritize leading indicators of business success.
- *Managing a globally diverse workforce:* The ability to attract employees from around the world and to enable global mobility in moving employees to the places where they will be able to contribute most effectively.
- *Adapting or changing:* The ability to respond quickly to emerging business opportunities and threats.
- *Building corporate social responsibility:* The ability to build a reputation as a "green organization" that supports responsibility for the planet, employees, and customers.
- *Collaborating or partnering across boundaries:* The ability to form alliances or partnerships both across functions inside the organization and with customers, competitors, and partners outside the organization.
- *Focusing on simplifying:* The ability to turn complexity into an elegant and well-coordinated process that concentrates attention on the critical few priorities.

Effective strategies focus attention on these sources of competitive uniqueness, as well as on any others that may be identified. Once strategic choices are made, plans can become more specific about actions, talent, and budgets. Through strategic choices, leaders invest time and money that make it possible to differentiate their company from competitors in the minds of targeted stakeholders.

HR Is Not Alone

Because of context, stakeholder, and strategic shifts, many business support functions have been undergoing transformation. Finance, operations, information technology (IT), and marketing are experiencing pressures that parallel those bearing on HR. Each of these functions is becoming more outside in by focusing more and adapting to contexts, stakeholders, and strategies. Managers in these areas are being asked to manage traditional duties and respond to future expectations. The HR profession is shifting in similar ways, so it is useful to take a look at other support functions.

For example, the traditional role of finance as financial gatekeeper remains but has been expanded to shape and challenge organizational strategies. McKinsey, the consulting firm, points out the increased expectations on finance functions sketched in Table 1.1.[4]

Table 1.1   *Views of the Finance Function*

Role	CEO View of Finance (Percentile)	Finance View of Finance (Percentile)
Active member of the leadership team	88%	40%
Contributes to company performance	84	34
Ensures efficiency of finance organization	70	80
Improves quality of financial organization	68	74
Challenges company strategy	52	29
Brings in a capital markets perspective	29	14

Likewise, over the past decade, a number of significant changes have challenged the role and competencies required of operations. As a result, the new competencies of operations leaders and professionals include the ones outlined in Table 1.2.[5]

The role of information technology leaders and professionals has also undergone significant changes to focus more emphatically on the key shifts outlined in Table 1.3.[6]

Last, consider the role of marketer and chief marketing officer. As David Court, a managing partner at McKinsey, puts it, "Many chief marketers still have narrowly defined roles that emphasize advertising, brand management and market research. They will have to spread their wings."[7]

Table 1.2   *The Changing Role of the Operations Leader*

Competency	From	To
Operations strategy	Incremental improvement	Set aggressive aspirations for operations; explore, develop, and implement breakaway strategies
Talent development	Develop outstanding operations professionals and leaders	Develop broader, transformative talent both for operations and for the larger organization; operations as a talent incubator and accelerator
Focus on growth	Manage production costs; drive cost efficiency	Facilitate growth and innovation; learn from and adapt best practices and across industries
Managing risk	Ensure quality; anticipate potential risks and take preventive action	Manage risk systematically, proactively, and cost-effectively; ensure organizational agility and flexibility in response to changing market and competitive dynamics
Breaking down the silos	Ensure excellent operational performance; communicate and coordinate with other functional groups	Contribute significantly to the alignment of operations, R&D, and commercial functions to common goals and strategy

Table 1.3   The Shifting IT Role

Current	Future
Keeping the engine running cost-efficiently and reliably	Shaping IT demand through participation in business strategy
Technical project management and execution	Building capability
Accountability for IT productivity	Educating management: helping the leadership team develop an informed view of future requirements
Serving business unit needs	Thinking about the enterprise: helping business leaders leverage IT assets and investments
Providing technical expert judgment	Sharing accountability for the business implications of technical decisions and investments
Managing legacy systems	Driving innovation
Leading technical change	Managing organizational change

According to Court, marketers need to develop competence in these areas:

- Taking greater initiative as a strategy activist
- Developing the skills to lead companywide change in response to changing customer buying patterns
- Assuming accountability for the company's external brand or profile as a whole; creating collaborative organizational relationships that align the organization's overall message to different stakeholders (customers, investors, communities)
- Building marketing capabilities throughout the organization as a whole
- Identifying the critical touch points for a customer and managing the complexity of a consistent customer experience
- Providing insight and strategic recommendations based on evidence-based analysis

HR has been undergoing a similar transformation so that effective HR professionals facilitate the creation and deployment of strategy. They help turn strategic choices into stories that resonate with key stakeholders. They turn the strategic directions into actions by aligning HR practices and leadership behaviors with the strategy. They also facilitate the processes of determining who participates in the creation of strategy. Effective HR professionals tell us not only what the strategy is but how it will be implemented.

The Business of Business: HR's New Normal and Its Implications

Effective HR professionals recognize, accept, and act on a new normal in business. When faced with "tell us about your business," they can respond by discussing global changes in context, stakeholders, and strategies. These shifts are not cyclical events that will return to a former state—they are a new normal grounded on enormous disruptive and evolutionary changes. Those who look backward for answers to future problems may be left behind.

Waves of HR Evolution

Business context, stakeholders, and strategies shift how HR work is conceived and performed. In the past half-century or so, the HR profession has been through three general waves (see Figure 1.2), and a fourth is emerging. Each wave follows a similar curve through time with start-up, learning, growth, and then stability.

Wave 1 emphasized the administrative work of HR, where HR personnel focused on terms and conditions of work, delivery of HR services, and regulatory compliance. HR was predominantly what we would describe as an "administrative and transactional utility." So long as HR consistently and cost-efficiently delivered the basics—employees were paid, pensions were administered, attendance was monitored, and employees were recruited—HR was seen as doing its job.

Wave 1 HR roles tended to be filled by people who did an excellent job of administration. This by no means implies that HR didn't also make other important contributions—training employees, auditing employee satisfaction and engagement, supporting talent planning. But the central tendency

Figure 1.2   *Evolution of HR work in waves*

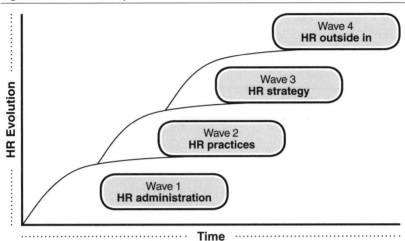

for these HR departments—the primary accountability—was administrative and transactional. The transaction and administrative work of HR continues today, but it is done differently through outsourcing and technology solutions. HR administration must continue to be done well, but when work becomes routine, it is time to move to other priorities. For example, Mercer has studied HR practices in the region known as EMEA (Europe, Mid East, and Africa) and found that although most HR departments there are moving beyond the administrative role, 16 percent still have no current interest in changing that role.[8] HR effectiveness in wave 1 is doing more with less, and HR credibility comes from flawless administration of transactions.

Wave 2 emphasized the design of innovative HR practices in sourcing, compensation or rewards, learning, communication, and so forth. For example, General Electric executives recognized that their future well-being was deeply influenced by how quickly and well the company could develop leaders at all levels able to support international and business unit growth. This led to the establishment of Crotonville, now the Jack Welch Leadership Center, a large campus outside New York City focused on developing the next generation of key functional managers and general managers. Faculty includes external experts, internal HR and organizational development staff, and senior executives of the company—starting with CEO Jeff Immelt. Similar innovations have occurred in rewards, communication, succession planning, and other HR practice areas. While each of these HR practice areas innovated in terms of what and how things were done, they also were interacted with each other to provide a consistent approach to HR. HR effectiveness in wave 2 is from innovating and integrating HR practices, and HR credibility derives from delivering best practices.

Wave 3 has focused on the connection of individual and integrated HR practices with business success through strategic HR. For the last 15 to 20 years, HR has worked to link its work to the strategy or purposes of a business. This work has expanded HR practices from the primary focus on talent to include contribution to culture and leadership. Given a business's strategy, HR professionals would be charged with assessing and improving talent, culture, and leadership to accomplish the strategy. In this wave, HR professionals turned strategies into HR priorities to deliver on strategic promises. To master strategic HR work, HR transformation occurred to upgrade HR professionals and to redesign HR departments. HR effectiveness in wave 3 creates a line of sight between business strategy and HR actions, and HR credibility comes from being at the table to engage in strategic conversations.

The worldwide economic crisis, globalization, technological innovations, and other changes in recent years have challenged the future of HR. Some HR leaders want to look back and reinforce HR administrative work by doing the basics well, while others want to return to focusing on targeted HR practices. Although we agree that the basics and practices of HR must still be done well, we would rather look forward to a new normal for HR.

Wave 4 uses HR practices to derive and respond to external business conditions. As discussed, we call this wave "HR from the outside in." Outside-in HR goes beyond strategy to align its work with business contexts and stakeholders. We acknowledge that the three earlier waves represent HR work that still has to be done well—HR administration must be flawless; HR practices must be innovative and integrated; and HR must turn strategic aspirations into HR actions. But rather than rely on these waves, we see future-facing HR professionals looking outside their organizations to customers, investors, and communities to define successful HR. Earlier, we gave examples of the implications for talent, culture, and leadership. HR effectiveness will show up in customer share, investor confidence, and community reputation, and HR credibility will be drawn from those outside the company as well as from those inside.

For HR to deliver the standards of the first three waves and the promises of the fourth (outside in), we believe that HR must learn to master six paradoxes. Paradoxes mean that HR people and departments are effective only when they can simultaneously deliver multiple outcomes. Instead of moving from one outcome to another, HR has to do both. In Figure 1.3, we list the paradoxes that will set the criteria for HR going forward.

These paradoxes may be described in detail as follows:

- *Outside and inside*: As we have discussed, a primary challenge for HR going forward is to turn external business trends and stakeholder expectations into

Figure 1.3   *Six paradoxes facing HR*

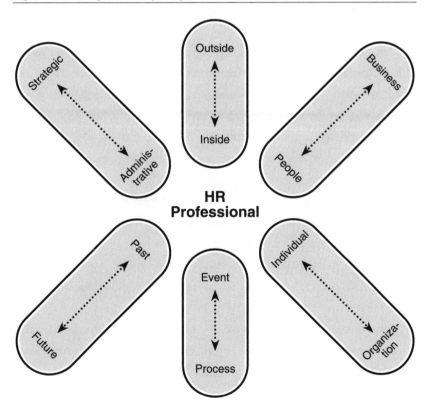

internal HR practices and actions. This will require that HR professionals simultaneously understand and operate in the marketplace and the workplace. HR professionals will likely spend time with customers, investors, and community leaders, and they will turn those experiences into HR innovations. To ride this paradox successfully is to be a strategic positioner who not only knows the business but can shape and position the business for success.

- *Business and people*: Traditionally, people went into HR because they "liked people." In wave 3, when strategic HR principles became popular, HR professionals were asked to become more business literate. Balancing the trade-offs between people and business is not always easy. HR professionals who go to either extreme create problems. Overemphasis on people turns business enterprises into social agencies that may lose the ability to meet market requirements. Overemphasis on business drives results without attention to how they are generated. To ride this paradox successfully is to be a credible activist who earns personal credibility and also takes an active position on business performance.

- *Organization and individual:* In recent years some people have suggested that HR rename itself to emphasize talent, often called human capital, workforce, or people. We completely agree that individual abilities have a significant impact on the success of a company. But we also believe that the way people work together, and the culture of the organization, is equally if not more critical to an organization's success. As often happens in sports, the teams with the superstars can lag behind teams with less individual talent but with great teamwork. So we suggest that the paradox is to manage the tensions between talent and teamwork, individual ability and organization capability, personal competence and organizational culture, and so forth. HR professionals should simultaneously assess and improve the flow of people in an organization, but they should also facilitate the creation and dissemination of an organization's culture that encourages them to work together. People both shape and are shaped by the culture. To ride this paradox successfully is to be a capability builder who can find the right mix of personal and organization development actions.

- *Process and event*: HR is not about an isolated activity (a training, communication, staffing, or compensation program) but about processes that generate sustainable and integrated solutions. Often HR professionals have focused on HR events. The field of HR has been plagued with panaceas, fads, and quick fixes. It's too easy to be mesmerized by the newest new things, and visitors in search of best practices examine a specific HR innovation without considering connected and surrounding programs. Faddish events create an emotional stir, but unless they are tied into sustainable processes, emotions turn to cynicism. Sustainability requires a long-term view, an integrated solution, and an ability to learn and evolve. To ride this paradox successfully is to be an HR innovator and integrator who weaves separate events into cohesive solutions.

- *Future and past*: As people age, they have more experiences to draw on that influence current choices, which can be both useful and constraining. When HR professionals rely on the past for their present choices, they fail to adapt. When they ignore the past, they relive it. When they are constantly preparing for the future, they may not have the luxury of waiting for it. Balancing the past and the future means learning principles from the past and then adapting those principles to future scenarios. It also means starting with a desired future state and then shaping present choices to create this future. To ride this paradox successfully is to be an HR change champion who connects the past to the future and who anticipates and manages individual, initiative, and institutional change.

- *Strategic and administrative*: When we ask non-HR colleagues, "What does HR mean to you?" we often get administration-centered responses: HR does my benefits; HR manages my pension; HR processes my payroll. These administrative actions do have to be flawlessly executed, on time, every time. But many of these routine HR actions are being done through technology to save time and increase efficiency. HR also has to become strategic in adapting to future business scenarios. To ride this paradox successfully involves using technology to flawlessly process administrative work while generating information for more strategic work.

Finding Out How You're Doing

To be effective, HR professionals need to master the challenges of these six paradoxes, being able as individuals and departments to manage the competing expectations. Exercise 1.1 is designed to help you assess where your HR department currently positions itself against these criteria. For example, if your department is wholly involved in getting people hired, paid, and into the pension plan, it would be at "1" on the administrative-strategic scale; if it has outsourced all of that kind of activity and focuses purely on the organization's long-term talent sourcing and training needs and setting its role in the community, it would be at "10" on that scale, Plot the results on the diagram that follows the scale and you will have a profile and image of your current HR department. The shape of Figure 1.4 shows how your HR department can focus to manage the paradoxes that will enable response to the new normal in HR.

Exercise 1.1   Auditing Your HR Department on Six Paradoxes

	To what extent does my HR department focus on:	
Inside	1 2 3 4 5 6 7 8 9 10	Outside
People	1 2 3 4 5 6 7 8 9 10	Business
Individual	1 2 3 4 5 6 7 8 9 10	Organization
Event	1 2 3 4 5 6 7 8 9 10	Process
Past	1 2 3 4 5 6 7 8 9 10	Future
Administrative	1 2 3 4 5 6 7 8 9 10	Strategic

Conclusion: What's Next for HR?

As we continue our work in HR, we will keep asking HR professionals to tell us about their business. Because of what we report in this book, we hope that the answers will increasingly include an informed and insightful discussion of business context, stakeholders, and strategy as well as an understanding of the

Figure 1.4   *Shape of HR department response to the new normal in HR*

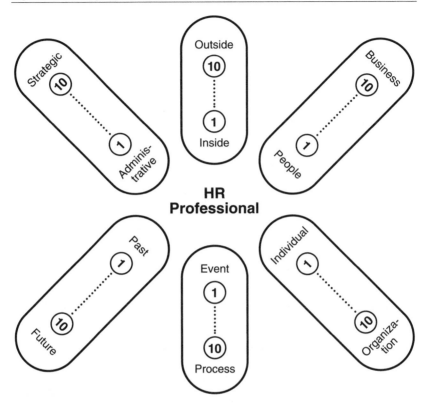

requirements for HR to deliver value. We also hope that this work provides frameworks and tools to build specific HR competencies. We are optimistic and confident that when HR professionals learn and adapt our research and ideas about HR from outside in, they will become even stronger contributors to business value.

CHAPTER 2

APPROACH AND FINDINGS

2

Effective HR professionals maintain the same high standards that companies expect of other key functional areas—that this, they must create specific and substantial value for customers and shareholders. And this is not a statement of simple hope or faith; it is a conclusion backed by 25 years of empirical research. Our Human Resource Competency Study (HRCS) has allowed us to assemble the world's largest global data set on the competencies of HR professionals. This chapter addresses five issues related to the research:

1. Purpose and vision
2. Development of the competency approach
3. Research methods
4. Evolution of the HR competency models
5. Overview of our 2012 findings

Purpose and Vision

Over the years of the HRCS, we have focused on contributing to the progress of the HR profession. We have two specific definitions of what we mean by *progress*, especially in the context of our research. At the individual level, progress is defined by improvement of the overall effectiveness of HR professionals. We help individual HR professionals understand which competencies to focus their professional development on so that they will be seen by others as competent and contributing. At the business level, progress is defined by the extent to which HR competencies and activities are applied to enhance business impact. We help HR professionals understand which competencies will allow them to contribute directly to business results.

In our mission to contribute to the progress of the HR profession, we initiated and sustained the HRCS to address five sets of questions:

1. At the most basic level, what are the competencies that exist within the HR profession? How are they bundled into useful categories for development and application?

2. What is the context? That is, which competencies have the greatest impact on individual effectiveness as seen by those who are most familiar with their functioning as HR professionals?

3. Which HR competencies have the greatest influence on business results? In selecting this focus, we differentiate between the competencies that are basic entrance requirements into the field and those that differentiate success. Most professional testing standards focus on the former and more or less ignore the latter. For example, passing the bar exam demonstrates that you have the knowledge required of an entry-level lawyer, but it does not tell you how effective a lawyer you will be. Our work focuses on the details that spell success.

4. How has the HR field evolved? What are the "areas of opportunity"? (These are activities that are rarely done well but are demonstrated in pockets of excellence to have the potential to offer a company a strong competitive advantage.)

5. What can individual HR professionals and departments do to raise the standards of the HR profession and add the greatest value to their individual careers and to the businesses they serve?

Throughout our work, we have sought to raise the standards of the HR profession. By helping HR professionals discover which competencies and activities add the greatest value to individual effectiveness and business success, we hope to inspire the field to add greater value—and we have provided specific suggestions for how this can be achieved.

BAE Systems

How all these purposes come together in a powerful way is exemplified by the experience of BAE Systems. British Aerospace and Marconi Electronic Systems merged to form BAE Systems, a defense contractor whose slogan is, "Protecting those who protect us." As a result of the merger, the firm's HR department was organized into three segments: shared services, corporate center, and client-facing HR professionals who work directly with line executives in their business. During the reorganization process, BAE's HR leadership recognized that the centrally important client-facing HR professionals had not developed the knowledge and skills that would be necessary to meet the demands of making greater contributions to the business. To address this issue, the HR leadership undertook a major developmental initiative for 63 of the key client-facing professionals.

The development team's first task was to build an HR competency model. The initial competency model was based on the team's personal experience and a consultant's anecdotal insights. As team members became aware of the HRCS research, they modified the competency model to reflect the HRCS competencies that were empirically associated with business results. They then created a customized developmental intervention that was exactly aligned with the components of the new competency model. The program included developing business knowledge, constructing a business-based HR strategy, building key organizational capabilities with a focus on cultural capabilities, managing change, and building best HR practices. The participants also completed two application projects in which the competency-based knowledge, skills, and tools from the classroom were applied to major business issues.

Prior to the intervention and unknown to the developmental vendor, the senior HR executive engaged an external auditor to conduct a pretest of HR's impact on business results. The information was gathered exclusively from line executives. A year later (and several months following the intervention), the auditor then conducted a posttest evaluation of HR effectiveness. The results were quite remarkable. In the opinion of line executives, HR's influence on business decisions and strategy more than doubled; HR's providing of innovative business solutions increased by 85 percent; HR's understanding of key performance indicators increased by 68 percent, and HR's provision of good general HR advice and support increased by 68 percent. (See Table 2.1.) To our knowledge this is the most rigorous measurement of any HR developmental intervention that has been published.

Table 2.1   *Internal HR Customer Satisfaction Audit Results and Improvement Scores*

	Pretest	Posttest	Perceived Increase
Influencing business decisions and strategy	30%	66%	+120%
Providing good general HR advice and support	51%	85%	+67%
Understanding key performance indicators	47%	79%	+68%
Providing innovative business solutions	33%	61%	+85%

The BAE Systems experience reveals the potential for applying the empirical research from HRCS in developing HR competencies that translate into business results. This is what we have tried to achieve with our competency research—and what we have accomplished.

Development of the Competency Approach

Early in our research, we made a conscious decision to apply competency logic to our study of HR professionals. This decision has proved so crucial to our success that it is useful to trace the evolution of the concept.

The competency approach began as a specialized and narrow application, but in the last 40 years it has grown into a leading logic for diagnosing, framing, and improving many aspects of HR management. Since its inception, its purposes, importance, and utility have expanded with the following observations:

1. Competencies enable the specification of what people need to know and do to perform better.[1]
2. Competencies can be communicated—and therefore can be taught and learned.[2]
3. Performance against competencies can be measured and monitored.[3]
4. In complex jobs, competencies are relatively more important in predicting superior performance than are task-related skills, intelligence, or credentials.[4]
5. Competencies facilitate the accurate matching of individuals with jobs.[5]
6. As they are strategically defined and created, competencies can be an important source of competitive advantage.[6]
7. Competencies can be a source of integration for otherwise potentially fragmented management and HR practices.[7]
8. Competencies can provide long-term ballast for organizational stability and flexibility.[8]
9. Since competencies can be measured, they can be framed as a key element of measuring the effectiveness of individual HR subfunctions or processes (for example, staffing, performance management, and development) as well as the effectiveness of HR as a whole.[9]
10. Competencies can also be used as the basis for developing more high-value-adding HR departments.[10]
11. Because competencies are ultimately expressed in what people do rather than what people are (actions rather than traits, predispositions, and the like), competencies can be an important element in diversity initiatives.[11]

As a result of all these benefits, the application of competencies continues to gain momentum. To some degree the competency approach for managing organizations has existed in the earliest records of organization and management. In fact, the Roman army actually practiced a competency approach:

attributes of excellent commanders were recorded, and these profiles were used to select soldiers and leaders with good prospects for success.[12]

In modern times, Frederick Taylor paved the way for HR competency studies as he popularized scientific management. In the search for standardization, one mechanism for enhancing human efficiency is specifying the task and behavioral requirements to complete the task and then ensuring that individuals were selected, trained, and rewarded according to these requirements.[13]

One of the first large-scale applications of competency to the work environment occurred during World War II; the U.S. Army Air Corps applied competency logic in selecting and training fighter pilots. The breakthrough occurred when the researchers modified their approach. Instead of asking people to identify the qualities of a good pilot, they asked pilots what behaviors and actions occurred in a specific situation in which they had witnessed exceptional flying. This resulted in information on what a good pilot did, as opposed to what people thought a good pilot should do. Following the war, a central figure in the air force's task force, John Flanagan, applied this approach on a large scale at the Delco-Remy division of General Motors.[14]

While the competency approach continued to evolve through the 1960s and 1970s, the competency approach as it is generally understood today was first conceptualized by David McClelland in a 1973 article.[15] His consulting company, McBer (started by David McClelland and David Berlow, hence the name), was hired by the U.S. Department of State to identify the behaviors and skills that determined superior performance in junior foreign service information officers.

In 1982 Richard Boyatzis of McBer Consulting published *The Competent Manager*. This work had substantial impact on the popularity of the competency approach because it was the most rigorous application of competencies to measure, predict, and build effective managerial performance.[16] Boyatzis's definition of competency has been generally accepted.[17] His definition is that "a competency is a characteristic of a person that results in consistently effective performance in a job."[18]

In parallel, many companies including BP, Manchester Airport, Cadbury, and Shell Canada developed managerial competency models specifically tailored for internal use.[19] During this period, as the use of competency models for managers proliferated in application, the technique began to be used for HR practitioners.

While it is difficult to trace the first application of the competency approach to the HR function, early studies include work of the Ontario Society for Training and Development in 1976,[20] as well as a 1967 study sponsored by the American Society of Training and Development that set out to identify the different roles and necessary skills of training directors.[21] One of the first extensive studies of HR competencies was conducted by Patricia McLagan for the American Society for Training and Development in 1983.[22] This important study documented the variety of possible roles for HR professionals and examined the detailed competencies of those involved in human resource development (coordinated integration of training, development, organization development, and career development).

In 1987, McLagan again collaborated with the American Society of Training and Development in developing a competency model for HR. This time, her focus was broader. She focused on HR's general developmental function and included most of the roles of HR (excluding HR research and information services, union relations, employee assistance, and compensation and benefits). This study offered extensive research based on evaluations from two surveys each involving over a thousand "field experts." The results of this competency study were printed in *Models for HRD Practice: The Research Report.*[23]

It was at this time that our Human Resource Competency Study began to take shape. In 1987, Dave Ulrich, Wayne Brockbank, and their colleagues developed a model of HR competencies based on interviews with 600 HR professionals.[24] This work became the foundation of the HR competency study, which began at the University of Michigan in the following year. Much of the subsequent HR competency work built on this model.

Towers and Perrin teamed up with IBM in 1991 to interview 3,000 HR professionals, line executives, consultants, and business scholars. Towers and Perrin found that line executives wanted HR to be computer literate, scholars wanted HR to show knowledge of and vision for HR, consultants wanted HR to predict the effects of change, and HR professionals thought that educating and influencing line managers was their most important competency.[25]

In 1996, Arthur Yeung, Patty Woolcock, and some of their associates from the California Strategic Human Resource Partnership developed an HR competency model based on interviews with 10 HR executives from 10 different companies.[26] The resulting model stressed the importance of competencies in four main areas: leadership, HR expertise, consulting, and core competencies. This study was focused on what competencies would be necessary in the future for HR.

Meanwhile Wright, Stewart, and Moore of Cornell Advanced HR Studies (CAHRS) surveyed 56 chief HR officers (CHROs) in 2009, 72 in 2010, and 172 in 2011.[27] For the 2011 data, both European and U.S. CHROs suggested talent as the most critical challenge, followed by cost control, succession planning, culture, and employee engagement (responses vary somewhat between European and U.S. CHROs). They also found that building HR competencies is the largest obstacle to achieving the CEO's agenda for HR. The practices most likely used to increase CHRO effectiveness include learning from an external network, having a business focus, engaging in self-development activities, and constructing effective HR processes. They also identified eight roles for CHROs and the amount of time spent on each role: strategic advisor; counselor, confidant, and coach; board liaison; talent architect; HR function leader; workforce sensor; and firm representative.

Boston Consulting Group has conducted annual studies of the HR profession in collaboration with the World Federation of People Management Associations and the European Association of People Management Associations.[28] In their 2011 study, they received surveys from 2,039 executives in 35 European countries. Based on executive assessments of "current capability" and "future importance," the four most critical topics for HR were managing talent (recruiting, developing, retaining), improving leadership development, transforming HR into a strategic partner, and strategic workforce planning. They identified five critical HR capabilities (what we would call competencies) to address these topics: transforming HR into a strategic partner, mastering HR processes, delivering on recruiting, restructuring the organization, and improving leadership development. They also highlighted the importance of technology and social media.

The Center for Effective Organizations has studied HR effectiveness over the past few years.[29, 30, 31] In recent work based on its experiences, it suggests six trends or shifts facing HR professionals:

- Hero leadership to collective leadership
- Intellectual property to agile cocreation
- Employment value proposition to personal value proposition
- Sameness to segmentation
- Fatigue to sustainability
- Persuasion to education

They suggest that these six themes respond to external trends as well as organization processes. They also propose that HR structure and competencies change to respond to these trends.

Consulting firm Deloitte summarizes its recommendations for HR competencies into three broad requirements: business (commercial awareness, business acumen, customer focus, aligned business to HR), HR (employee relations, get the basics right, HR expertise, HR metrics, change delivery), and consulting capabilities (brokering, trusted advisor, impact and influence, facilitation and coaching, leadership, project delivery).[32] Deloitte argues that when HR professionals master these competencies, they are able to be business partners who help their business be successful. It bases its recommendations on case experiences with clients.

Hewitt, another consulting firm, surveyed 85 individuals from different firms to find out how their firms managed their HR priorities and competencies.[33] It suggests that HR professionals need competencies in organization design, service delivery and technology, governance and metrics, and strategy and program design. When HR professionals master these four skill sets, they are able to help their companies manage their businesses.

Roffey Park Institute, a research organization in London, surveyed 171 HR professionals and interviewed 7 subject matter experts and 6 line managers to review the validity and relevance of the business partnering model for HR.[34] It suggests that HR skills in interpersonal relationship and business knowledge are key to success for HR professionals. It also identifies 14 specific behavioral HR competencies and suggests that demonstrating consistent delivery and building HR credibility are perceived as top predictors of HR success.

The Society for Human Resource Management (SHRM) has conducted a number of studies using different approaches over several years. In 1990 SHRM engaged Tom Lawson to interview 20 CEOs and 50 HR administrators about what HR was doing and what needed to change in HR for it to be a more valued contributor.[35] Lawson found that HR needed to focus on building management abilities including leadership, influence, business knowledge, and proficiency with new technologies.[36] In 1998, SHRM sponsored another study of HR competencies by Stephen Schoonover. SHRM's new competency model was based on 300 interviews with HR professionals from 21 companies over a 7-year period. This study found three main areas of HR competency: core competencies, which consisted of personal attributes, management, leadership, and functional knowledge and skills; level-specific competencies, which were composed of executive, team leader and manager, and individual contributors; and role-specific competencies, which included HR generalists, HR strategists, and HR product and service specialists.

The Chartered Institute for Personnel and Development (CIPD) has created an HR profession map that offers a comprehensive view of how HR professionals can provide insights and solutions to their businesses.[37] This map is organized around how HR can provide leadership and insights in eight HR practice areas: organization design; organization development; resourcing and talent planning, learning, and development; performance and rewards; employee engagement; employee relations; service delivery; and information.

These studies all have strengths and limitations. In general, a major strength of these studies is that they have helped the field focus on the importance of understanding and developing what HR professionals need to be, know, and do. However, these studies share four shortcomings. First, with a few exceptions most of these approaches to HR competencies rely on self-perception instead of other-perception. They ask HR professionals to report on what they think they need to know and do to be effective. Second, many of them rely on such small numbers that generalizing their findings to larger populations is problematic at best. Third, they are limited in geographic scope—usually North America. They assume that best HR practices and professionals are located uniquely in North America. Fourth, they are limited to one point in time. They tend to underappreciate the dynamic nature of competencies and their need to change as the context of business changes.

These are the problems we have addressed in the HRCS over the past 25 years. In creating the world's most comprehensive, global, and business-oriented competency study, we have attempted to capitalize on the advantages and mitigate the disadvantages of other work.

HRCS Research Methods

From its inception, the HRCS was designed to identify the cutting-edge practices and competencies of high-performing HR professionals. To maintain its cutting-edge relevance, an HR competency survey was designed in close cooperation with line managers and leading academicians, HR associations, and practitioners. It drew on the knowledge, skills, abilities, and experiences of HR and line leaders; the knowledge of emerging research, theories, and concepts of organization and HR held by leading academicians; and the ability of leading practitioners to test the applicability and relevance of emerging concepts and theories under alternative conditions.

Before the first round of the survey in 1987—as well as each subsequent round (in 1992, 1997, 2002, 2007, and 2012)—the research team went through a three-step process. First, we conducted a thorough examination of the relevant literature on business trends in HR practices and competencies. Second, we talked with hundreds of HR professionals, line executives, academics, and consultants in individual interviews or in semistructured focus groups. Third, in the rounds following 1987, we focused on those items that had been found to be most important in preceding years.

From these preparatory activities, we then constructed the survey for that round. Since we wanted to examine which competencies were related to both individual effectiveness and business success, we developed measures for two outcome variables. We measured individual or personal effectiveness by asking HR and non-HR associates of each HR participant the following question: *Compared to other HR professionals you have known, how does this participant compare?* Business success was measured using an aggregate index of seven dimensions: profitability, labor productivity, new product development, customer satisfaction, attraction of required employees, regulatory compliance, and relative standing. Relative standing was covered by asking, *Compared to major competitors in your industry, how has your business performed financially for the last three years?*

What's a Business?

In the survey, the term *business* is used to describe the organizational units in which the HR participants generally provide services. Businesses are "identifiable units that are commonly understood within the firm." Thus *business* could refer to the corporate office, a group (household products group), a division (software division), a plant (Ann Arbor manufacturing), a function (financial services), or a physical territory (Asia-Pacific region).

We avoided the term *business unit* because it has different meanings in different firms. For example, in some companies the Asia-Pacific region may be referred to as the business an HR professional serves, even though the region is not actually a "business unit" in the vernacular of that firm. The research team decided to focus on the participants' business rather than on the corporation as a whole because it seemed probable that the HR practices and competencies important for one business may be less so for another even if they are part of the same corporation.

We also asked questions concerning HR department issues: Which stakeholders receive the greatest focus from the HR department? What are the focal activities for the HR department? What is the overall effectiveness of the HR department? What is the influence of the HR department relative to other functions?

In addition, we asked two contextual questions that examined different aspects of change: the rate of change in the relevant industry and the rate of change within the participant's company. Given the state of environmental turbulence, we wanted to evaluate the relationship of HR competencies to personal effectiveness and business success under different conditions of change.

In every round of the study we have applied a 360-degree methodology. HR participants were sent one "participant survey" to complete on themselves. They were also sent nine surveys to distribute to their "associates": peers, subordinates, supervisors, internal clients, or others familiar with the "participant's functioning as an HR professional." Some of the associate raters were HR professionals; many were non-HR clients, including line executives. Thus we ended up with three categories of respondents: HR participants who completed a survey on themselves, HR associates who completed a survey on HR participants, and non-HR associates who completed a survey on HR participants.

In the early rounds of the study (1987, 1992, and 1997), participants came largely from North America. Beginning in 2002, we sought partners in other parts of the world. The first of the regions to be involved were India, Europe, and Latin America. Since 2002 the survey has become increasingly global. We have been honored with involvement of outstanding colleagues from around the world. Our 2012 research advances the global range of the study to include the leading HR professional organizations in Australia (AHRI), China (51Job), India (NHRD), Latin America (IAE), the Middle East (ASHRM), Northern Europe (HR Norge), South Africa (IPM), and Turkey (SCP). We also tapped into our own extensive networks in North America, including the Ross School of Business at the University of Michigan.

Thus far, we have collected information from more than 55,000 participants representing more than 3,000 businesses. The 2012 work, which is the focus of this volume, includes more than 20,000 individual respondents. (See Table 2.2.)

Table 2.2   *HRCS Response Rates*

	1987	1992	1997	2002	2007	2012
Individuals	10,291	4,556	3,229	7,082	10,063	20,013
Business units	1,200	441	678	692	413	635
Respondents: combined HR and non-HR associates	8,884	3,805	2,565	5,890	8,414	17,385
Participants	1,407	751	664	1,192	1,671	2,628

Over the years we have seen distinct and useful trends in respondent characteristics, as shown in Table 2.3.

Table 2.3 permits the following conclusions concerning participant characteristics. The number of women in the HR profession continues to grow steadily. We have seen an increase in the number of participants who have graduate degrees, who are individual contributors (i.e., who have no direct reports and who have fewer years in HR. Hence our sample is increasingly female, more educated with less work experience, and individual contributors. The number of functional HR specialists in the sample has increased, while the number of HR generalists has decreased. The proportion of individuals from smaller and medium-sized companies has grown. This gives a better mix of participants from different-sized companies, so we are able to generalize the implications of the study for HR professionals from companies of all sizes.

Table 2.4 reports respondent roles for the 2012 HRCS. It indicates that the newest data set includes self-reports (HR participants), the perceptions of HR colleagues (HR associates), and those of line managers, peers, and clients (non-HR associates). Thus the results don't just represent HR people talking about what they think matters; they also include insights from those outside HR. This table also clarifies that in the last 15 years (from 1997 to 2012), males in our data set have dropped from 70 percent to 38 percent, and females have increased from 30 to 62 percent. It is also interesting to note that the non-HR associates are 69 percent males, which means that often female HR professionals in our data set are working with male associates.

Table 2.3   Characteristics of the Human Resource Competency Data Set, Rounds 1–6

Round	Round 1 1987	Round 2 1992	Round 3 1997	Round 4 2002	Round 5 2007	Round 6 2012
Gender of HR participant:						
• Male	77%	78%	70%	57%	46%	38%
• Female	23	22	30	43	54	62
Education of HR participant:						
• High school degree	3%	7%	4%	4%	9%	3%
• Associate college degree	5	7	6	9	12	7
• Bachelor's degree	48	43	42	42	37	39
• Graduate degree	44	43	48	45	41	51
Level of the HR participant:						
• Individual contributor	20%	24%	29%	24%	28%	34%
• Manager of individual contributors	36	41	34	34	30	39
• Director of managers	36	29	30	31	20	19
• Top manager	8	6	7	11	21	7
Company size for HR participant:						
• 1–499	15%	17%	22%	25%	31%	19%
• 500–999	10	9	13	15	14	33
• 1,000–4,999	25	22	34	33	28	10
• 5,000–9,999	11	12	11	9	6	10
• Over 10,000	39	40	20	18	20	28

(continued on next page)

Table 2.3   Characteristics of the Human Resource Competency Data Set, Rounds 1–6 (continued)

Round	Round 1 1987	Round 2 1992	Round 3 1997	Round 4 2002	Round 5 2007	Round 6 2012
Years in HR for HR participant						
• 5 years or less	10%	14%	13%	25%	24%	25%
• 6–9 years	14	19	15	18	20	18
• 10–14 years	26	24	21	22	23	25
• 15 or more years	50	43	51	35	32	32
Primary role of HR participant:						
Benefits/medical/safety	6%	5%	5%	4%	3%	3%
Compensation	5	4	4	6	6	7
HR planning, strategy, affirmative action	6	8	5	8	14	14
Labor relations	6	8	5	6	5	4
Org. development, research, effectiveness	2	5	3	13	7	9
Recruiting	3	6	4	4	6	11
Training, communication	7	14	6	12	9	11
Generalist	61	45	60	48	49	40

Table 2.4   Respondents in the 2012 Data Set

Respondent Role	Definition	Number of Total Respondents F = % Female M = % Male
All respondents	All respondents who completed a majority of the 139 competency items	20,013
HR associates	All respondents and associate raters who work in HR	**9,897** F 65% M 35%
Non-HR associates	All respondents and associate raters who are not part of the HR organization	**7,488** F 31% M 69%
Participants	HR participants who elected to participate. Each participant has associate raters as well.	**2,638** F 62% M 38%

Table 2.5 gives the response rate by region. Several implications of this table are reasonably important. The data set is representative of every major part of the world. While the data set is tilted disproportionately toward North America, it nonetheless constitutes the largest database of its kind in every geographical region—even those with only relatively modest response rates—and is the largest of its kind in the world.

Table 2.5   Percent of Respondents by Geographical Region

Region	% of Total Respondents (20,013)
North America (United States and Canada)	35%
Latin America	16%
Europe	12%
China	7%
Australia/New Zealand	6%
India	8%
Turkey	3%
Africa	1%
East Asia	7%
Middle East	2%

Table 2.6 examines the ratio of employees to HR professionals in different industries. It is interesting to note the differences across industries, from 163:1 in agriculture to 43:1 in mining.

Table 2.6   Ratio of Employees to HR Professionals

Industry	Agriculture	Banking	Chemicals	Construction	Food	Manufacturing	Mining	Pharmaceuticals	Public Administration	Services	Utilities	Wholesale/Retail
Employee to HR ratio	163	83	80	75	103	110	43	67	65	81	56	92

We have also been able to break down the respondent rate by industry in each global region in Table 2.7. The data set has strong representation from service, manufacturing, and banking, but the regional differences are interesting. The Middle East sample is strongest in the chemical industry (including petrochemicals). Australia is strongest in public administration. Europe and Asia are strongest in the banking sector. Africa is strongest in services. Finally Turkey is strongest by far in the wholesale and retail sectors.

With these data in hand we then set to work on the analytical processes. To achieve the objectives of the study, we took these seven steps:

1. We calculated the average scores for individual competency items, departmental issues, demographics, and other context issues.
2. We then factor-analyzed the 139 individual competency items. Out of this initial factor analysis, we identified six factors that we refer to as domains.
3. Then we further factor-analyzed the items in each domain. This second level of analysis also identified powerful and important patterns in the data

Table 2.7 Respondent Percentage by Industry and by Region

Industry	Total 100%	United States and Canada	Latin America	Europe	China	Australia and New Zealand	India	Turkey	Africa	Asia	Middle East
Agriculture	1	1	1	1	0	2	1	0	1	0	1
Banking	15	6	14	28	10	14	2	11	16	26	12
Chemicals	3	3	2	5	5	1	2	1	1	1	20
Construction	3	1	6	6	3	2	3	1	0	1	1
Food	4	6	7	4	1	4	2	6	4	0	2
Manufacturing	20	22	14	14	29	5	31	26	12	13	17
Mining	3	2	9	1	0	1	0	0	4	0	8
Pharmaceuticals	5	9	8	2	3	1	3	24	37	2	0
Public administration	4	3	0	6	1	28	0	0	7	2	1
Services	31	37	29	19	36	31	43	3	51	45	32
Utilities	5	4	5	3	2	6	10	1	3	1	3
Wholesale/retail	7	7	5	9	11	6	1	25	1	7	1

set. For ease of communications, we refer to the first level as competency domains and the second level as factors of those domains.

4. For each competency domain and factor, we calculated the average score. These mean scores tell us how effectively HR participants in the study were exhibiting the patterns of competencies as categorized into domains and factors as well as the specific competencies that were reflected in individual questionnaire items.

5. Through the application of regression analysis, we then examined how much influence each competency domain and each competency factor had on business outcomes.

6. Through additional application of regression analysis, we examined also how much influence each competency domain and competency factor had on the perception of overall competency of the HR participants in the minds of HR and non-HR associates.

7. For ease of interpreting the relative impact of competency domains and factors on individual effectiveness and business success, we then scaled the regression beta weights to 100 points for ease of interpretation.

Evolution of the Human Resource Competency Model

Over time our findings have evolved. Business dynamics have changed and HR has changed along with them. As a result our basic competency model has also evolved.

In the 1987 model, three main categories of HR competency emerged from the data: knowledge of the business, delivery of HR practices, and management of change. HR was stepping out of its traditional role of driving HR transactions and pursuing functional practices, and practitioners were beginning to engage in the business and in helping business to manage the turbulence that was just beginning to make itself felt. (See Figure 2.1.)

In 1992 personal credibility emerged as an important domain for HR professionals. To be allowed onto the business playing field, personal credibility became mandatory. Credibility was a function of being able to work well with

Figure 2.1   *1987 HR competency model*

senior leaders, communicating with excellence, and delivering results with integrity. As the world passed through the fall of centralized economic models in India, China, and Russia, change management became more heavily weighted. In the more globally competitive business environment, HR professionals in high-performing firms were spending increasingly more time and effort on strategic HR issues, whereas those in low-performing firms continued to focus more heavily on operational HR issues. (See Figure 2.2.)

In 1997, cultural management made its debut in the human resource competency model. As a critical capability, cultural management addressed the organization's collective knowledge, thought patterns, and integrated actions. In high-performing firms, HR professionals played a central role in identifying and implementing organizational cultures that helped the firm win in the marketplace and successfully implement its business strategy.

As culture emerged, so did another important empirical trend that gave substance and direction to culture and became a harbinger of the future direction of the HR field. We were able to verify that HR professionals in general

Figure 2.2   1992 HR competency model

had relatively low knowledge of external market dynamics. However, HR professionals in high-performing firms knew significantly more about external business realities (that is, customers, competitors, industry trends, and globalization) than did HR professionals in low-performing firms. We were able to verify the importance of HR having an external line of sight and not merely an internal one. (See Figure 2.3.)

In 2002 HR's role as a strategic contributor asserted itself. The strategic contributor competency domain consisted of an integration of fast change, strategic decision making, and market-driven connectivity. Market-driven connectivity was a new concept to the HR field. As far as we know, this category had not been identified by any previous competency work. This factor consisted of HR professionals' identifying important information from the business environment, amplifying that information across the organization, providing the tools that unify the organization around key market information, and reducing the presence of the types of less important information that frequently block attention to more critical market information. By so doing, HR professionals help their organizations successfully navigate changing customer, competitive, and shareholder requirements.

Figure 2.3   *1997 HR competency model*

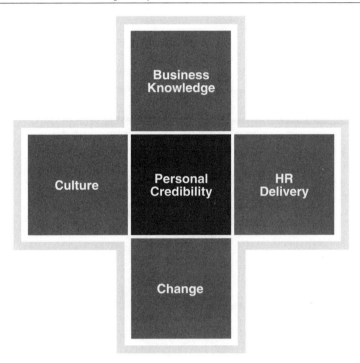

Another trend that occurred in this round was the nature of business knowledge that HR professionals should have. Prior to this round, HR's business knowledge was organized around various business functions (finance, marketing, IT, and so on). In this round business knowledge became organized around the firm's value proposition and the integrated value chain. HR professionals were beginning to organize their business knowledge into more usable formats. (See Figure 2.4.)

In 2007 we found that building organization capabilities became a defining feature. The process of building organizational capabilities was an integration of three domains. First, as strategic architects HR professionals helped formulate and implement the customer-centric business strategy. Second, they built organizational capabilities as empirically represented by culture and change management. Third, they aligned talent and organization design activities with the organizational capabilities that were, in turn, required by the customer-centric business strategy. We found that to optimize this inte-

Figure 2.4   2002 HR compentency model

gration, HR professionals had to excel more than ever before as credible activists in driving business results. Interestingly, non-HR associates had greater expectations for HR professionals to be focused on the external customer than HR professionals did of themselves. We also found an important integration between talent management and organization design. Thus the current trend toward framing the HR agenda entirely in terms of talent management to the exclusion of organization design will probably result in a suboptimal contribution to the business. (See Figure 2.5.)

Overview of the 2012 Findings

As in past years, the 2012 survey sought to answer four questions:

1. What are the primary competency domains and factors for HR professionals?

Figure 2.5   *2007 HR competency mode*

2. How well do HR professionals perform each competency domain and factor?

3. Which competencies have greatest impact on the individual effectiveness of HR professionals as perceived by their HR and non-HR associates?

4. Which competencies have the greatest impact on business success?

In 2012, we identified six domains of HR competency. These are represented in Figure 2.6 and explained in more detail in the list following.

• *Credible activist*: HR professionals in high-performing firms function as credible activists. They do what they say they will do. Such results-based integrity serves as the foundation of personal trust that, in turn, translates into professional credibility. They have effective interpersonal skills. They are flexible in developing positive chemistry with key stakeholders. They translate this positive chemistry into influence that contributes to business results. They take strong positions about business issues that are grounded in sound data and thoughtful opinions.

Figure 2.6   2012 HR competency model

- *Strategic positioner:* High-performing HR professionals understand the global business context—the social, political, economic, environmental, technological, and demographic trends that bear on their business—and translate these trends into business implications. They understand the structure and logic of their own industries and the underlying competitive dynamics of the markets they serve, including customer, competitor, and supplier trends. They then apply this knowledge to developing a personal vision for the future of their own company. They participate in developing customer-focused business strategies and in translating the business strategy into annual business plans and goals.
- *Capability builder:* At the organization level, an effective HR professional creates, audits, and orchestrates an effective and strong organization by helping define and build its organization capabilities. Capability represents what the organization is good at and known for. These capabilities outlast the behavior or performance of any individual manager or system. Such

capabilities might include innovation, speed, customer focus, efficiency, and the creation of meaning and purpose at work. HR professionals can help line managers create meaning so that the capability of the organization reflects the deeper values of the employees.

- *Change champion*: Effective HR professionals develop their organizations' capacity for change and then translate that capacity into effective change processes and structures. They ensure a seamless integration of change processes that builds sustainable competitive advantage. They build the case for change based on market and business reality, and they overcome resistance to change by engaging key stakeholders in key decisions and building their commitment to full implementation. They sustain change by ensuring the availability of necessary resources including time, people, capital, and information, and by capturing the lessons of both success and failure.

- *Human resource innovator and integrator*: At the organization level, a major competency of effective HR professionals is the ability to innovate and integrate HR practices around a few critical business issues. The challenge is to make the HR whole more effective than the sum of its parts. High-performing HR professionals ensure that desired business results are clearly and precisely prioritized, that the necessary organization capabilities are powerfully conceptualized and operationalized, and that the appropriate HR practices, processes, structures, and procedures are aligned to create and sustain the identified organizational capabilities. As they do so with discipline and consistency, they help collective HR practices to reach the tipping point of impact on business results. The innovation and integration of HR practices, processes, and structures directs HR more fully toward impacting business results.

- *Technology proponent*: For many years, HR professionals have applied technology to basic HR work. HR information systems have been applied to enhance the efficiency of HR processes including benefits, payroll processing, healthcare funding, record keeping, and other administrative services. In this HRCS round, we see a dramatic change in the implications of technology for HR professionals. At the organization level, high-performing HR professionals are now involved in two additional categories of technological application. First, HR professionals are applying social networking technology to help people stay connected with one another. They help guide the connectedness of people within the firm and the connectedness between people outside firms (especially customers) with employees inside the firm. Second, in the high-performing firms, HR professionals are increasing their role in the management of information. This includes identifying the information that should receive focus, bundling that information into usable knowledge, leveraging that knowledge into key decisions, and then ensuring that these decision are clearly communicated and acted upon. This updates the operational efficiency competency and will add substantive value to their organizations.

Performance

How well do HR professionals perform in each of the primary competency domains?

In Table 2.8, the remaining three research questions are answered. The table tracks HR performance in each competency domain and the relative impact of HR competences on individual effectiveness and business success.

In the first data column in Table 2.8, we see the performance of HR professionals in the various competency domains. It is clear that HR professionals function best as credible activists. They are effective at building their credibility by establishing relationships of trust, by effectively communicating key business and HR issues, and by actively advocating insightful opinions that move the business forward.

They perform the core of the competency domains of strategic positioner, capability builder, change champion, and HR innovator and integrator at somewhat lower levels of effectiveness. In high-performing firms, HR professionals contribute to the establishment of a customer-centric business strategy; they translate the business strategy into important organizational capabilities; they build and sustain organizational capabilities though the disciplined and integrated application of HR innovations; and they create organizations that are flexible and adaptable at achieving business results.

Table 2.8   *HR Perceived Performance*

	Mean Score on This Competency Domain (1 to 5)	Impact on Perceived Individual Effectiveness (Beta Weights Scaled to 100%)	Business Impact (Beta Weights Scaled to 100%)
Credible activist	4.23	22%	14%
Strategic positioner	3.89	17%	15%
Capability builder	3.97	16%	18%
Change champion	3.93	16%	16%
Human resource innovator and integrator	3.90	17%	19%
Technology proponent	3.74	12%	18%
		Multiple R^2 42.5%	Multiple R^2 8.4%

The domain in which HR tends to be the weakest is in understanding and applying technology to build HR efficiency, to leverage social networking, and to manage the flow of strategic information.

Impact of Competencies on Perceived Effectiveness

Which competencies have the greatest impact on individual effectiveness of HR professionals as perceived by their line and HR associates?

In the second data column of Table 2.8, we identify the relative impact of the six competency domains on the individual effectiveness of HR professionals as seen by their respective HR and non-HR associates. To be perceived as competent, the HR professional should exhibit the competencies of a credible activist as described earlier in this chapter. The other core HR activities are closely bundled together. This implies that to be seen as competent across the board, HR professionals must exhibit these core HR competency domains in an integrated manner.

Excelling as a technology proponent has least influence on associates' perceptions of HR professionals. This may partially be the result of low expectations and lack of experience that HR professionals have in this domain.

Business Impact of HR Competencies

Which HR competencies have the greatest business impact?

The third data column of Table 2.8 expresses some interesting and, to some degree, unexpected results. The close results of HR professionals as capability builders (18 percent) and HR innovators and integrators (19 percent) reinforce the logic that HR practices must integrate to create and sustain key organizational capabilities in order to significantly impact business success. It turns out that the technology proponent domain has the same level of impact on business success as the capability builder and the innovator and integrator domains. This speaks to HR in a new information-intense context as exemplified by emerging social media.

To discern more detail of what makes an impactful HR professional, we also looked at 20 factors that characterize the competencies of HR professionals. (See Table 2.9.)

From these results we can derive even more insights into which competencies are done best at the factor level and which contribute most to individual effectiveness and business impact.

For the strategic positioner domain, cocrafting the strategic agenda is most important for being seen by associates as a competent contributor. However, decoding customer expectations has greater impact on business success.

Virtually all the credible activist factors are done at a relatively high level and have the greatest impact on individual effectiveness as seen by associates. But they systematically have much less impact on the business.

For the capability builder, capitalizing on organizational capability and creating a meaningful work environment have average impact on business success, but aligning strategy, culture, behavior, and practices has the second-greatest impact on business of any of the factors—and it is done at only a modest level of effectiveness. This indicates an obvious area for HR to focus its efforts.

Table 2.9   *Factors for HR Competence on Individual Effectiveness and*
Business Impact

HR Competency Domain Factors	Mean (1 to 5)	Individual Effectiveness Percentage	Business Impact Percentage
Strategic positioner:			
• Interpreting global business context	3.83	4.4	4.2
• Decoding customer expectations	3.83	4.4	5.2
• Cocrafting a strategic agenda	3.96	6.3	4.6
Credible activist:			
• Earning trust through results	4.36	6.9	4.0
• Influencing and relating to others	4.24	7.0	4.1
• Improving through self-awareness	4.08	6.5	4.7
• Shaping the HR profession	4.13	4.4	2.9
Capability builder:			
• Capitalizing on organizational capability	4.03	5.4	5.3
• Aligning strategy, culture, practices, and behavior	3.94	5.3	6.1
• Creating a meaningful work environment	3.94	4.1	5.2
Change champion:			
• Initiating change	3.94	5.4	4.8
• Sustaining change	3.91	4.7	5.7
HR innovator and integrator:			
• Optimizing human capital through workforce planning and analytics	3.95	5.5	5.6
• Developing talent	3.83	4.0	5.3
• Shaping organization and communication practices	3.94	5.8	5.6
• Driving performance	3.87	4.7	5.2
• Building leadership brand	3.87	4.9	5.4
Technology proponent:			
• Improving utility of HR operations	3.72	2.9	5.0
• Leveraging social media tools	3.68	2.7	4.7
• Connecting people through technology	3.77	4.6	6.3
Overall R^2		.431	.108*

*The slight differences in R^2 are because the data are factored into either 6 or 20 scales, which shifts somewhat the variance explained, but the ratios are similar with regressions of either 6 or 20 items.

The change champion results at the factor level are likewise interesting. To be seen as a competent individual contributor, the HR professional should initiate change. However, to contribute to business performance, sustaining change is more important.

The HR innovator and integrator domain has substantial influence on both individual effectiveness and business impact. The average influence of its factors on business success is the highest among all domains. Its factors are second only to the credible activist factors in influence on perceptions of individual effectiveness. The factors have similar influence on business success. The message is clear: HR professionals must make sure that their collective practices are innovative and integrated.

At the factor level the technology proponent is interesting. The average effectiveness scores of these factors are the lowest among all domains. Yet the collective impact of these factors on business success is second only to the influence of the collective factors of the HR innovator and integrator domain on business success. And one factor, connecting people through technology, has more influence on business success than any other factor across all domains. This finding is profound. In today's information-intensive world, HR professionals in high-performing firms are becoming masters at managing the message. They are excelling at connecting stakeholders on the outside with people on the inside in meaningful ways through technology.

It is useful to chart these results as shown in Figure 2.7.

This matrix provides a vivid representation of the relationship between current HR effectiveness and business success. Note that the personal credibility factors are in the upper left-hand corner, indicating that they are done at a high level of effectiveness but have relatively little influence on business success. HR professionals should therefore be cautious in continuing to focus on building additional strength in personal credibility. Our data indicate that they need to move on to the agendas that add greater value. As indicated earlier, the seductive danger is that while being a credible activist has the lowest impact on business performance, it has the highest impact on being seen as being effective by others. Thus the knowledge, skills, and abilities that create the appearance of competence are not what actually create business impact.

Figure 2.7   Prioritizing HR compentency actions

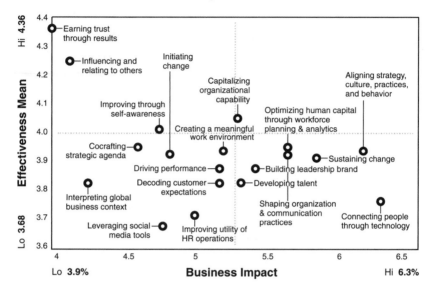

Prioritizing HR Competence Actions: Based on Current Effectiveness and Business Impact

The factors that have the greatest impact on business success are, in order of importance:

- Connecting people though technology
- Aligning strategy, culture, practices, and behavior
- Sustaining change

Furthermore, HR professionals exhibit these competencies at medium to low levels of effectiveness. The opportunity for HR professionals to add greater value to their organizations' success is by focusing on these three.

Conclusion: Developing Competence with Competencies

It has been and continues to be our opportunity to track and contribute to the evolution of the HR field. We have tracked and will continue to track the field by empirically verifying major trends in the competencies of the HR profession. However, we also hope we have promoted the positive evolution of the field by identifying the competencies that contribute most to individual effectiveness and business impact. Our work has enabled us and our global partners to provide models, tools, and practices that help translate the aspirations of those in the HR field to be business contributors into a verifiable reality.

CHAPTER 3

STRATEGIC
POSITIONER

3

Strategic positioning can make a huge difference in the effectiveness of a company's HR efforts. Three examples follow.

MOL Group

MOL, an integrated oil and gas company in Eastern Europe (Hungary, Slovakia, and Croatia), faces talent challenges.[1] It employs around 34,000 people, but its workforce has been aging over the last 20 years. With negative perceptions about work in this industry widespread among younger people, it was hard to keep up with natural attrition—especially as those willing to consider working for an energy company were rarely qualified to do so.

Members of the HR team wanted to find more effective ways of recruiting young employees. They knew that they had to change the attractiveness of natural sciences among secondary school students, who would then go into natural science studies at university. They pursued a number of activities to support natural science education and attract future employees to their industry and firm:

- They launched a "Freshhh" brand to attract and engage future employees. They held an online contest called "Junior Freshhh" in which 900 teams (2,500 pupils from five countries) competed on math, chemistry, and physics problems. These contests were done through Facebook, LinkedIn, and other modern social media.
- They created award programs for natural science teachers. More than 300 nominations of science and math teachers came from 120 different schools.

- They created online teaching tools for science topics (called Freshhh EDU) for both teachers and students.
- They formed strategic partnerships with teacher associations and created scholarships at targeted universities.
- They sponsored a dialogue conference where those interested in natural science education shared teaching methods with secondary schools and universities.
- At universities, they funded science and math studies through faculty sponsorship, internships (more than 200 students), and more student contests (with more than 3,500 participants from 60 countries).
- They invited winners of the Freshhh University competition to join MOL's fresh graduate program (called GROWWW), where they have unique career opportunities within MOL (300 employees a year).

These talent-enhancing activities cost €374,000—but they gave good value. They touch more than 25,000 students, so it costs only €14 per pupil. Based on MOL's research after these initiatives, 30 percent of secondary students would like to apply for engineering and earth science programs, a huge improvement. For Freshhh, MOL spends about €32 per participant. and it hires at least the 10 most talented candidates. The company has 30 times more applications per year since starting these initiatives. Those new employees who go through the GROWWW program have a retention rate of 92 percent, and in four years, 25 percent have moved into management positions. MOL's HR leaders calculate that they have saved at least €50,000 because they did not have to use search firms to fill these positions. Finally, they have increased the engagement level throughout their workforce.

Singapore Housing Development Board

When visiting Singapore recently, we were impressed with the country's incredible multiculturalism. We found people happily celebrating religious holidays from faiths other than their own. At Christmas, we found Muslims and Hindus singing Christmas songs. At Ramadan and Eid, we found Buddhists and Christians recognizing these Muslim holidays. This translates to remarkably easygoing and constructive relationships in the workplace.

How could Singapore capture such unity of focus (helping it grow as a country) with such diversity of background? We learned that Singapore is an island city-state with relatively few natural resources. Government, industry, and education leaders realized that human capital would become a critical source of the country's ability to compete. With birthrates of about 1.1 per woman (well below the replacement level of 2.1), leaders knew that human capital growth would have to be through immigration. The country has about 5.2 million inhabitants—about 3.8 million citizens and 1.4 million immigrant foreigners. Its cultural heritage is mixed in national origin (Chinese 74 percent, Malay 13 percent, and Indian 9 percent); religion (Buddhism 33 percent, Christianity 18 percent, no religion 17 percent, Islam 15 percent, Taoism 11 percent, Hinduism 5 percent); and language (English, Mandarin, Malay, and Tamil are all official, and many others are spoken as well).

In many countries with such multicultural tendencies, people isolate themselves into their own social networks. Since 85 percent of people in Singapore live in public housing, the Housing Development Board—essentially the HR department for the island nation—has encouraged multiculturalism by requiring that each housing area reflect the ethnic diversity of the overall population. The policy sets upper limits on block-level and neighborhood-level ethnic proportions and encourages residential desegregation. Because people of different backgrounds live together, they socialize more and break down cultural barriers.[2] Singapore maintains that part of its incredible progress has come from desegregation and acceptance of diverse cultures.

Novartis

Novartis, a global pharmaceutical firm, has a strategy for growth that varies in each country. Its emerging-market operations span more than 50 countries on four continents, each with its own diverse needs, priorities, and challenges. Its

HR leaders have to evaluate the issues that hinder operations success in each nation. Political instability in the Middle East, lack of funding in Jamaica, and extensive corruption in the CIS countries (the former Soviet Union) are prominent examples. Macroeconomic problems like local protectionism and currency volatility also pose external challenges. In addition, a lot of the emerging markets in the Middle East, Asia, the CIS, Central America, and the Caribbean rely heavily on public healthcare; the private market is small, and Novartis must work primarily with governments. Other than regulatory matters, a lot of governments are focused on job creation chiefly through manufacturing.

The company has had a good share of success. For example, in Nigeria it identified a valuable private market segment among the roughly 10 million people who were relatively affluent as a result of the oil industry boom. However, it was dealing with a lot of corruption within the country in the context of the operating environment and faced several internal challenges, including having a number of key local managers with blood ties to tribal warlords, resulting in rampant nepotism! Novartis management decided to clean house and build from scratch and put professional contracts in place. It streamlined the portfolio to target the market segment, cleaned up and expanded the distribution network, assessed and streamlined the local organization, and significantly upgraded local management by bringing in locals who knew the business and who adhered to international standards. The resulting operation ended up being 40 percent ahead of projections in the first 18 months.

In emerging markets Novartis must look outside-in and have key strategic imperatives to build capability both collectively and individually. This means strengthening local talent and moving away from reliance on expatriates. HR executives have seen that if a process isn't owned locally, it won't happen. In addition, in the course of leading the transition to high performance across the board, from the sales team to the management, its HR professionals have found it necessary to keep refining their approach to the market and to be flexible in organizational design to meet particular needs.[3]

What We Mean by Strategic Positioner

In each of the cases described here, the approach to organization practices has a definite outside-in flow. MOL recognized that its talent deficit could be partially solved by investing in secondary and university education, by changing the image of natural sciences, and by creating an enticing employee value proposition. Singapore government leaders recognized that their human capital challenge would be partly solved through immigration—but that would bring in diverse groups that would have to learn to collaborate with each other to be productive. Their public housing policy sets the foundation for this collaboration. Novartis recognized that its global growth strategy required awareness and sensitivity to local conditions. However, its leaders had to bring their values to the local setting and to make sure that their HR work both adapted to and shaped local conditions.

High-performing HR professionals think and act from the outside in. In the past 25 years, the outside-in concept has evolved from knowing the business financials to adapting strategy to serving stakeholders to responding to business conditions.

From 1987 through 2007, our research found (as others have advocated) that HR needs to know the business to be effective. We proposed a business literacy test for HR professionals that would confirm they had the basis for informed dialogues with their business colleagues. These are the questions it addressed:

- Who is our largest competitor and why do people buy from them?
- What is our stock price?
- What is our P/E (profit to earnings) ratio?
- What was the profit and revenue of our division/company last year?
- Who sits on the board of directors? What are the priorities and interests of the different board members?
- What is our market share?
- Is our market segment growing or shrinking?
- What are the emerging technology trends facing our industry?

- What are the top two or three priorities for our business leaders this year?
- Who is our largest customer and why does it buy from us?
- Who are our primary competitors? What do they do better than we do? What do we do better than they do? Which do customers value most?
- What social and political trends might be disruptive to our industry?

We also found that HR professionals did not score high on business knowledge (a mean of 3.37 out of 5.0 in 2002 and 3.39 in 2007). Many, including our group of researchers, have suggested that HR professionals will never be full business partners unless and until they master the business. Without business knowledge, HR professionals cannot fully engage in business-related conversations.

In the 2012 round of research, "knowing the business" evolved into being a strategic positioner. We choose the word *positioner* intentionally. People are often asked about different aspects of their position:

- *What is your position in the family?* This implies your formal birth order among siblings, but also implies the informal role you play in your family.
- *What is your position on a team?* This might refer to your formal assignment, but it also may refer to the informal contribution you make to your team.
- *How do you position yourself for financial security in the future?* In this case, *position* refers to today's investments for tomorrow's opportunities.
- *What position do you hold in your career?* (For example, what is your position at the university?) This may refer to a role or title, but it also may refer to your status or standing in the community.
- *How well are you positioned for success?* This often refers to preparing yourself for future career prospects.

HR professionals acting as strategic positioners help place their organization in the business context in which they operate. *Positioning* here refers to formal products and services as well as informal reputation. Positioning focuses on creating the future as you recognize, anticipate, and take advantage of emerging trends. Positioning requires flexibility and adaptation to discover and then respond to opportunities. Positioning is more than merely transforming your organization; it is about transforming it to fit with and shape future opportunities as defined by your selected markets.

We see four phases of becoming a strategic positioner: acquiring a grasp of finance, strategy, stakeholders, and context (see Figure 3.1). These phases are not discrete; they capture an increasingly complete definition of business, and they developed through several of our research rounds. In our early work, business knowledge emphasized the language of business, which generally focuses on finance but includes any category of business knowledge that is central to a company's business success. Many HR professionals have avoided learning the basics of finance because of fear of or discomfort with math or financial equations. Like people coping with a second language, they must know enough in the new language to get by, even if they don't speak as a native with flawless accent and extensive vocabulary. HR professionals must learn the language of business and pass the business literacy test given earlier. Business knowledge also means a core technical knowledge of the business that can require advanced training (that is, automotive engineering for GM, electrical engineering for Intel, or statistics and logistics for Walmart).

Our work evolved in phase 2 to making sure that *business* also meant a company's strategy and how the organization created a distinct competitive

Figure 3.1   Building blocks of strategic positioning

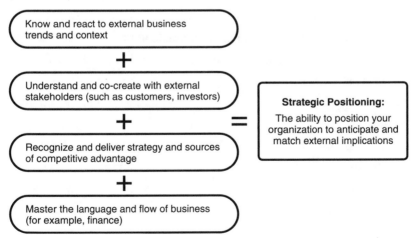

advantage. In 2002, we called this *strategic contribution*, a constellation that consisted of culture management, strategic decision making, fast change, and infrastructure design. In 2002, strategic contribution scored a mean 3.67 out of 5.0 and had a higher impact on business performance than on individual effectiveness. In 2007, we called this domain *being a strategic architect*; at that time it scored a mean of 3.62 and had a moderate impact on both individual effectiveness and business performance.

We furthered our work in phase 3 by focusing HR on external stakeholders: customers, investors, communities, and regulators.[4] HR learned to rely on these external stakeholders to set criteria for effective HR. Customer expectations could shape who is hired and promoted, how performance management is defined, what training and development accomplish, and how leaders behave. We have done a lot of work to validate and demonstrate that collaboration with targeted customers results in sustainable value. In addition to customers, we have advocated that investor confidence ties to intangibles around leadership, talent, and organization. Our research with investors has found that about a third of their confidence in a firm's future earnings derives from their perception of the quality of leadership.[5]

We now move to phase 4, which focuses on what happens when HR professionals know and translate external business trends into internal decisions and actions. They understand the general business conditions (including technological, political, and demographic trends) that affect their industries and geographical regions. Like MOL, the Singapore government, and Novartis, they translate these trends into organization actions.

By mastering these four phases of strategic positioning (know business fundamentals, contribute to and architect strategy, align with external stakeholders, and anticipate external trends), HR professionals contribute to their business not just by being involved in discussions but by proactively positioning their organization to win in the future. Strategic positioning significantly raises the bar for HR professionals. At this point, an HR professional who cannot read and interpret financial statements, contribute to strategy, recognize and serve external stakeholders, and anticipate and react to business trends simply will not fully contribute to business discussions. It is not enough to just learn finance or strategy.

At MOL, the Singapore government, and Novartis, the talent and organization initiatives were successful because HR professionals mastered all four levels of strategic positioning.

The Factors of Strategic Positioner

Based on our legacy studies and current research, we have identified 35 specific knowledge and behavior items that characterize the strategic positioner domain; these 35 items turn out to cluster statistically into three factors (see Table 3.1).

Table 3.1   *Strategic Positioner: Factors, Mean Scores, and Individual Effectiveness and Business Impact*

Factor	Mean Score (Out of 5.0)	Individual Effectiveness	Business Impact
Interpreting the global context	3.83	29%	30%
Decoding customer expectations	3.83	29%	37%
Co-crafting a strategic agenda	3.96	42%	33%
R^2		.332	.062

This table highlights that HR professionals are generally better at cocrafting a strategic agenda (3.96) than at interpreting the global context or decoding customer expectations (3.83). It also shows that cocrafting a strategic agenda is more important to be seen as personally effective than it is in driving business impact (42 percent to 33 percent). Business impact comes more from HR professionals being able to decode customer expectations (37 percent). The strategic positioning typology we present in Figure 3.1 suggests that HR professionals may be personally effective by knowing finance and strategy, but they drive business results more when they work with stakeholders (particularly customers) and business context.

We now turn to the insights and actions of each of these three factors.

Factor 1: Interpreting the Global Context

The traditional media adage, "All news is local," has dramatically and irreversibly shifted. Facebook has become the world's third-largest country, with access to technology replacing geographic proximity as the primary defining boundary. News of the Arab spring, the Occupy Wall Street movement, Greek debt, or Iranian oil policies instantaneously reverberates around the world. Global news flows rapidly along social media. The BBC estimated that when a student shot other students at a U.S. university, about 70 percent of 18- to 25-year-olds worldwide learned about the incident through social media, not traditional media. While people are still interested in what their neighbors are doing, it is increasingly clear that global villages shape their personal lives. Anyone who doubts the reality of the global village should just ask people in their twenties to name their personal and professional friends. Inevitably, the personal cohorts of the rising generation are multicultural and have been generated and sustained through social networking.

HR professionals need to be acutely aware of the complex, changing, and sometimes overwhelming global business settings in which their organizations operate. It is not enough to know your department, your firm, or even your industry. HR professionals need to know the context in which they work so that they can position their organization for the future. These days this requires being business literate, connecting with key stakeholders, and mastering the context.

Being Business Literate

It is difficult to position an organization for the future without fully understanding how the organization operates. Since finance is the universal language of business, any discussions of business literacy must be grounded in finance. HR professionals should be able to interpret an income statement, balance sheet, and financial analyst's report on their organization. They should know how their company creates wealth and how to track wealth creation. Increasing business literacy, like learning a new language, includes many small steps:

- Start every staff meeting by reviewing financial performance data, not just to review the data but to subtly enhance financial literacy among the HR staff. It is also useful to review competitor financials in detail.
- Share the annual industry and competitive presentation presented at the board of directors meeting with the HR team so that team members can master the same information as company leaders.
- Develop a course on "finance for the nonfinancial manager" and invite the HR leaders to teach this course so that they become more comfortable with financial information.
- Record and play the quarterly investor call for the HR staff meeting and other HR professionals.
- Place HR professionals on the distribution list for financial reports and industry trends sent to business leaders.
- Ensure that HR professionals master the logic of their particular business so that they know its core technical requirements.
- Require all HR professionals to enroll in financial training courses and then certify them at least in finance and accounting standards.

For 25 years, we have been somewhat confused by the way HR professionals tend to shy away from mastering the language and logic of business. Like those who move into a new country but avoid learning the local language and logic, these HR professionals will always remain isolated within their own enclave.

Connecting with Key Stakeholders

With business literacy, HR professionals can engage in conversations about the business not only with employees and leaders but with outside stakeholders. In Chapter 1, we propose a stakeholder map for HR professionals to use to guide these conversations. To be a strategic positioner, the HR professional should also connect with customers, investors, and communities in which the organization operates.

Research has shown that about 50 percent of a firm's market value comes from what are broadly called *intangibles*.[6] In our research we have created an architecture for intangibles that includes meeting goals consistently, having a clear strategy, delivering technical competence, and creating organization capabilities. More recently, we have surveyed investors to discover that 29 percent of their investment decisions are based on "quality of leadership" of the companies they invest in—even though they don't have suitable ways to define, operationalize, or track this quality.[7] We believe that an emerging metric for HR will be ROI (meaning *return on intangibles*) because HR professionals position their organization with their investors.

HR professionals can learn about investor expectations in many ways. They can educate themselves by attending investor calls or presentations, by reading analyst's reports on their firm and industry, and by interviewing key industry analysts to find out how they make investment decisions and how they evaluate the firm. More actively, they can include key analysts in the design of training sessions (which both enhances the content taught and increases the analysts' confidence in future earnings). They can also pay attention to how rating agencies (such as Moody's or Institutional Shareholder Services) rate their company—and they can make this information more meaningful to themselves by owning stock in their own company and its competitors.

We have helped HR professionals become more adept at investor positioning by plotting their firm's price/earnings ratio and comparing it to those of competitors over a 10-year period. This is a high-level and somewhat unsophisticated approach to investor insights, but it signals how investors see a company. Table 3.2 reports this price/earnings (P/E) audit of a large global company (XYZ) compared to its top five competitors (A through E). This table shows that this firm's P/E ratio is about 30 percent behind industry average (10 versus 13) and that with a market capitalization of $30 billion, this firm was experiencing about a $9 billion loss from intangible valuation. We often use these types of data as a litmus test for management's commitment to change. Sometimes, when we share these data, leaders are defensive, often blaming the metric or us for sharing it. These leaders will be unlikely to position their firms for future investor confidence. In many cases, however, leaders respond constructively by acknowledging the data and then asking, "How can I make significant improvements?"

Table 3.2   Assessing a Firm's P/E Ratio Versus Its Competitors'

	2002	2003	2004	2005	2006	2007	2008	2009	2010	2011	Average
XYZ	32.6	n/m	n/m	n/m	13.2	7.7	n/m	25.6	13.3	10.1	10.25
A	15.6	15.5	13.1	14.1	13.4	13.6	8.4	18.1	12.0	10.6	13.44
B	16.0	14.0	14.4	14.7	14.7	12.4	11.0	14.8	14.5	11.0	13.75
C	14.1	14.0	15.1	17.5	15.4	12.0	10.8	21.8	15.0	11.7	14.74
D	n/m	28.6	14.7	19.2	11.0	12.6	9.1	18.9	14.5	11.9	14.05
E	14.8	13.0	12.2	12.3	12.8	16.2	6.7	12.2	11.5	10.5	12.22
XYZ Market Capitalization of $30.6 billion								Industry Average			13.075

To do investor positioning, we utilize what we call an intangibles audit. In an intangibles audit, investors and customers are interviewed to find out how well the organization meets commitments, follows a clear strategy, deploys technical competence, and builds organization capabilities.[8] When HR professionals contract for, lead, or facilitate an intangibles audit, they not only learn about finance and investor expectations, they also help leaders position their organization for positive intangible results. In one company, senior executives thought they had outstanding intangibles because they felt they kept promises, had a clear strategy, invested in strong technical core competencies, and developed organization capabilities. However, when they collected information from customers and investors, they found that they grossly overrated themselves as compared to customer and investor perceptions. After initial defensiveness, the CEO focused on building the capabilities most desired by the investors and customers.

Mastering Context

Ultimately, HR professionals who are strategic positioners need the ability to anticipate and prepare for the future. We cocoached (with HR) a leader with responsibility for operations in over 150 countries. He spent a lot of time visiting countries, but he often felt that he did not add value on these visits because he was not grounded in the country. He asked us to help him prepare a template of questions he should ask to diagnose the context of the business in each country. Based on work by Lynda Gratton and others who study the future of work, we framed the six areas outlined in Table 3.3 where he could ask questions and learn about business conditions in that market or industry.[9]

Table 3.3   Assessment and Insights on Business Context

Area of Interest	Diagnostic Questions
Social	What are the social trends (lifestyle, religion, urbanization, family patterns) in this country or industry?
Technological	What ways will technology change this country or industry?
Economic	What are the economic indicators (GDP, unemployment, debt) of a country and how do they affect a particular industry?
Political	What is the political and regulatory climate for a country or industry?
Environmental	What are the environmental trends that shape this country or industry (such as carbon footprint or social responsibility)?
Demographic	What demographic shifts are happening in a country or industry (age, education, global diversity)?

HR professionals can address these questions in a variety of ways. They can help prepare presentations to the governing board about external trends, read industry association forecasts and publications, and study top competitors and anticipate what they will do. They can also keep current with general business publications (such as the *Wall Street Journal*, the *Economist*, or the *Financial Times*), and they can follow the best observers of industry trends (for example, Fareed Zakaria, editor of *Time International* and leader of the TV show *GPS*; Al Jazeera—an excellent source of information on the Middle East—and Mohamed El-Elarian, a frequent commentator on the economy and co-CEO of PIMCO).

Being business literate, connecting with stakeholders, and mastering context help interpret global business context that positions the company in the global marketplace.

Factor 2: Decoding Customer Expectations

Of all potential external stakeholders (investors, regulators, suppliers, and so forth), our research showed that customers deserve unique attention. Obviously, without customers who want and buy products or services, organizations cease to exist. In our research, we observed that HR professionals should decode customer expectations by mastering the following behaviors:

- Understand customer buying criteria.
- Help articulate a customer value proposition that guides internal organization actions.
- Contribute to building the brand of the company with customers, shareholders, and employees.
- Ensure that the culture (firm brand) of the business is recognized by external stakeholders (customers, shareholders, and so on).
- Focus the culture on meeting the needs of external customers.

It turns out that the more customers participate in organization practices and the more organization practices are designed and delivered with a line of sight to the customer, the greater customer intimacy and share. In Table 3.4, we propose a hierarchy of customer-centric organization actions, each of which further binds and bonds organizations with customers.

HR professionals cocreate customer intimacy and guide their organization to customer share by addressing three questions:

1. *Who are our targeted customers?* HR professionals can partner with marketing and sales to segment customers based on revenue, buying patterns, channels, size, and opportunity. We have worked with HR professionals

Table 3.4   *Stages of Customer Intimacy and Organization Actions*

Phases of Customer Connection	Outcome and Application to Gain Customer Share	Impact on Customer Intimacy
6—Culture	*Shared mindset:* Firm brand in the marketplace shapes culture or values in the workplace.	Anticipating or foretelling
5—Leadership	*Leadership brand:* Customer expectations become the foundation of leadership.	Leading or branding
4—HR practices	*HR value added:* Customers participate in managing people, performance, communication, and organization practices.	Aligning or governing
3—Technology	*Technology collaboration:* Customers connect with the company through shared technology.	Information sharing or networking
2—Strategy	*Strategic unity:* Customers help shape strategy or unique sources of competitive advantage.	Partnering or cooperating
1—Product or service	*Market share:* Customers help define products or services of interest to them.	Researching or listening

who build marketing segmentation into training programs so that participants throughout the organization can recognize target customers.

2. *What do the targeted customers value? That is, what are their buying criteria?* HR professionals can help define target customers' value proposition
(price, speed, service, quality, innovation, or value). HR professionals have
trained marketing and sales professionals to do market research and collect
customer value data. When internal employees learn to do market research
(rather than calling in market research consultants), the employees become
more sensitive to customer buying criteria.

3. *How does the organization build sustainable relationships with targeted customers?* HR professionals can facilitate each of the six stages of customer
intimacy outlined in Table 3.4. In particular, HR professionals can audit
and tailor their HR practices to be customer-centric. Customer-centric
HR comes when customers participate in setting hiring standards, interviewing potential job candidates (particularly at senior levels), defining

performance measures, attending training as participants or presenters, allocating financial rewards, participating in communication forums, and governing organization decision making.

To build customer connection, HR professionals partner with sales, marketing, and other functional areas so that the organization offers a unified approach to customer share. We have observed and coached HR professionals to better decode customer expectations by engaging in the following activities:

- Conduct a value chain analysis of your major customers. Include a definition of who the customers are. What are their buying criteria? Whom do they currently buy from? Where are you strongest and weakest compared to key competitors?
- Serve on a cross-functional team whose task is to identify customer buying habits and recommend steps to improve market share.
- Spend time with customers—and their customers. If this is not possible, spend time with sales and marketing staff, review customer feedback, and sit in regularly on call center calls to develop an informed view of what customers are thinking and concerned about. We recommend that HR professionals dedicate about 5 percent of their time to working with customers or their surrogates.
- Review customer performance data to sense customer expectations.
- Work with the marketing department to involve employees more extensively in market research efforts. Ensure that information gathered through such efforts is used to solve customer problems and to improve customer satisfaction indicators.
- Reduce the focus on low-value-added information (internal reports, approvals, paperwork, and meetings) and increase the focus on customer-centric information.
- Buy and use your company's products or services.
- Audit your HR practices and see the extent to which they reflect customer expectations.
- Share customer information throughout the company.

When HR professionals understand customers and decode their expectations to drive organization actions, they help position their organization for future success. As the research reported in Table 3.1 indicates, when HR professionals improve in these areas, they are more likely to help their business be successful.

Factor 3: Cocrafting a Strategic Agenda

As strategic positioners, HR professionals participate in strategic discussions. For many years, HR professionals sought access to strategy forums. They got invited to these meetings, and they talked about how HR would implement strategy; now they have to add value when they cocraft a strategic agenda. A few years ago, an insurance firm sold four major businesses for about $1 billion cash. It was clear the company could not leave $1 billion on the balance sheet or it would be vulnerable to a takeover. It was also clear that the company would likely invest the money in dividends, stock buybacks, or acquisitions. At that point, the HR team could have begun to prepare an acquisition due diligence around organization and talent issues. However, the HR leader focused the HR strategic discussions on reengineering current HR practices. The HR team had not been asked to consider an acquisition possibility, and it didn't bring up the matter on its own. Not surprisingly, a few months later, the company pursued an acquisition. HR was not invited to the early acquisition dialogues, in part because it had not anticipated and prepared for them. The acquisition went forward, but HR was on the outside looking in and wondering why it was not an active partner in business discussions.

As we work with business leaders shaping strategy, we see some common challenges:

- Maintaining strategic simplicity in the face of business complexity
- Preserving strategic agility inside a company in the face of enormous volatility outside
- Encouraging diversity of thinking and unity of action

- Keeping up broad, global, and general strategies alongside granular, local, and specific actions
- Ensuring that strategy implementation is at least as demanding as strategy formulation

As HR professionals contribute to strategy discussions, they need to master competencies that will overcome these challenges and enable strategic work. Our research has identified specific be, know, and do insights that HR brings to strategic dialogues. The chief contribution to business strategy formulation involves helping shape the vision of the future of the business. HR professionals spot opportunities for business success, framing complex ideas in simple and useful ways. In the process, they help identify and manage risk and provide alternative insights on business issues. They translate business strategy into a talent (workforce) or culture (workplace) set of initiatives.

In helping HR professionals turn these personal competencies into the ability to cocraft a strategic agenda, we have found that HR professionals play three roles:

- Storyteller
- Strategy interpreter
- Strategic facilitator

Storyteller

You can do a great deal to create strategic unity with appropriate stories. To simplify strategy so that it creates intellectual direction and emotional support, complex demands need to be stated simply and clearly. Unfortunately, there's a tendency to think that if you can get something onto one page, it is simple and clear—but that's just not the case. We once worked with a company in which the senior team had spent six months hard at work, finally preparing a one-page document that covered vision, mission, values, strategy, goals, objectives, and priorities: some hundreds of words in small print. The team sent this document to more than 50,000 people with a workbook and video to guide its use. Nothing happened. People glanced at it and went on with business as usual. And that company is far from alone. A recent global study of 450 enterprises found that 80 percent felt that their people did not understand their strategies very well.[10]

Rather than trying to list everything that matters, you can make use of one of the most powerful unifying tools—tell strategic stories. Well-told stories make memorable points that lead to action. Stories have a setting (a place and a time to help the audience picture the events), a protagonist (a customer or employee affected by the strategy), an incident (something happens that may be a challenge, a danger, or an opportunity), an outcome (how the protagonist was affected), and a plot line (how the characters in the story got where they were going).[11] Old Navy (part of Gap) has done a marvelous job creating a prototype customer named Jenny, a woman who is in her late twenties or early thirties, shops on a budget, and wants to be smartly dressed. When the company considers product choices, it asks, "How will this affect Jenny?"

HR professionals as storytellers go beyond PowerPoint slides and road shows to craft personal messages that communicate both to the head and to the heart. People often remember the stories more than the facts. This requires having and knowing the company's vision and then turning this vision into a specific experience. CIBC, a leading Canadian bank, is working to improve customer service. It has the requisite customer service statistics and the tagline, "For What Matters." But its communications have far more impact when customers tell their own stories: how the bank helped a newlyweds get their loan for their first house, a business leader receive financial and other support for a start-up company, a major company fund its acquisition strategy.

Strategy Interpreter

In strategy interpretation, the goal of HR is to turn strategy into talent, culture, and leadership—but that takes active participation. After months of striving for access to strategic conversations, an HR professional we know got invited. At the first meeting, the discussion was on capital structure and financial covenants; the second was on globalization strategy in emerging markets; the third was on the stages of innovation to commercialization. All three sessions interested our HR colleague, but he was not sure what to contribute, so he was silent. He was not invited to the fourth session. What could the HR professional have talked about in these sessions? He wasn't an expert on any of the topics under consideration, but he could have been an active contributor by asking insightful questions and probing alternatives about talent, culture, and leadership required to interpret and enact strategy. Any strategy requires the right talent in the right positions to make it happen.

HR professionals can identify the key wealth-creating positions in the company and the requirements for filling these positions. They can open a discussion of the talent risks and opportunities associated with any strategy initiative. A life insurance firm wanted to do business in Vietnam, but the HR professional in charge of staffing the initiative realized that there were very few local Vietnamese actuaries who could help them enter the market. His insights helped the company recognize the talent requirements. Other companies can examine their talent as a way to enter new businesses, discovering what they have to offer to meet previously unrecognized needs. UPS Supply Chain Solutions, for example, grew out of UPS leaders' recognition that their transportation services were an integral part of the computer repair business, so they invested in this talent to build future businesses. UPS now offers all types of services to improve customer supply chains.

But talent is only part of the picture. Some HR professionals are moving to call themselves "human capital specialists" and focus exclusively on talent. We strongly disagree with this approach. We believe that culture, broadly defined, matters as much as talent to sustained business success, if not more. The talent agenda focuses on putting smart individuals in place; culture focuses on building smart organizations that can make optimal use of smart individuals. HR professionals should be cultural anthropologists who observe and shape a work environment that sustains the strategy. They can then weave HR practices around the culture by hiring, promoting, paying, and training employees in ways that reinforce the cultural values. For example, we know of one bank that doubled in size in a two-year window through organic growth and diverse application. The CHRO and her staff were very worried about maintaining and evolving the desired culture. They worked to articulate what culture, or identity, they wanted, how to share this culture with new employees, and how to weave it into all HR practices.

Finally, leadership is a unique subset of talent and a driver of culture. C-suite executives, the top leadership cadre, and high-potential employees set and sustain a direction that others follow. HR professionals can examine the types of leaders required, their skills, their availability, and the ways to increase the pool of leaders.

We now advocate and advise that HR professionals interpret strategy by probing the implications of any strategic discussion on talent, culture, and leadership. When they do so, they cocraft the strategic agenda.

Strategic Facilitator

Managing the strategic process requires care and attention. In the recent economic downturn, most leaders felt increased pressure to perform. Under difficult circumstances, leaders often turn to their primary instincts. Many companies had leaders retreating into increasingly smaller trusted cohorts and making strategic choices with little engagement from others. Those choices had a distressing tendency to fail even when they were well justified and well thought out. Sometimes the process of creating a strategy is as important as the strategy itself. When leaders isolate themselves and issue edicts, they often signal that they are isolating their company from their customers and investors.

At times, this kind of isolation may be necessary for the creation of bold new directions that avoid group-think. But more often, the more people who are appropriately involved in the strategy-making process, the more likely it is that they will be committed to it and thus the better results it will bring.

HR professionals who facilitate strategic processes are very attuned to good governance. Building on a solid foundation of customer and competitive insights, they have clear protocols about what decisions need to be made, who needs to make them, and when they need to be made. They have excellent organization facilitation skills to know when to involve which groups of people. They have insightful political savvy to talk to the right people at the right time to garner support. They have team-building skills to ensure that team members have a clear purpose and strong relationships to facilitate a strategy.

We advise HR professionals who are invited into strategic discussions to be very aware of the processes connected to these forums:

- Are the right people in the room?
- Are the strategic decisions grounded in the empirical reality of customers and competitors?
- Are the conversations in the room the same as those outside the room? (For example, do people talk in hallways or at breaks about different issues than during a formal session?)
- Are the choices being made balancing aspiration and stretch with accomplishment and realism?
- Is the group focused on strategic choices or decisions rather than vague ideals?
- Is there a rational process for taking ideas conceived in the discussion into the organization?
- Who else needs to participate at what level of strategic thinking (for example, creating, implementing, tracking, and investing in the strategy)?
- What follow-up and accountability will there be to make sure that people deliver what they promise?

As HR professionals facilitate strategy, they become ever more integral to the process. The process of strategic positioning communicates the position. When one executive we know demanded that his employees engage in participative management practices, people laughed behind their hands and continued with business as usual; the hypocrisy of this edict created more cynicism than support.

Conclusion: HR Professionals as Strategic Positioners

Most of us have used some version of a global positioning system to find out where we are on the face of the earth. Likewise, as strategic positioners, HR professionals help their organizations know where they fit in the context of

business trends and stakeholders; how they can identify, anticipate, and identify customer expectations; and how they can facilitate the creation of strategy. When HR professionals master these competencies, they gain personal
credibility.

CHAPTER 4

CREDIBLE
ACTIVIST

4

To appreciate credible activism, it's necessary to look at a few examples.

Humana

Humana, headquartered in Louisville, Kentucky, is a leading healthcare company with 40,000 associates in the United States and Puerto Rico. It offers a wide range of insurance products and health and wellness services that incorporate an integrated approach to lifelong well-being. Humana has seized opportunities throughout its history to reinvent itself to meet changing customer needs.

In 2000, Humana had emerged from a failed merger; its stock had plummeted, and costs were rising exponentially. The new CEO, Mike McCallister, called on Bonnie Hathcock, Humana's CHRO, to help create a new strategy to turn things around. Hathcock proved a credible activist indeed. She worked closely with the senior team to create the Humana Leadership Institute, bringing Humana's senior leaders together in a learning forum that engaged them in defining "Humana's dream," an aspiration to be a leader in lifelong well-being that appealed to employees emotionally as well as intellectually, thus evoking excitement and commitment. The dream has become a movement within the company that has energized associates to pursue their own well-being, provided positive outcomes, and become a guiding force for how people are thinking about engaging their customers.

A number of HR-led initiatives in Humana have since demonstrated the power of well-being as a driver of engagement and positive health outcomes. For example, one program demonstrated an increase in associate well-being that reduced obesity over time. The focus on well-being has also led to changes in the workplace and design of workspaces. It has inspired associates to introduce grassroots initiatives ranging from well-being fairs to physical exercise challenges such as stairs and steps campaigns. As a result of these initiatives, Humana engagement scores were above 75 percent. Says Hathcock, "We know that a focus on well-being can bring powerful results to our business, and the research supports this."

The focus on lifelong well-being is now a cornerstone of Humana's new brand identity, and Humana has broadened its focus beyond healthcare costs to preventive care and improving well-being. Said McCallister in a recent interview with *Fortune* magazine (March 2011), "This idea of helping people get to a better spot from the standpoint of well-being is what's going to drive us, and we think that's a business for us."

Olsson Associates

Olsson Associates is an engineering consulting firm. It was founded in 1955 in Lincoln, Nebraska, and by 1987 had grown to approximately 40 employees who provided consulting services to small municipalities throughout its state.

It had also reached a crossroads. It had won its largest project to date— the expansion of a major water treatment plant. This project provided a springboard for growth. Roger Severin, the company's new president, took the opportunity and set about creating a new type of company, combining the best traditions of the firm with new attitudes and practices, effectively, a new culture. Patty McManus Corcoran, the firm's HR director, interviewed consulting firm clients (Olsson's and others) to help define the practices and behaviors that constituted great service. Together with Severin, she embarked on a project to define the kind of company that would most readily attract and retain the individuals who most naturally give great service to clients.

Over the next 10 years, Severin and McManus Corcoran made significant changes, working together. They established a strong team environment. They created opportunities for young high performers to begin to lead projects and services. Even as the company grew rapidly, they preserved the small-firm feel, an open-book financial system, and a profit-sharing and a stock ownership program open to all employees. The results? Throughout the decade of the 1990s the firm made the changes that set the stage for the 2000s. The company now has more than 600 employees, operates nationally through a network of 20 offices, and 88 percent of the firm's work stems from repeat business.

The changes made to create a great service company set the foundation for success, and McManus Corcoran played a critical role; she was named president of the company in 2005. She later took on a new challenge, creating the OA Institute, a training program to help employees become better leaders, understand Olsson values and culture, and obtain everything needed to succeed in their jobs.

What We Mean by Credible Activist

Effective HR professionals are credible activists. Credibility comes when HR professionals focus their time and attention on the issues that matter to the business, do what they promise, meet their obligations and commitments, communicate effectively and build relationships of trust with line managers and other colleagues, and demonstrate a willingness to take professional and personal risks to create value for the business. Hathcock at Humana and McManus Corcoran at Olsson Associates are both excellent examples of the credible activist domain:

- They delivered strong results.
- They built trusting relationships with the CEO and senior team.
- They accepted risk, stepping outside their safety zone to challenge current practices and contribute to a new strategy and priorities for the organization.
- They took an outside-in perspective, identifying opportunities and threats arising from external trends and showing how to take advantage of them. In the case of Humana it was well-being. For Olsson it was creating a higher service culture.
- They contributed actively and directly.
- They continued to grow in contributions as HR professionals and leaders.

Being a trusted advisor helps HR professionals have more productive and satisfying professional relationships; more importantly, without building trust, it is difficult for anyone to have real impact. As activists, HR professionals have a point of view, not only about current HR activities but about the expectations of customers, investors, and other stakeholders and about the role HR can play in meeting these expectations. Credible activists are skilled at influencing others. They do so through homework and analysis—externally and internally—that prepare them to identify key priorities for improvement based on an assessment of opportunity, threat, and vulnerability. They effectively relate the facts and facilitate agreement on a course of action through clear, consistent, and high-impact communications.

Credible activists demonstrate pride in the contribution they make as HR professionals, and they invest in the profession to stay in touch with new ideas and innovations in the field, and to find better ways to improve talent, culture, and leadership. They are identified with the profession and give as much as they get. They are likely to be actively involved in the HR association of their industry or community.

Credibility and Activism

It is the combination of credibility and activism that enables HR professionals to establish trusting relationships with line managers and other colleagues. Individuals who are credible but not activists may be admired for their insight and expertise, but they won't have much impact. Those who are activists but not credible may have good ideas, but no one will pay much attention to them.

The Development of Credible Activism as a Competency Domain

Over the last 25 years, we have seen an intriguing shift in what establishes and preserves HR professional credibility. We can identify three distinct phases:

1. In phase 1, credibility is personal and based on personal relationships with line managers. HR professionals who had good chemistry with line managers and were responsive to managers' needs were the ones seen as having personal credibility. Personal credibility was the central competency in HRCS rounds completed in the 1980s and 1990s.

2. In phase 2, personal credibility moved from the center of perceived competence to a subordinate role in strategic contribution—the new center of HR competence in 2002. It remained important to build positive relationships with line managers and colleagues, but the quality of relationship alone was not sufficient; increasingly, credibility was based on business contribution.

3. Phase 3 began with the credible activist of the 2007 round, or credible activist 1.0. By 2007 performance expectations for HR professionals had evolved and reflected the challenge of operating in a more complex, competitive, and challenging global economic environment. The domain moved from personal credibility to credible *activism*, emphasizing the degree to which HR professionals took greater initiative in setting the HR agenda and contributing to business priorities, based on an understanding of external and internal needs and challenges. Both Humana and Olsson provide excellent examples of credible activism for the business and not just HR by demonstrating HR courage and leadership in taking initiative.

An additional factor was what we called "HR with an attitude," which means that HR professionals take an informed and proactive position about business and HR issues. This proactive stance indicates an increased professional pride in HR, a recognition of the increasingly strategic role that HR plays in business results, and a sense of the opportunities for performance, growth, and development that follows. Both cases demonstrate increased contribution, as well as greater willingness to accept the risk and reward of greater strategic contribution.

We think of the current research as a revising and refining of credible activism for a "new normal." Credible activist 2.0 is a more nuanced description of the domain. The emphasis is plainly focused on building trust by delivering results. Supporting factors support the primacy of performance and initiative in creating business impact: doing the right thing in the right way at the right time with the right people. In addition, the importance of continuous improvement, self-awareness, and self-development has increased and now includes the value of active participation in professional associations. It is not enough to identify oneself with HR; there is a call to greater involvement in progressing the field and staying in touch with innovations in other organizations, regions, and industries. Beyond playing a more strategic role and building better relationships with line managers and HR colleagues, HR professionals need to build their self-awareness of strengths and needs as well as take advantage of opportunities for growth, development, and skills improvement as Corcoran did.

The Elements of Credible Activism

In the last round of the HRCS, the credible activist domain was central to developing a reputation as an HR high performer. In that research, four factors contributed to the category:

1. *Delivering results with integrity:* HR professionals develop a track record by demonstrating the judgment required to define the right priorities along with the skill to address priorities in the right way.
2. *Sharing information:* Sharing information starts with the ability to communicate effectively in person and in writing. It also required building a broad and deep network of relationships across the organization and certainly beyond HR.
3. *Building trust:* Building trust focused on building strong relationships with line and HR colleagues.
4. *HR with attitude:* Activism was the new message of the 2007 research, and it indicated the importance of both credibility and activism or initiative in contributing to the organization.

The Factors of Credible Activism

In the 2012 round, credible activism was again identified as a crucial competency for high performance in HR. However, we also observed some meaningful shifts in what credible activism means and requires. Table 4.1 sets out the constituents of credible activism that emerged in the 2012 results.

Table 4.1   Credible Activist Competency Factors

Factor	Mean	Individual Effectiveness	Business Performance
Earning trust through results	4.36	28%	25%
Influencing and relating to others	4.24	28%	26%
Improving through self-awareness	4.08	26%	30%
Shaping the HR profession	4.13	18%	19%
Overall R²		.405	.056

The most important element of building a reputation for credible activism is earning trust through results, followed closely by influencing and relating to others effectively. Not far behind is the perception of continuous personal and professional improvement: improving through self-awareness and taking action to continue to grow and develop functional and interpersonal skills. Finally, high-performing HR professionals are seen not only to do effective HR but to move their own effectiveness forward in their team, in their organization, and in the broader professional community.

The impact of credible activism on ratings of HR professional performance is, as noted in Chapter 2, significant. This is the domain in which HR professionals in our population score highest. It has the highest mean among the six competencies. We know that the high scores for credible activism are consistent for both HR and non-HR (line) respondents; both HR and line participants recognize its importance.

The position of credible activist as the highest-rated HR professional competency was consistent across regions: it was at the top in every region, in the roles played by HR professionals, and in the ratings of different levels of respondents, and it accounted for the greatest variance in assessing the professional effectiveness of HR professionals. It is the factor that is most associated with personal effectiveness, but it is not the principal correlate with business success; for that, we must look to other competency domains. However, credible activism is the doorway to competency, necessary but not sufficient, the foundation but not the home. As credible activists, HR professionals have access and relationships of trust with their business leaders. The other five domains suggest what HR professionals need to contribute once they engage with business leaders.

Factor 1: Earning Trust Through Results

Perceived professional effectiveness starts and ends with results. High-performing HR professionals earn trust by meeting commitments. Among the four elements that compose the credible activist, this is the factor on which individuals score highest. Evidently, HR professionals around the world have earned trust with their business leaders.

Strong performers in any field understand that meeting commitments is always a balancing act between clarity and consistency of goals on one the hand, and flexibility and agility in responding to change on the other. This is particularly true in HR, where agility is critical: HR professionals operate in a dynamic environment and must both deliver on established goals and also respond to changing priorities; the loss of a major contract may require a sharp right turn in priorities in order to make the organizational and staffing changes needed within a demanding time frame. And when an acquisition is made or the company is purchased, it's all hands on deck.

Earning trust through results has three elements:

1. Set clear expectations
2. Meet commitments
3. Display integrity

Set Clear Performance and Goal Expectations

Results are based on plans, and plans are necessarily dynamic. Effective HR professionals use some form of service-level agreements to preserve consistency and flexibility through regular discussion and feedback. Such an agreement need not be legalistic; in fact, it may be a straightforward as a single sentence: "We will meet monthly to jointly review performance, revise priorities, and identify together ways to improve our performance."

Meet Commitments

Credible activists meet their commitments. They build confidence by keeping their promises, delivering the right solution on deadline. Jane Wakely, chief marketing officer of the Mars Chocolate business, tells the story of a contract HR employee working on a key strategic project who stayed on a key conference call until 15 minutes before going into surgery. An extreme case, but one that built a strong reputation for commitment. Credible activists want feedback, regularly and specifically. They recognize that meeting commitments is in part in the eyes of the receiver. Strong HR professionals are eager to know how they are evaluated and want frequent feedback in order to know how to improve their services and the quality of their relationships.

Credible activists understand that building trust through results is not just focused on the big things; the details matter. Meeting commitments includes basics such as being on time, preparing appropriately, being attentive, and taking the initiative in solving problems or overcoming obstacles.

Display Integrity

Earning trust through results means "doing the right thing in the right way at the right time with the right people." But dig deeper, and integrity—ethics—becomes a critical dimension. As enablers of the culture, HR professionals have a special obligation to act as models of the cultural aspirations of the organization—how employees should act toward customers, suppliers and partners, and one another. Demonstrating personal integrity is a key dimension of credible activism. Business partners who are not confident that HR professionals will conduct themselves with integrity won't give critical or sensitive assignments to HR, and they will tend to limit the relationship to transactional or administrative issues. For strategic issues, people outside HR want to work with professionals they trust and on whose judgment they can rely.

Here are some of the things HR professionals can do to reinforce the ethical principles of the organization:

- Write a code of conduct or statement of ethical values
- Openly identify and discuss *gray-zone issues*. These are ethical issues for which people may not be clear about company policy or the most appropriate behavior, or situations for which there are legitimate differences in point of view about what is most appropriate.
- Regularly review the ethical principles or values of the organization and help people apply them to real situations. Bring up the behavior of other organizations and review their actions through the prism of your company's values. As Kurt Lewin was fond of saying, "There is nothing more practical than a good theory."
- Help individuals understand the consequences of violations to the organization and to colleagues. This has the additional benefit of helping HR professionals (and others) develop a more thoughtful and insightful perspective on the right response, how to deal with similar situations in the future, and what to do if they see problematic behavior.
- Review the behavior of individuals in other companies—competitors and also those in other industries—to help individuals understand the practical implications of ethical principles. For example, show how a lack of teamwork between BP and its contractors, and a lack of rigor in applying company values, led BP to the worst oil spill in Gulf of Mexico history. Or how the drive for return and a lack of focus on its core values led to bankruptcy.

Build Trust

The new research reinforces the fundamental message that trust is a critical dimension of building strong relationships with internal and external stakeholders. For example, David Maister has made a career of understanding the constituents of trust in his work with professional services.[1] He and his colleagues found that building trusted advisory service relationships depended on four elements:

$$\text{Trust} = \frac{\text{Credibility} + \text{Reliability} + \text{Intimacy}}{\text{Perception of Self-interest}}$$

Maister's work nicely combines with the concept of trust through results. Effective HR professionals earn trust by demonstrating the insight, skills, and expertise needed to contribute to business and functional goals (*credibility*), building a reputation and track record for meeting commitments and keeping promises by performing well on accountabilities (*reliability*), establishing effective interpersonal relationships (*intimacy*), and ensuring honesty and clarity in communication. They avoid even the appearance of being manipulative or self-serving in what they do and how they do it.

Test yourself in Exercise 4.1. Using the trust formula, rate yourself and then interview colleagues both in HR and in other departments. It may be difficult for people to answer these questions candidly, but the exercise creates an opportunity to model candor and a willingness to take some risk to improve. As you review the results, identify what you see to be opportunities for improvement on a prioritized basis.

Exercise 4.1   *Evaluating Trust*

Trust Element	Self-Rating (1 = low; 5 = high)	Stakeholder Ratings (1 = low; 5 = high)	Opportunity for Improvement
Credibility			
Reliability			
Intimacy (personal relationships)			
Perception of self-interest			
Average			

For example, many HR professionals find themselves in a situation in which they feel pressured to sell a corporate HR solution. A typical example is a policy that is appropriate in one region but may create problems in another. Here are several ways to deal with the conflict more productively:

- Be clear and explicit about the areas of agreement and disagreement with local preferences.
- Help line management understand the practical implications of the change and realistically assess the problems it may cause, their severity and impact.
- Work with line management to clearly identify the areas where HR may need to revisit aspects of the decision and advocate for a proper review.
- Help line management understands the bigger picture and the corporate logic for the change.
- Ensure corporate HR understands the concerns of local management to the change and advise on what response or change might be most helpful.
- Avoid taking sides. The HR role is to balance enterprise and local needs, not choose one over the other.
- Assess 60, 90, or 180 days after the decision is made and the actions have been taken. Inform both.

Factor 2: Influencing and Relating to Others

Tracy Chastain, divisional HR vice president at McKesson under CHRO Jorge Figuerdo, offers a good example of the second dimension of credible activism in action: influencing and relating to others. Her division of the company identified the need to eliminate 200 information technology jobs. The reduction was necessary, but she wanted to avoid the probable consequences: loss of talented employees, impact on the company's employment brand, a blow to organizational morale (as people wondered, Am I next?), and the stiff financial cost of several millions of dollars in severance. Rather than grit their teeth and send out severance notices, Chastain and her team worked closely with other divisions of McKesson that employed IT staff of their own and identified positions for almost all displaced employees. The cost of relocating people was a fraction of expected severance costs, saving the company almost $10 million. At the same time, employees appreciated the flexibility of the organization and its commitment to people, and the business disruption was minimized. The plan had its challenges and detractors, but Chastain and her team prevailed, addressed the concerns, demonstrated the savings, and persuaded company and business leaders of the positive impact for employees and the community. In the process, she and her team demonstrated the following competencies:

- They took the risk of proposing a more difficult and complex but more effective enterprise solution.
- They did their homework on what would be involved in the plan and reviewed the benefits and costs.
- They anticipated problems and offered and implemented feasible solutions.
- They anticipated obstacles and proposed ways to overcome them practically.
- They took responsibility and accountability.

The trust formula illustrates the importance of building effective relationships with line and functional colleagues. Had Chastain not developed a relationship of trust with the leaders of her business, it is unlikely that they would have taken on the additional demands of finding places for almost 200 people. And had she not built strong relationships with HR colleagues, it is likely that they would have been less helpful in the placement process or less confident that the newly available IT people were good performers.

After earning trust through results, the next most important factor is influencing and relating to others. As the data suggest, high-performing HR professionals build broad and deep relationships up, down, and across the organization and also beyond the organization so as to develop an outside-in perspective on challenges. These relationships are based on the principle of give and get. A sustainable relationship implies consideration on both sides, as would any contract between individuals. HR professionals who build strong reputations as trusted advisors tend to be described as:

- Being committed to the performance of the line managers and teams they work with, demonstrating a genuine, ongoing interest by staying in contact; volunteering useful information; and offering help.

- Providing insight by developing an outside-in perspective and by helping line managers understand the human capital implications of their plans and priorities. They collect information on how competitors are dealing with similar issues as well as the pros and cons of different approaches. They also provide perspective on how top companies deal with similar issues, and they are up to date and attentive to data. For example, they would pay close attention to industry-specific or broader studies of key issues, using databases such as the RBL/Hewitt "top companies for leaders" research to identify needs for improvement in their talent management and leadership development practices.

- Respecting the time of the people they work with, conserving the most precious commodity in organization life today. It is particularly important for HR professionals seeking to influence to articulately and succinctly communicate both in writing and in presentations. If necessary, they make use of organizations such as Toastmasters as a no-risk way to improve their communications skills.

- Working well with others. It's easy to work well with people you like; working with individuals who are challenging or disagreeable is much more difficult. High performers find ways to disagree without being disagreeable. They don't avoid conflict but manage it in a way that preserves and, in fact, builds the relationship. We often say that development is benefited by building on strengths that strengthen others. Working effectively with others and modeling good teamwork certainly fits that category.

- Being willing to take appropriate risk on behalf of the organization. Conflict often implies personal risk, particularly when one challenges the point of view of one's boss or a senior line manager. This risk should not be avoided, but it can be reduced by planning and anticipating areas of disagreement. Risk can be determined by the will to win divided by the fear of failure. Increased risk comes from increasing drive and desire to win and reducing the fear of failure by learning from not punishing mistakes.

Risk can be further reduced when HR professionals demonstrate that they understand the line managers' interests and perspectives, summarize benefits and potential problems, and suggest ways to maximize success for their approach and alternative courses of action. And risk can be additionally reduced when one does the homework to talk in facts rather than hypotheses and biases. Listening and demonstrating understanding through summarizing, paraphrasing, and identifying implications also reduces risk. It should be clear that the goal is the best solution, not winning or losing the argument. This can be demonstrated by focusing on how to make each of the options work.

When it comes to developing relationships that lead to influence, a stakeholder relationship audit is a useful tool. Good HR professionals have a broad base of relationships among HR colleagues, line managers, and other key staff members. The purpose of the map is straightforward: With whom do you have relationships? What relationships do you need that are either absent or not sufficiently strong? And what are your priorities for improvement? Table 4.2 provides an example of what the map might look like for a hypothetical group.

When you make up your own stakeholder relationship map, remember to take the following actions:

- *Seek guidance in identifying the relationships you need to develop and maintain*: You may not have perfect vision—few people know all the individuals who are critical to their performance. Coaching will help, as will checking in with more experienced line and HR colleagues.
- *Ask for regular feedback in improving the quality of your relationships*: Don't assume that because you are in regular contact with someone, your relationship is one of a trusted business partner. Ask yourself, Is my name top of mind when the business partner needs help? And is my circle of influence—invitations to be involved, range of issues—expanding?
- *Think ahead*: Don't focus only on the relationships you need now. Think ahead. Ask yourself: Over the next year or two, what additional relationships will be helpful? How do I best start to build each of these relationships?
- *Define the plan:* How often is contact required? What are the critical agenda items? Do discussions produce results that are implemented and with what

Table 4.2   Stakeholder Relationship Map

Individual	Why Important	Status of Relationship	Improvement Ideas
Bill Smith	Key business partner	Strong	Keep in regular touch
Kermit Havens	CFO	Good	Lunch monthly per his request
Julia Mai	Head of manufacturing	Poor	Attend her monthly staff meeting
Jacqueline Filo	Sales chief	OK but needs to improve given 2012 priorities	Agree on the priorities to address and work with her team to build a shared and supported game plan
Mark Tomosic	Senior R&D pro; not a manager but very influential	Need to establish	Propose a monthly conversation
Jeff Ng	Strong supporter of HR	Strong	Send articles in areas of his interest
Aurelia Lopez	Vocal critic of HR	OK	Help her address her top priority for change

impact? Having identified relationships that need to be reinforced, what does "good enough" look like?

- *Make sure each relationship is two-way:* Consider a partnership agreement that defines what is expected and required on both sides—but with a view toward creating a strong business partnership. For example, Aramco, the Saudi energy giant, recently completed an innovative experiment to reinforce this aspect of credible activism. Having invested in building the business partner skills in HR, the company is now training managers to be effective partners with HR. Aramco has learned that partnership is a two-way process, requiring a two-way skill set.

- *Finally, ask yourself: How do I continue to build a network over time?* A variety of tools can help here. How often do you reinforce your network—for example, by providing information, or articles of interest, or examples of innovative HR practices from other companies? A network is a living organism and must be nourished through sustenance and exercise. In networks we do this through information sharing, interaction, and mutual support.

Factor 3: Improving Self-Awareness

Improving self-awareness is a new factor in the credible activist domain. This is an important addition to the findings of this round. Self-awareness is an obvious benefit in improvement and key to building trust through results and to building stronger relationships as evidenced in ideas like emotional intelligence. But there is a second value: HR takes responsibility for modeling and reinforcing the importance of continuing development and individual career ownership.

Self-improvement is hard. Consider the numbers of people who commit to losing weight or exercising in the new year and the tiny proportion (12 percent) that succeeds.[2] A successful self-improvement plan has five elements:

1. Recognition of the need for change
2. A specific goal, time frame, and plan of action for changing
3. Support before, during, and after taking action
4. Rigorous monitoring of progress
5. Help from a spotter or admired individual who reinforces and supports change motivation and commitment

Self-improvement requires self-awareness and a gut-deep belief in the need to change. But self-awareness is not the same as humility. It is a thoughtful and informed understanding of one's strengths and weaknesses now, and the longer-term strengths that are required to fulfill an ambition. Nietzsche famously wrote, "What doesn't kill us makes us stronger." Less dramatical but no less true is that development always involves risk—time risk, cost risk, performance risk, and career risk. Just as with other forms of innovation, self-development challenges the status quo and arouses suspicion.

Risk needs to be embraced emotionally. But it also needs to be managed and contained. A good rule of thumb is to start where the system is. Risk/

reward analysis teaches us that high risks for indefinite rewards are unlikely to gain traction. There are several ways to reduce the risk of innovation, whether you are innovating in the course of self-awareness development or innovating on behalf of the business:

- *Test the value of the effort:* Ask whether this is what we want to spend precious time and effort on.
- *Be specific and explicit about the goals:* Use "SMART" as an acronym for good goal setting: specific, measurable, ambitious, realistic, time-bound.
- *Collect the right data to get traction on the problem.*
- *Consider contingencies and anticipate areas of difficulty, challenge, and suspicion:* Then recruit help from the stakeholders who will be affected by implementation.
- *Ask for help from business partners:* There is power in asking for help or feedback and in engaging line managers with whom you work by saying, "I am working on improving my business knowledge and would like your help. Would you involve me in pertinent meetings or direct me to colleagues who can help me understand the business and where and how HR can be helpful on a more proactive basis?" This kind of request is rarely refused, and it is doubly useful. Besides the specific information it evokes, it engages line leaders with you and helps build your relationship with them.
- *Celebrate small wins:* Herb Shepard in his "Rules of Thumb for Change Agents" wrote that change means many small fires or small steps.[3] It is much the same in managing your own personal growth and development. These small steps—or as some call them, *small wins*—should be reflected upon and celebrated. They are a source of learning and also a source of strength and conviction.

Personal and professional development is a contact sport, a version of skill acrobatics. And, as in any contact sport, those of us on the field benefit from having a spotter who helps us learn, grow, and keep our balance. Most of the research of the last 20 years points to the virtues of having a mentor. If you have no mentor, get one—someone who can help you translate conditions and make sense of where to put your energies for the benefit of the organization. This is why executive coaching has become a growth industry; this is not at all surprising given the challenge of leadership in these economically dynamic times.

Top organizations use several tools to ensure that HR professionals are aware of their own strengths and needs and that they take active steps to improve and develop. We describe these tools in greater detail in Chapter 9, which focuses on HR professional development strategies. However, it is useful to note some of the most useful tools here:

- *Competency frameworks:* Self-awareness starts with an understanding of a performance standard. The RBL Group/Hewitt research published by *Fortune* magazine points out that over 70 percent of organizations have a competency model.[4] It is essential to make sure that such a standard is in place, used by the organization, and well communicated.
- *Individual development plans:* Performance improvement is a team sport as much as a solitary endeavor. Top organizations ensure high-quality discussions between managers and HR professionals leading to recognition of strengths, identification of specific priorities for improvement, development of plans, and agreement on outcomes.
- *Training:* Training is an integral aspect of ensuring improvement through self-awareness. The best training is active, engaging, and focused on the application of concepts and tools to real situations the professional will face.
- *Communities of practice:* Communities of practice bring together professionals—physically or virtually—with common interests and roles for shared learning.
- *Feedback:* Processes such as 360-degree feedback or the use of tools such as the Myers-Briggs Type Inventory provide self-awareness. When teamed with development planning, this type of information provides a strong foundation for improvement.
- *Coaching and mentorship:* Many organizations are now using internal or external coaches to assist leaders and other professionals as they work to understand how to improve their effectiveness.

- *After-action review (AAR).* AARs were invented by the armed forces to review the impact of an action, identify what went right or wrong, and what could and should be done differently next time. Good AARs use descriptive rather than evaluative terms (that is, "So and so did X," rather than, "So and so failed.") to focus on the behavior of individuals and groups and provide a useful venue for improvement through self-awareness.

- *External experiences.* Finally, external experiences are a critical element of self-awareness. Serving on the board of one's religious institution or a local charity or joining a committee or agency of one's local community can offer a rich source of self-development.

Table 4.3 summarizes the competencies involved in self-awareness and the actions that can be taken to enhance it.

Factor 4: Strengthening the HR Profession

As earlier sections imply, credible activism—like the other competency domains—reflects the outside-in orientation. Knowing "how we do HR in our company" is essential to performance in one organization, but a career that spans multiple companies and industries benefits from an investment in learning how HR professionals in other organizations address problems similar to yours, how they are innovating on behalf of the organization, and the implications of the environmental challenges faced by other businesses and their HR professionals. Without such knowledge, it is unfortunately easy for a star in one company to fail in another, as Harvard professor Boris Groysberg observed of finance professionals.[5]

Strengthening the HR profession involves four actions:

1. *Participating in HR professional organizations.* Strong HR professionals recognize that professional organizations are a unique and rich source of ideas and innovations that can be brought into their organizations and either adapted or adopted as is. We also encourage a mix of physical and

Table 4.3   *Improving Self-Awareness*

Awareness and Self-Improvement Discipline	Potential Actions for HR Professionals	Potential Actions for HR Leaders and Teams
Learning from both successes and failures	Establish a discipline of personal after-action review.	Institute after-action review as a key performance discipline in HR.
Taking appropriate risks (based on a solid awareness of the costs and benefits)	Improve your assessment of risk: what must go right for this to be successful, what could go wrong, ways to monitor and track results, what actions are most likely to put things back on track if a problem occurs.	Practice the discipline of potential problem analysis.
Developing awareness of impact on others, both HR and line colleagues	Utilize 360-degree feedback or another method to improve your knowledge of how others experience you.	Install a data-based competency model and employ 360-degree feedback on an annual basis as part of the overall performance management and development process in HR.
Having a personal leadership brand that helps focus learning and self-improvement	Define how you want to be perceived by HR and line colleagues, and use your definition to help you focus on priorities for improvement.	Make sure every HR team member has a personal leadership brand and an associated development and improvement plan.

virtual membership. For example, websites like RecruitingBlogs.com offer social networking opportunities for individuals who focus on staffing and recruiting.

2. *Improving the skills of HR colleagues.* The best learners are also teachers. Investing in building the skills of HR colleagues requires individuals to be clear and disciplined about a topical area, tool, or technology.

3. *Building a strong external network of relationships.* How robust is your network? Do you have the range and depth of relationships that allow you to quickly collect the information you need and feel confident of its accuracy? If not, you may wish to work on your network, enhancing your understanding of how HR in other organizations is innovating.

4. *Becoming involved in key HR community events.* It is rare that a week or two goes by without an opportunity for HR professionals to listen to well-known human capital writers or senior HR executives speak about their work and challenges. Beyond public sessions, TED or other news media present a variety of online or virtual opportunities. We encourage you to participate, and to do so with colleagues—allowing the event to inspire a discussion of the implications and applications of what the speaker said. Cast a wide net: websites and blogs abound, authored in a variety of countries and enabling HR professionals to learn firsthand how strategic HR is practiced in different industries and different parts of the world. Some websites include:

- TED for video speeches and interviews with entrepreneurs and experts in a variety of fields
- EO—Entrepreneurs' Organization for perspective on what entrepreneurs are thinking
- *McKinsey Quarterly*, a good source of new ideas from the consultants and leaders at McKinsey (and most other firms have equivalent sites)
- *Marketwatch*, a top business website
- *Frontline*, an excellent business show
- *Hoovers'*, for information on company news and key events
- *Career Journal,* which provides a perspective on who's hiring, and for what
- *Motley Fool*, an entertaining but also serious website with information about companies from an investment perspective
- *Vault*, for perspective on how people describe their companies as employers
- *Multexinvestor.com*, for information on research reports

Psychologist Stanley Milgram offers an interesting metaphor for involvement in the larger community of HR practitioners. He completed a well-known series of experiments to identify the "degrees of separation" between individuals: how many relationships it would take to get a postcard from one person to another across the country whom the originator did not know.[6] Facebook recently revisited the research and found that social media had further reduced the "degrees of separation" between individuals from an average of 5.5 or 6 connections (hence, "six degrees of separation") to under 5 connections. Through utilities like Facebook and LinkedIn, the world is becoming smaller. The question for HR professionals: Is your world small enough and your professional network robust enough to enable you to find the information and guidance you need quickly and accurately? If not, reduce your professional "degrees of separation" by investing in expanding your external network.

Conclusion

HR professionals need to be credible activists if they are to excel in their work. In particular, the strategic positioner domain more or less requires strength in the credible activist domain too, so that people will pay attention when HR professionals set out to help their organizations understand and identify the key external trends that shape business opportunity and threats. Effective HR professionals build credibility through results, establishing relationships of trust, and growing the self-awareness to know when, how, and with whom to act.

CHAPTER 5

CAPABILITY BUILDER

5

How long does it take to get a feel for the atmosphere of a restaurant, grocery store, church, or bank—or business unit of your organization—when you walk through the door? Moments, usually. This intuitive feel may be labeled many things: culture, climate, work environment, expectations, unwritten rules, ambiance, brand, identity. Regardless of what it's called, it is real, and it affects both how customers feel about doing business with a place and how employees feel about working there.

HR professionals can key into this informal intuition and help create the right organization—that is, an effective and engaging organization that does what is needed—by becoming what we call "capability builders." In the last 20 years, we have worked with leaders from dozens of companies to define and deliver the right organization. Examples come from around the world and across the gamut of business:

- The International Labor Organization (a specialized agency in the United Nations system) has worked to instill a sense of performance accountability so that associates do what they promise and meet deliverable deadlines.
- General Electric leaders have worked to create an identity of innovation, imagination, and invention across the company's wide array of businesses.
- Harrah's has worked to build a customer service mentality among all employees that distinguishes the customer experience from that in other casinos.
- NAB, a leading Australian bank, has focused on building a reputation for "fair value" in terms of products and prices.
- Quintiles, a pharmaceutical firm doing clinical research and consulting, has emphasized corporate social responsibility and customer connection as its cultural differentiators.

- MTN, a leading African telecommunications provider, has focused in the one- to three-year time frame on the capabilities of speed and talent, and in the longer term on shifting to leadership and learning.

All organizations—big and small, public and private sector, global and local, corporate and divisional—find value in defining and delivering a distinct atmosphere that affects employees, customers, and investors. This chapter reviews the history and power of the concept, clarifies and defines it, and shares our research findings. Then it offers specific actions HR professionals can take to become capability builders in their own right.

What We Mean by "Capability Builder"

In *The Visible Hand,* business historian Alfred Chandler captures the role of management in creating organizations that respond to invisible market forces. He points out that since the industrial revolution, organizations have been essential in shaping and delivering a business's strategy.[1] To help HR professionals build the right organization, it is useful to ground their understanding of the "right organization" in a brief historical review of organization thinking. This is given in Table 5.1.

Following the logic in Table 5.1, HR professionals help create the right organization by making it more efficient through reengineering work, by clarifying roles and responsibilities through organization design choices, by aligning and integrating systems through organization audits, or by defining and delivering the right capabilities through cultural audits.

Organization capabilities represent what the organization is known for, what it is good at doing, and how it patterns activities to deliver value. We admire organizations less for their efficiency, morphology, or systems than for their capabilities. The capability approach to organizations builds on other approaches. For the systems movement, capabilities represent the unifying maypole that joins separate systems. For the morphology or bureaucracy movement, capabilities represent the outcomes of the organization design.

Table 5.1 Approaches to Creating the Right Organization

Theme of the Organization Movement	Founding Authors	How to Characterize an Organization	Focus of Organization Improvement	Current Applications
Efficient →	Frederick Taylor	Machine with parts	Standard operating procedures	Reengineering to drive efficiency
Bureaucracy →	Max Weber, Alfred Sloan	Morphology and shape defined by looking at clear roles and specialization	Clear accountability with roles and responsibilities	Multidivisional firm; strategic business units; matrix; delayering
Systems thinking →	Bob Katz and Daniel Kahn, Jay Galbraith, Dave Nadler and Mike Tushman, Dave Hanna	Organization aligned to environment; integrated systems within the organization aligned	Systems connected to each other (as with sociotech); organization diagnosis of systems	Customer-centric organizations, horizontal organization, organization audits
Capability	C. K. Prahalad, George Stalk, Bob Kaplan and Dave Norton, Dave Ulrich and Norm Smallwood	Capabilities within the organization	Diagnosing and investing in key capabilities	Cultural audits, process improvements

For the efficiency movement, the capability logic broadens the outcomes of organizations beyond efficiency. Shaping the right organization through a capability lens synthesizes four current approaches to organization assessment (see Figure 5.1).

Creating the right organization through a culture perspective means finding the right organization values, norms, or patterns (see Table 5.2 for examples of a culture view of organizations).[2] Creating the right organization through a process lens means identifying and improving key processes such as new product development, continuous improvement, product diversification, orders to remittance, innovation, and so forth. These processes often stand out through balanced scorecard assessments of organization alignment.[3,4,5] Creating the right organization through core-competencies logic focuses on upgrading functional activities like R&D, manufacturing, quality, marketing, supply chain, HR, and information technology.[6] Creating the right organization through a resource view means identifying key resources that an organization possesses to create value.[7] The capability logic synthesizes and advances these approaches to enable HR to create the right organization.[8]

Figure 5.1   *Organization capability synthesis*

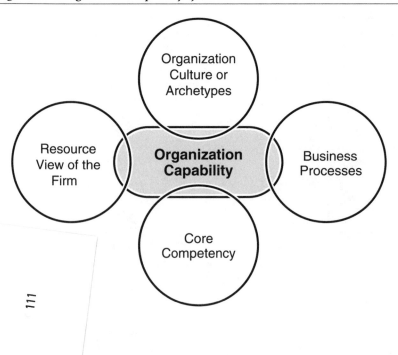

Table 5.2   *Organization Cultures or Archetypes*

Dan Denison	Bob Quinn	Henry Mintzberg
Four major cultures (and, not shown, twelve subcultures): • Mission • Consistency • Involved (people) • Adaptability	Four competing values: • Create (adhocracy) • Compete (market) • Control (hierarchy) • Collaborate (clan)	Five major archetypes: • Entrepreneurial • Bureaucratic • Professional • Divisional (diversified) • Innovative ("adhocracy")

The capability perspective was introduced in the 1990s and has evolved since to become a top priority for HR professionals and business leaders.[9,10] In this perspective, HR professionals define, audit, and improve the key capabilities required for success. Nearly 60 percent of 1,440 respondents to a 2011 McKinsey survey of senior business leaders say that building organizational capabilities is a top-three priority for their companies.

Companies can gain a competitive advantage by building foundational capabilities. . . . Companies need to be more deliberate in understanding which capabilities truly impact business performance.

—*McKinsey Quarterly*

In recent years, several lists of generic and possible capabilities have been published. George Stalk has proposed that organizations might have capabilities of speed, consistency, acuity (ability to see the competitive landscape), agility, and innovativeness.[11] Korn Ferry, the consulting firm, proposes that capabilities build strategic effectiveness and has boiled down 20 capabilities into seven categories[12]:

• Strategy execution
• Managing innovation and change
• Attracting, retaining, and motivating talent

- Leveraging a productive culture
- Managing profitability and delivering value
- Developing future leaders
- Governance

Ulrich and Smallwood identified 10 core capabilities that organizations might possess and subsequently have added to this list.[13]

HR professionals create the right organization when they define, diagnose, and deliver the right organization capabilities. Being a capability builder matters because capabilities outlast any individual leader, and they establish an organization's identity that endures over time.

The Factors of Capability Builder

For 20 years we have been studying organization capabilities. In this round of the research, we identified possible capabilities (or cultures) that an HR professional might foster. In all, we found 18 competencies clustered into three factors that defined how to become a capability builder. These factors, their mean scores, and their impact on individual effectiveness and business success are outlined in Table 5.3.

Table 5.3   Capability Builder: Factors, Mean, Individual Effectiveness, and Business Impact

Factor	Mean Score (out of 5.0)	Individual Effectiveness	Business Impact
Capitalizing organization capability (7 items)	4.03	36%	32%
Aligning strategy, culture, practices, and behavior (8 items)	3.94	36%	37%
Creating a meaningful work environment (3 items)	3.94	28%	31%
R^2		.31	.074

These results indicate three areas where HR professionals can improve to become capability builders and help create the right organization. First, they can capitalize on organization capability, which means that they do capability (organization) audits to determine which capabilities are the most important given the organization's strategy, stakeholders, and context. This ability helps HR professionals be seen as individually effective, and it contributes to business success. Second, they can create a line of sight between strategy, culture, and individual behavior. Our research shows that this ability has even more impact on business success. Third, and possibly an emerging trend, HR professionals can help create a meaningful work environment. At present, HR professionals are somewhat better at diagnosing required capabilities than establishing them or creating meaningful work settings. The results also show that the ability to align strategy to culture to behavior has the most impact on business performance.

The following sections discuss processes and tools to improve in each of these areas.

Factor 1: Capitalizing on Organization Capability

Organizations must be designed to help deliver strategy. To do so, HR professionals and business leaders should focus on an organization as a set of capabilities rather than as processes, structures, or systems. As leaders define their strategic direction, they should also be disciplined about the capabilities required to get there. Focusing on organization capabilities ensures that desired strategies are realized. HR professionals should be able to do organization audits through five steps:

1. *Select the organization element in which the organization audit should occur.* This element might be the entire organization or a business unit, region, or plant. Any group that has a strategy with financial and customer results can and should do an organization audit—but it can't be a bottom-up effort. An organization audit must be sponsored by the leadership team of that element. For example, if you want to audit the entire company, you need the

board of directors or a senior leadership team to sponsor the project. HR executives may be the architects of the audit, but it needs to be owned and sponsored by the unit's leader or a transformation team.

2. *Create the content of the audit.* Content deals with the dimensions that should be audited. We have proposed 13 generic capabilities (see Exercise 5.1). The team designing the audit should take these generic capabilities and adapt them to the requirements of the organization. Identify the range of organizational capabilities required for delivering on strategic promises that go beyond the 13 we delineate. One approach to capturing the espoused capabilities involves reviewing company public documents, executive speeches, minutes of executive committee meetings, advertising, and media reputation indexes. Doing content analysis of these public documents enables the HR professional to document the existing espoused capabilities. This list needs to be put into words and phrases tailored to the organization. The result of this effort will be an organization audit template that suggests specific capabilities related to the organization unit being audited.

3. *Collect data from multiple groups on the current and desired status of the capabilities being assessed.* This information may be collected by pursuing a variety of patterns:

   - *90 degree.* Collect data from only the leadership team of the unit being audited. This is the quickest method, but it is often deceptive because the leadership team's self-report may be biased.

   - *360 degree.* Collect data from many groups within the company. The assessment of different groups may tell a very different story depending on how each group sees the information.

   - *720 degree.* Collect information not only from inside the company but from groups outside the company. External assessors might include investors, customers, or suppliers. These external groups become important because, ultimately, they are the groups that will determine if the organization has intangible value. We particularly like to interview key customers to determine the capabilities they desire and the capabilities they observe in the company.

Exercise 5.1   *Capability Audit of Generic Capabilities*

How effectively do we currently perform on each of the following 13 capabilities?	How Effective Currently (1 = low; 5 = high)					2–3 Most Critical (Check which)
	1	2	3	4	5	
Talent: We are good at attracting, motivating, and retaining competent and committed people.	☐	☐	☐	☐	☐	☐
Speed: We are good at doing things fast, with agility, adaptability, flexibility, cycle time, responsiveness.	☐	☐	☐	☐	☐	☐
Shared mindset: We are good at managing or changing our culture, which may involve doing transformation of firm identity, firm equity, firm brand, shared agenda.	☐	☐	☐	☐	☐	☐
Learning: We are good at generating and generalizing ideas with impact through knowledge management and sharing best practices.	☐	☐	☐	☐	☐	☐
Collaboration: We are good at teamwork, working across boundaries, doing merger integration, and sharing information.	☐	☐	☐	☐	☐	☐
Innovation: We are good at administrative, product, channel, or strategic innovation.	☐	☐	☐	☐	☐	☐
Accountability: We are good at establishing rigorous performance principles that set clear performance expectations and hold people accountable for results.	☐	☐	☐	☐	☐	☐
Leadership: We are good at building leadership depth through the company and embedding leaders at all levels who build confidence in the future.	☐	☐	☐	☐	☐	☐
Strategic unity: We are good at articulating and sharing a strategic point of view, a strategic agenda, and shared strategic priorities.	☐	☐	☐	☐	☐	☐
Efficiency: We are good at reducing costs without affecting quality through redesign, reengineering, or restructuring.	☐	☐	☐	☐	☐	☐
Customer connectivity: We are good at customer relationships with a customer-focused organization and customer intimacy.	☐	☐	☐	☐	☐	☐
Social responsibility: We demonstrate good corporate citizenship by managing our carbon footprint, philanthropy, and values.	☐	☐	☐	☐	☐	☐
Risk: We are good at managing risk by attending to disruption, unpredictability, and variance.	☐	☐	☐	☐	☐	☐

4. *Synthesize the data to identify the most critical capabilities requiring managerial attention.* The data from the audit need to be condensed into key messages and then translated to action. This requires looking for patterns in the data and picking no more than three capabilities that require leadership attention to deliver strategy goals. Getting to a few focused capabilities requires prioritizing and identifying which capabilities will have the most impact and be the easiest to implement.

5. *Assign teams to deliver critical capabilities by putting together an action plan with steps to take and measures to monitor.* This capability plan should be focused and timely. Once the critical capabilities are identified, design a consistent process for defining and delivering that capability. We have seen companies bring the senior team together for a half-day meeting (often facilitated by HR) to cover the following points on critical capabilities:

   - *Definition of capability:* What must we accomplish through the capability of speed, talent, or collaboration? This should be a statement with a clear outcome that can be measured and tracked.

   - *Decisions about accomplishing capability:* What are the decisions we can make immediately to foster this capability?

   - *Measures to track and monitor capability:* How will we monitor our progress in attaining this capability?

   - *Actions that can be taken to deliver capability:* What can we as leaders do to invest in this capability? Our menu of actions might include education or training events, staffing and assigning key people to a project or task force, setting performance standards for those responsible for the capability, creating task forces or other organization units for those doing the capability work, sharing information across boundaries, and investing in technology to sustain the capability.

We have found that the best capability plans have a 90-day window. That is, they identify specific actions and results that will happen within 90 days to demonstrate that capability development is under way and ensure a disciplined gate process that encourages accomplishment. This rapid-cycle action will drive significant and immediate progress in the organization.

Lessons Learned from Capability Audits

As we have worked with dozens of companies to do capability audits, we have learned some practical lessons that will help HR professionals become capability builders. No two audits will look exactly the same, but our experience has shown us that, in general, there are good and bad ways to approach the process. We recommend a few guidelines:

- *Get focused.* It's better to excel at a few targeted capabilities than to diffuse energy over many capabilities. This means identifying which capabilities will have the most impact considering the resources required and prioritizing accordingly. The remaining capabilities identified in the audit should meet standards of industry parity. Investors seldom seek assurance that an organization is average or slightly above average in every area; rather, they want the organization to have a distinct identity that aligns with its strategy.
- *Learn from the best.* Compare your organization with companies that have world-class performance in your target capabilities. It's often helpful to look for analogous industries where companies may have developed extraordinary strength in the capability you desire. For example, lodging businesses and airlines have many differences, but they're comparable when it comes to several driving forces: stretching capital assets, pleasing travelers, employing direct-service workers, and so on. The advantage of looking outside your own industry for models is that you can emulate them without competing with them. People in those industries are far more likely than your top competitors to share insights with you.
- *Create a virtuous cycle of assessment and investment.* A rigorous assessment helps company executives figure out what capabilities will be required for success, which helps them determine where to invest. Over time, repeating the assess-invest cycle results in a baseline for benchmarking.
- *Compare capability perceptions.* Like 360-degree feedback in leadership assessments, organizational audits may reveal differing views of the organization. It's instructive, for example, when top leaders perceive a shared mindset, but employees or customers do not. Involve stakeholders in improvement plans. If investors rank the firm low on a particular capabil-

ity, the CEO or CFO may meet with the investors to discuss specific action plans for moving forward.

- *Avoid underinvestment in organization intangibles.* Often, leaders fall into the trap of focusing on what is easy to measure instead of what is most in need of repair. They read balance sheets that report earnings, economic value added (EVA), or other economic data, but they miss the underlying organizational factors that would add value.

- *Don't confuse capabilities with activities.* An organizational capability is a bundle of activities, not any single pursuit. So leadership training, for instance, needs to be understood in terms of the capability to which it contributes, not just the activity that takes place. Instead of asking what percentage of leaders received 40 hours of training, ask what capabilities the leadership training created. Attending to capabilities helps leaders avoid looking for single, simple solutions to complex business problems.

Looking Ahead

HR professionals become capability builders when they can do organization audits that have clear capability results. Like any skills development effort, organization audits often start small, allowing their sponsors to learn from experience. This means that early capability-building efforts might focus on a smaller division or function, or on an external organization (such as a non-profit or community organization).

Factor 2: Aligning Strategy, Culture, Practices, and Behavior

Most aspiring HR professionals want to contribute value, and they work hard to do so, attempting to align their personal work with business goals. In both our research and our professional work, however, we have found that having a line of sight from business context to strategy to capability to HR practice to individual behavior to metrics is easier said than done. After years of experimenting and practicing, we have found a seven-step process that works—something HR professionals can follow to gain strategic alignment. At the heart of this process is the definition of capability. The process follows the seven steps shown in Table 5.4. The seven steps are described in the table in terms that make a generic template for strategic HR alignment. However, they can be tweaked to include specifics, depending on the situation.

Table 5.4 *Steps to Aligning Strategy, Culture, HR Practices, and Behavior*

Steps/Questions	Activities	Outcomes
1. **Business:** Where will we do a strategic HR linkage?	Select the business for which you want to create a strategic HR linkage. This business probably has a unique strategy and set of performance indicators.	Specify a business where a strategy-HR linkage can occur.
2. **Environment:** What are the business trends?	Define the business context: • Identify major trends in the environment that will affect your organization in the future. • Examine expectations of each of the key stakeholders.	Articulate the external environmental and stakeholder conditions that will shape the industry and organization.
3. **Strategy:** What are the strategic drivers for the business?	Specify the strategy required to respond to external conditions: • What is your business trying to accomplish? • How will your business best serve customers? • What are the strategic choices and scorecards that you will have to guide those choices?	Prepare a clear and simple statement of forward-looking strategy with vision, mission, goals, and priorities.
4. **Organization:** What do we need to be good at as an organization?	Identify, audit, prioritize, and define key organization capabilities: • Select the top two or three capabilities. • Prepare behavioral descriptors for each one.	Prioritize the top two or three capabilities for strategic success.
5. **HR investment:** What are HR priorities?	Prioritize and invest in key HR practices: • Create a typology or menu of HR practices that can be used to reach outcomes. • Generate alternative HR practices. • Prioritize critical HR practices. • Make investment choices on critical practices (cost-benefit analysis).	Prepare a set of critical HR practices that must be implemented in order to accomplish the deliverables.

(continued on next page)

Table 5.4   *Steps to Aligning Strategy, Culture, HR Practices, and Behavior (continued)*

Steps/Questions	Activities	Outcomes
6. **Action plans:** Who will do what, when, where, and how?	Prepare specific action plans (who, what, when, where) for accomplishing HR priorities.	Commit to an action plan with detailed tasks, responsibilities, resources required, time frames, and so on.
7. **Measures or metrics:** How will we measure our progress?	Define a scorecard with measures and metrics to track success, particularly about key capabilities.	Ensure that measures are in place to track progress on both activity and the results of the activity.

As HR professionals lead their management teams through the seven steps provided in Table 5.4, it is important for them to make sure that they facilitate informed and candid conversations that lead to the outcomes for each step. Often, this means a one- or two-day workshop where line managers and HR professionals create a clear line of sight between business context and managerial actions. It is also important to go sequentially and *not* jump into the HR priorities without performing the earlier steps. Our research and experience show that gaining management buy-in to the importance of capabilities (or culture) is at the heart of this process.

We have taken hundreds of management teams through these seven steps. Here are some tips for making the process work:

1. *Business:* Where will we do a strategic HR linkage?
   - Require clarity about the business strategy and structure: is the business a single entity, holding company, or diversified company?
   - Get the management team to agree to where the business is today and where it is headed in the future.

2. *Environment:* What are the business trends?
   - Invite in, read, or learn from industry or country futurists who can anticipate what might happen in the future.
   - Prioritize environmental trends in terms of probability of occurrence and impact on the business.

- Consider second- and third-order consequences of the trends.

3. *Strategy:* What are strategic drivers for the business?
    - Gain clarity around vision by asking each team member to answer the question, "In 20 words or less, where is our business headed?" Work to gain consensus.
    - Identify key choices that must be made concerning products, customers, finance, operations, and organization given the future direction.
    - *Organization:* What do we need to be good at as an organization?
    - Do an organization audit with the senior company leaders by asking them what the organization needs to be good at and known for.
    - Also collect data from key customers and investors outside the company.
    - Prioritize the top two or three capabilities and then offer behavioral descriptors for them.

4. *HR investment:* What are HR priorities?
    - Have a methodology to prioritize HR practices. One useful grid is to plot the HR initiatives on impact (low to high) and ease of implementation (also low to high). You can then see which initiatives should get the most attention.
    - Have members of the management team divide 100 points into the possible HR priorities.
    - Sequence the priorities to see which should come first.

5. *Action plans:* Who will do what, when, where, and how?
    - Make sure that individuals all recognize how their own behavior will change as a result of the strategic HR work. Ask people to be very concrete about what they will stop, start, and continue.
    - For the prioritized HR initiatives, create clear accountabilities with deadlines and consequences.

6. *Measures or metrics:* How will we measure progress?
    - Ask team members what they would see more of and less of if the HR priority were implemented. Turn these statements into standards.
    - Invite all members of the management team to publicly declare what they will do and how they will be measured on it.
    - Track and post key metrics so that there is follow-up and accountability.

HR professionals who facilitate an alignment process have the ability to build capability because the desired capabilities become the lynchpin of the strategy HR process.

Factor 3: Creating a Meaningful Work Environment

We are both surprised and not surprised that in this research the capability of creating a meaningful work environment was a unique factor in becoming a capability builder. It was a new development, but the concepts associated with meaning are becoming pervasive in the individual psychology and marketing literature. In Table 5.6 we show that on the psychology side, thought leaders like Marlin Seligman at the University of Pennsylvania are demonstrating that lasting happiness comes from finding meaning, not just performing activities. In the marketing world, thought leader Phil Kotler has a very similar evolution of marketing toward values-driven marketing, where the goal of a campaign is to make the world a better place. We show the parallels of these works on employee connection in Table 5.5. In Table 5.6 we summarize thought leaders who are moving beyond engaging employees with concepts like wellbeing, flourish, drive, mojo, and the why of work.

Table 5.5   *Pervasiveness of Meaning*

Psychologist Happiness Factors How do we help people find happiness?	Employee Connection Factors How do we help employees feel connected to work?	Marketing Customer Connection How do we build customer intimacy?
Martin Seligman	Dave and Wendy Ulrich	Phil Kotler
Pleasure Sensual enjoyment	Satisfaction Like your job or work	Product Sell products (market share)
Engagement Lost in the flow of an activity	Engagement Give discretionary energy to the job	Customer Satisfy and serve key customers (customer share)
Meaning Connected to deeper values	Meaning Find purpose and abundance at work	Value-driven Make the world a better place (emotional share)

Table 5.6   Illustrative Drivers of Meaning at Work

	Daniel Pink	Tom Rath (Gallup)	Martin Seligman	Marshall Goldsmith	Dave and Wendy Ulrich
Core book	Drive	Well-being	Flourish	Mojo	The Why of Work
Core premise or question	What motivates people?	What would your best possible future look like?	How do people find happiness in their lives?	How do we attain a balanced life and career?	How do people find abundance in their professional and personal lives?
Key factors	Autonomy Mastery Purpose	Career Social Financial Physical Community	Positive emotion Engagement Relationships Meaning Accomplishment	Identity Achievement Reputation Acceptance	Identity Purpose Relationships Work environment Work challenge Learning Delight

The meta-message is increasingly clear: people today in countries around the world want more from their jobs than work; they want work with a purpose. HR professionals, who build sustainable capabilities, need to help all employees find personal meaning from the work that they do.

To create meaning as a capability, we suggest that HR professionals assess the current abundance in their organization using a scale like the one in Exercise 5.2 below. Once the meaning benchmark is set, they can engage in the following activities to increase it:

- Shape an identity by helping people recognize what they want to be known for and to connect that identity with the corporate identity.
- Prepare a compelling purpose by articulating the organization's aspirations in emotional terms.
- Encourage positive relationships at work by helping employees make and form relationships, which may focus on common interests, managing conflict, and cooperation.
- Create a positive work environment by sharing information, being transparent, and setting clear standards.
- Establish the appropriate work challenges around what work is done, where it is done, and how it is done.
- Help people learn from successes and failures.
- Urge people to have fun and find delight at work.

HR professionals can have conversations around these issues and then coach leaders in being meaning makers. They can also design and deliver HR practices with these criteria in mind—and then role-model these meaning-making activities.

Think of the organization in which you work as you complete the assessment in Exercise 5.2. In a small company, this would be the entire organization; in a large company, it would be a division, plant, geography, or other work unit.

If your score is between 85 and 105, you are in an abundant work setting. Relish it, and work to make it last.

Exercise 5.2   Assessment of the Abundant Organization

Principles of Abundant Organizations	Abundant Organization Questions To what extent does my organization:	Assessment (1 = low; 5 = high; circle which applies)
Identity: What are we known for? Build on strengths (capabilities in an organization) that strengthen others.	1. Have a clear identity concerning what we are known for that is shared by those inside and outside the organization.	1 2 3 4 5
	2. Focus on key individual strengths (or organization capabilities) that distinguish us in our markets.	1 2 3 4 5
	3. Encourage employees to use their signature strengths at work to strengthen others.	1 2 3 4 5
Purpose and direction: Where are we going? Have purposes that sustain both social and fiscal responsibility.	1. Communicate its social purpose and organizational direction with clarity and consistency.	1 2 3 4 5
	2. Match employees' personal goals with the organization purpose.	1 2 3 4 5
	3. Help employees achieve what motivates them.	1 2 3 4 5
Teamwork and relationships: How well do we travel together? Go beyond high-performing teams to high-relating teams.	1. Bring team members together to solve problems and make decisions.	1 2 3 4 5
	2. Foster teamwork that delivers creative outcomes.	1 2 3 4 5
	3. Enable people to form positive relationships and resolve conflict.	1 2 3 4 5
Engagement and challenging work: What challenges interest employees? Engage not only employees' heads (competence) and hands (commitment) but also their hearts (contribution).	1. Encourage employees to choose work projects that challenge them.	1 2 3 4 5
	2. Allow flexibility in how work is done.	1 2 3 4 5
	3. Help employees see how their work positively impacts others.	1 2 3 4 5

(continued on next page)

Exercise 5.2   Assessment of the Abundant Organization (continued)

Principles of Abundant Organizations	Abundant Organization Questions To what extent does my organization:	Assessment (1 = low; 5 = high; circle which applies)
Effective connections: How do we demonstrate a positive work environment?	1. Demonstrate a positive rather than a cynical work environment.	1 2 3 4 5
Create work cultures that affirm and connect people throughout the organization.	2. Use time and space to build patterns of affirmation and connection.	1 2 3 4 5
	3. Provide resources to help all employees meet the demands of their jobs.	1 2 3 4 5
Resilience: How do we learn and grow from change?	1. Persevere to develop people and products.	1 2 3 4 5
Respond to change by mastering principles of growth, learning, and resilience.	2. Encourage learning from both successes and setbacks.	1 2 3 4 5
	3. Recover when things go wrong	1 2 3 4 5
Civility and delight: How do we bring delight into our organization?	1. Feel like a friendly place.	1 2 3 4 5
Attend to what helps individuals feel happy, cared for, and excited about life.	2. Encourage employees to have fun at work.	1 2 3 4 5
	3. Demonstrate respect and civility for all.	1 2 3 4 5

128

If your score is between 70 and 84, your work setting is on track to make abundance happen. Identify the questions where you score lower and focus on those areas.

If your score is between 55 and 69, you are close to losing it.

If your score is less than 54, your organization's journey to abundance may be impossible at the present time. If you are committed to staying at your organization, find one or two areas where you can make progress. Don't try to do everything at once.

Conclusion: HR Professionals as Capability Builders

Establishing the right organization leads to strategic and business success. Defining the right organization through a capability lens requires that HR professionals perform capability audits, align strategy to capability to individual behavior, and establish a capability of meaning throughout the organization. As capability builders, HR professionals see how the whole is greater than the parts and establish organization identities that outlive any individual leader. The ambiance you feel when walking into an organization need not be accidental but a thoughtful application of these ideas.

CHAPTER 6

CHANGE CHAMPION

6

As the pace of change increases in every aspect of our lives, HR professionals have become change champions in many companies around the world, and this has generally been much to their employers' advantage.[1] We begin with two examples.

Hilton Worldwide

Hilton Worldwide is one of the world's largest hospitality companies: 10 leading brands, 3,750 properties (865 hotels under development), 620,000 rooms in 89 countries, 142,000 team members, and 360,000 franchise team members. The year 2011 marked the largest global pipeline in Hilton Worldwide's 93-year history, with key growth in China, Russia, Egypt, Jordan, Turkey, and Saudi Arabia. To compete in this globally changing world, Hilton leaders have focused on growth in emerging markets and driving group and transient travel sales in an increasingly competitive landscape.

To meet these business demands, Hilton has had to face and manage a number of change challenges: It moved its headquarters from California to Virginia in 2010, replacing 90 percent of the headquarters staff and integrating 70 new leaders into the top hundred. It introduced two new brands, Hilton Worldwide and Home2 Suites, while rehabilitating existing brands like Hilton Hotels and Waldorf Astoria and ensuring growth rates that match potential through new properties in emerging markets.

As CHRO since July 2009, Matt Schuyler recognizes that the company's ability to manage change is critical, because the organizational structure is a matrix between brands, shared service functions, and hotel operations—with each focused on shared accountabilities of operations, guest service, and growth. To anticipate, cope with, and deal with change, members of the HR team facilitated a number of initiatives:

- They framed a concise, compelling, and inspiring vision ("To fill the earth with the light and warmth of hospitality"), mission ("We will be the preeminent global hospitality company—the first choice of guests, Team Members, and owners alike"), and values ("Hospitality, Integrity, Leadership, Teamwork, Ownership, Now"—which produces the acronym "HILTON").
- They surveyed the business for areas where HR process could add significant value, settling on recruitment, movement, development, assessment, outplacement, rewards, and recognition.
- They inventoried overall HR processes and vendors to simplify offerings and improve cost structure.
- They simplified, automated, and created flexible HR policies and practices, going from more than 300 HR policies to 3 that are aligned with the needs of the business.
- They designed and implemented leadership measurement systems based on business objectives and incorporated leadership behaviors into the compensation system.
- They developed robust and rigorous executive talent assessments and introduced a new succession planning system, and in the process they updated change skills of HR professionals to become change masters, agents of change, and experts in common sense.

In part because of these efforts, team members are more engaged, and Hilton Worldwide has had remarkable results—increased guest satisfaction and a compounded annual growth rate of 30 percent from 2009 to 2011—while adding more than 150,000 rooms and 500 properties. Hilton Worldwide now enjoys the highest pipeline of new properties and rooms in the industry. As Schuyler and the HR team reflect on their experience, they have learned that leadership, with the right direction, is incredibly adaptable to change—

and what gets measured gets done with the right support structure from HR and other functions.

Viterra

In 2000, Saskatchewan Wheat Pool was a small provincial co-op with $1.5 million in unsecured debt, but by 2011 it had become the largest Canadian-owned agricultural business. In the process, it had acquired Agricore United, renamed itself Viterra, and undergone a major transformation.

To make this change, Mayo Schmidt, CEO of the Wheat Pool, began by working to reduce the size of the company radically by selling off underperforming businesses, raising new capital, and dissolving its board. He was doing the job he was hired to do. However, his personal coach pointed out that he was not going to "reduce the company to success," and he began to develop a growth process. He decided to create a new company with the goal of being the most capable organization of its kind in Canada. With his personal coach, he pursued the following interventions:

- Schmidt prepared himself to be the leader he needed to be by employing the resources of his coach, joining Harvard's agricultural case studies program, doing a 360-degree feedback round with all his top personnel, and acquiring new personnel to complement his own skills.
- He developed a new vision and worked through the commitment process with all the top executives until he had buy-in throughout the firm.
- He expanded his strategic planning from a single office to the entire top group. This group went through a creative problem-solving workshop and developed an entirely new strategy.
- He employed an outside firm to remove several million dollars of corporate waste and bureaucracy.
- He created an office of the CEO, which he shared with his top operations person and the head of HR.

- He oversaw the insertion of several new information technologies and developed a new performance management system to hold people accountable for objectives and values.
- He directly intervened with the culture, values, and guiding principles to help people separate from the old co-op mentality to the new business reality.
- Finally, he put in place temporary systems responsible for continuous change and a playbook for acquisitions.

Today Viterra is the world's largest industrial oat miller. It has entered the canola-crushing business, and it manufactures feed for cattle, poultry, and pigs. The company has the respect of the financial community because of substantial cash inflows. Schmidt has been elected CEO of the year within Canada, and Viterra employee turnover is very low even though the company competes with the shale oil business for personnel. This success was evident in a 2009 Regina press release: "Viterra generated net income of $288.3 million for the year, up sharply from the $116.5 million earned during the same period in 2007." Schmidt commented, "Our continued focus on operational excellence, together with our integration efforts led to record performance this year.'"

What We Mean by Change Champion

We are privileged to have firsthand experiences with line managers and HR change champions like those just described. They continually teach us about how to turn change theory into practice. They do what others talk about. They exemplify the theory and research on change. There are literally millions of books, articles, studies, and theories of change. Collectively, as authors, we have over a hundred years of experience studying and applying organization change. Wayne began his career as an internal Organization Development (OD) consultant helping a company face and manage change before doing his Ph.D. One of Dave's earliest papers was, "When, Why, and How Will OD OD?" Jon led change as an internal and external consultant and as a business executive. Over the years, we have been privileged to work with some of the most perceptive and relevant thought leaders in the change field.[2] As we mull over this body of work, we propose 10 succinct insights on change that shape how HR professionals become change champions. Table 6.1 lists these 10 insights and summarizes their organization and personal implications for HR professionals as change champions, and the following sections explore them in more detail.

Table 6.1   Implications of Change Insights

Insight	Organization Implications To what extent does our organization . . .	Individual Implications To what extent am I able to . . .
1. Change happens.	Recognize and accept the pressure and realities of change?	Feel comfortable dealing with pressures for change rather than ignoring or avoiding change?
2. Change requires response.	Build an internal capacity to respond to change that equals external demands for change?	Demonstrate new behaviors consistent with changing business demands?
3. Most change attempts fail.	Learn from change failures and transfer those lessons to future change efforts?	Face and learn from my failures so that I don't make the same mistakes twice?
4. Change matters.	Increase, measure, and track our capacity to change and share this information with employees, customers, and investors?	Monitor my personal ability to learn, adapt, and change?
5. Change enables.	Move more quickly than competitors on key organizational initiatives?	See change as a significant element of my ability to accomplish my personal goals?
6. Change demands closing the know-do gap.	Recognize the latest research and best practices on change and then apply and adapt those findings to our organization?	Study change theory and practices and adapt them to my work setting?

(continued on next page)

Table 6.1   Implications of Change Insights (continued)

Insight	Organization Implications To what extent does our organization . . .	Individual Implications To what extent am I able to . . .
7. Change arises from both evolution and revolution.	Balance change though continuous improvement or advocate bold and dramatic change?	Continuously improve on my past and act on my desired future?
8. Change can be pushed or pulled.	Start with a compelling future vision and fold the present into the future or start with the present and take incremental steps to go forward (tipping point)?	Envision an aspiring future for my work and take daily actions to approach that future?
9. Change occurs at multiple levels.	Focus change on individual, initiative, or institutional efforts?	See how my personal changes model what I want to see in the culture of my organization?
10. Change follows a common process.	Have a disciplined process that we apply to change initiatives?	Have a regular and routine process of making personal changes?

Change Happens

The pace of change is rising exponentially. Change occurs in every part of personal and professional life. Customization, information flow, customer and employee expectations, and organizational transformation are all increasing, fueled by technology. Knowledge has an ever-shorter half-life as change emanates from newer knowledge made more accessible through the Internet. Organizations also go through dramatic changes. Of the original Fortune 500 list published in 1955, only 70 companies exist independently 56 years later. In just a decade, from 2000 to 2010, about half of these large and seemingly stable companies disappeared. Obviously change happens in all our personal and professional lives.

HR professionals should help their companies face, accept, and be open to the pressures for change rather than hide from them.

Change Requires Response

Organizations (and individuals) have varying abilities to respond to change. If an organization cannot change as fast as the pace of change in its environment, the organization will fall behind, decline, and disappear. Change in an organization should at least match the pace of change of the environment. Gary Hamel, a renowned business thinker and professor at the London Business School, suggests that managers have to continually ask, *How do you build organizations that change as fast as change itself?*

HR professionals conceptualize and design organizational agility, flexibility, and responsiveness to external changes.

Most Change Attempts Fail

There are a lot of statistics about the failure of personal and organizational changes. At a personal level, 98 percent of New Year's resolutions fail, 70 percent of Americans who pay off credit card debt with a home equity loan end up with the same or higher debt in two years, and despite the $40 billion a year Americans spend on diets, 19 out of 20 lose nothing but their money. Marriage counseling saves fewer than one in five couples on the brink of divorce. Only a quarter of those who have experienced heart attacks make behavioral changes. Efforts to overcome personal problems like eating disorders, depression, anxiety, or a sedentary lifestyle also have low long-term success rates.

Organizational changes are not much more successful. It turns out that only 20 to 25 percent of initiatives (attempts to improve in areas such as quality, customer service, or cycle time) are successfully implemented. Most corporate transformations start with enthusiasm and end with cynicism, and leaders' tenure in top jobs has consistently fallen.

HR professionals have to face the challenge of change failures and work to improve these bleak numbers, which means diagnosing why changes fail and learning from past failures.

Change Matters

Leaders and organizations that do manage to change tend to reach their goals. In the leadership research, leaders who have learning agility are more likely to be seen as effective and to have longer tenure in their roles.[3] The leadership research also shows that effective leaders help make organizational changes that enable strategy.[4] Organizational research on change suggests that if companies change, they are likely to survive; if they don't change, they wither and die.[5, 6]

HR professionals help build individual and organizational capacity for change into regular discussions because these capacities enhance performance.

Change Enables

For some, *change* becomes the outcome or goal of a leader or an organization. More often the capacity for change is best seen as an adjunct that enables other business goals; thus change operates as a means, not as an end. So we see leaders working to build *fast* innovation, *rapid* globalization, *agile* customer service, *flexible* collaboration, *shifting* brand identity, or *rapid* strategy. In a world of precipitous change, organizations must not only define the right outcomes but move quickly to get there. In the consumer products industry, for example, the adage is that the first mover in new products or services gets about half the market, while the next four players split the rest.

HR professionals can help leaders focus their strategies to be clear and precise about what they are working to do and then build in a capacity for change to rapidly deliver each outcome. For example, after reducing its debt, Viterra transformed its strategy from being a grain transporter to a company that helps farmers solve problems at every step of the crop production process. Thus, when the farmer needs money to buy crop inputs and seed from Viterra, the company developed a partnership with banks to extend credit, to provide the farmer with best harvest times, to transport the extracted grain, and to connect the farmer to customers in other countries.

Change Demands Closing the Know-Do Gap

Most people who eat more than they should know they should lose weight. They even know how to lose weight—eat less, eat right, and exercise more—but they don't do it. The same applies to other unfortunate habits, both personal and organizational. We often ask seminar participants to brainstorm for 60 seconds on the topic of, "What do you know about effective organizational change?" We generally find that the group generates the same measures listed in leading change books. We know what to do, but we don't often do it.[7]

HR professionals bring discipline to change processes so that what people know, they do. They create and use a change pilot's checklist to help keep the organization on course.

Change Arises from Both Evolution and Revolution

Change can be initiated in many ways. Evolutionary change suggests continuous improvement, small steps, transactional actions, rigorous planning, and reaching a tipping point. Revolutionary change implies discontinuous change, bold moves, transformational outcomes, immediate action, and anticipating a new future.

HR professionals need to help line managers determine when to initiate evolutionary change and when to go for revolutionary change.

Change Can Be Pushed or Pulled

Sometimes, change begins with a clear destination—a specific strategy, goal, or outcome—supported by concrete plans to help move from the present to the future endpoint. At other times, change begins with a direction—an aspiration, value set, or orientation—followed by taking early steps to move from the present into the future. Destination change requires an engineering mentality to stipulate the end state and the steps toward it. Direction change requires a pioneering mentality to articulate a future and then act quickly to move forward.

HR professionals can help craft aspirations and define actions to link the present to the future.

Change Occurs at Multiple Levels

We classify three targets of change: individual, initiative, and institutional. Individual change helps people improve on their behaviors and performance. Initiative change means accomplishing specific projects (aimed at quality, innovation, cost, service, teamwork, and so forth) in a timely way. Institutional change implies transforming a culture or work environment to sustain change.

HR professionals can be coaches for individual improvement, agents for initiative changes, and stewards for cultural transformation.

Change Follows a Common Process

In the change literature, many programs, initiatives, tools, and actions have been proposed as common processes for making change happen. Table 6.2 summarizes some of the leading approaches. They often include creating a case for change, defining the future state, building commitment to moving forward, and finding ways to institutionalize the change.

HR professionals need to create an accepted, shared, and wisely used process for implementing initiatives throughout the organization.

The Factors of Change Champion

We have identified 11 specific knowledge and behavior items that characterize the change champion domain. These 11 items statistically cluster into two factors as shown in Table 6.3.

These data offer additional insights into the process of change. By statistically separating the initiating change factor from sustaining change, the data suggest that HR professionals have to do more than get change started; they have to be persistent at sustaining change. One of the reasons we label this

Table 6.2 Change Processes

Author	Warner Burke	John Kotter	Dale Lake	Price Pritchett
Example of work	*Organization Change*	*Leading Change*	*Change Manual[6]*	*Quantum Leap*
Change processes	• Be self-aware. • Monitor external environment. • Establish a need for change. • Provide clear vision or direction. • Communicate the need. • Deal with resistance. • Leverage multiple actions. • Have consistency and persistence.	• Establish sense of urgency. • Create guiding coalition. • Develop vision or strategy. • Communicate change vision. • Empower employees for action. • Generate short-term wins. • Consolidate gains and produce more change. • Anchor new approaches in culture.	• Design a change agenda. • Assess the current situation. • Create dissatisfaction or need for change. • Activate change champions. • Influence stakeholders. • Assess and overcome resistance. • Build team and network. • Create structure for success. • Do project management. • Monitor progress. • Have continuous learning.	• Give clear marching orders. • Nail down each job. • Manage resistance to change. • Encourage risk taking. • Create supportive work environment. • Attend to transition and change. • Take care of "me" issues. • Communicate over and over again.

(continued on next page)

Table 6.2 Change Processes (continued)

Author	Michael Beer	Hay Group	GE Change Acceleration Process[9]	P&G Organization Development	Your Company
Example of work	*Organization Change and Development*	*Hay Model for Change*	*Change Acceleration Process*	*Organization Systems Design Model*	
Change processes	Dissatisfaction. • Model or purpose of change. • Success or outcomes. • Cost of change • Resistance to change.	• Ensure reasons for change • Identify "change agents" • Assess stakeholders and sponsors. • Plan project activities. • Communicate changes. • Assess impact on people and structure. • Address the impacts of the change. • Share process change. • Support changes. • Train for new skills. • Measure and report on progress	• Lead change. • Create a felt need. • Define a direction or shape a vision. • Mobilize commitment. • Make decisions. • Dedicate resources. • Learn, adapt, and monitor.	• Start with results required. • Align leadership. • Define culture needed to deliver results. • Integrate organization systems to reinforce culture.	

Table 6.3   Change Champion Factors: Mean, Individual Effectiveness, and Business Impact

Factor	Mean Score (out of 5.0)	Individual Effectiveness	Business Impact
Initiating change	3.94	53%	46%
Sustaining change	3.91	47%	54%
R^2		.296	.066

domain "change champion" and not "change agent" (a more common term) is that the agent of change often initiates change but does not follow through. An agent acts on behalf of someone else and does not take personal ownership of the need to make something happen. Based on these data, we envision change champions as people who both start and follow through with change.

The data in Table 6.2 also suggest that for HR professionals to be seen as personally effective, they have to initiate change. However, to drive business success, they also need to sustain change over time. At present, most HR professionals seem to have more experience at initiating or starting change than at making sure the desired changes survive.

Factor 1: Initiating Change

Initiating change means getting started, turning pressure for change into change initiatives, and the taking first steps to move change forward. Our research showed that six competencies define the extent to which HR professionals initiate change:

1. Ensure that key leaders are supportive of major change initiatives.
2. Help people understand why change is important—create a sense of urgency.
3. Identify and overcome sources of resistance to change.
4. Help set the direction of change with clear intended outcomes.
5. Build commitment from key people to support change efforts.
6. Articulate the key decisions and actions that must happen for change to progress.

As change agents who initiate change, HR professionals help define why change matters, what should be changed, and who supports the change. In defining why change matters, HR professionals need to build a compelling intellectual and emotional case for change. The intellectual case often comes from empirical evidence that successful change will lead to positive personal or organizational outcomes. The emotional case for change comes when people see and feel the impact of the change on principles that matter to them.

To define what should be changed, HR professionals need to turn complex challenges into simple opportunities. They need to articulate change outcomes either as directions for the change or as destinations. These outcomes need to be communicated with visual images to capture the change, with verbal messages to enunciate the change, with stories to emotionally capture the change, and with metrics to track the change. As Bob Eichinger puts it:

> There is a magic bullet to change. The research is crystal clear. People are less afraid of change to the extent they participate in its design and execution. The more people are involved in the determination, planning, design and execution of the change, the less resistant they will be. Change leaders need to be patient and design as much participation into the process as is humanly possible.[10]

To build support for the change, HR professionals need to involve key people to participate in the change process. Bob Eichinger's magic bullet implies the need to figure out how to mobilize commitment by identifying and involving key stakeholders to a change. This may come from asking their opinions, making them into cosponsors (a process called *cooptation*), inviting them to make key decisions, and making them public advocates for the change.

To become better at initiating change, HR professionals need practice. They can coach business leaders in the midst of change and observe what they (the HR professionals) do well and what they do not do well. They can participate on teams charged with implementing business initiatives. They can investigate how well their organization has accomplished change in the past, synthesize lessons learned, and propose new actions for the future. They can help establish a tailored organizational change model that adapts lessons of and research on change to their organization. They can help build discipline to use this model on key initiatives.

They can examine how change has happened within the HR department as new practices or structures are implemented. Using the HR department as a test lab helps HR professionals become change-competent before working on business issues. They can also coach or consult with nonprofit community agencies going through change and observe how change processes apply in these settings.

Factor 2: Sustaining Change

Sustaining change means sticking with initiatives, making sure that desired changes happen, and delivering outcomes from the change. Our research identified three specific behaviors that HR professionals can demonstrate to help sustain change:

1. Ensure the availability of resources needed to stick with the change (money, information, technology, people).
2. Monitor and communicate progress of change processes.
3. Adapt learnings about change to new settings.

As change champions who sustain change, HR professionals have to make sure that changes last by implementing sustainable disciplines into their organization. In our work on leadership sustainability, we have identified seven principles of sustainability that HR professionals can master to make change stick.[11] They form the acronym "STARTME," which helps keep them in mind:

1. *Simplicity*. Simplicity means that the leaders focus on a few key behaviors that have high impact on the most important issues. Leadership sustainability requires that we find simplicity in the face of complexity and replace concept clutter with simple resolve. It entails prioritizing the behaviors that matter most, shifting from analytics with data to action with determination,

framing complex phenomena into simple patterns, and sequencing change. HR professionals should help prioritize and simplify change priorities.

2. *Time.* Leaders put their desired behaviors into their calendar, and this shows up in how they spend their time. Employees pay far more attention to what they see leaders do than to what they hear leaders say. Leadership sustainability shows up in whom we spend time with, what issues we spend time on, where we spend our time, and how we spend our time. HR professionals should monitor how leaders invest their time as carefully as their money.

3. *Accountability.* Leadership sustainability requires accountability, where leaders take personal responsibility for making sure that they do what they say they will do. Accountability increases when leaders also require personal commitments from others and follow up on those commitments. HR professionals ensure accountability comes by making personal commitments public, by following up on commitments, and by giving feedback on the change efforts.

4. *Resources.* Leaders dedicate resources to support their desired changes with coaching and infrastructure. At all levels, when people have ongoing coaching, they are much more likely to enact desired behavioral change. Marshall Goldsmith demonstrated the use of coaching with leaders, and we have found that a mix of self-coaching, expert coaching, peer coaching, and boss coaching can be woven together as a resource for sustained change. Selection, promotion, career development, succession planning, performance reviews, communication, policies, and organization design should also be aligned to support leadership change. HR professionals can serve as coaches and architects for sustaining change.

5. *Tracking.* Unless desired leadership behaviors and changes are operationalized, quantified, and tracked, they are nice to do—but are not likely to be done. Effective metrics for leadership behavior need to be transparent, easy to measure, timely, and tied to consequences. Leadership sustainability should be woven into existing scorecards and can even become its own scorecard to ensure that leaders monitor how they are doing. HR professionals help create and manage these scorecards.

6. *Melioration.* Leaders *meliorate*—make themselves and their environment better—when they improve by learning from mistakes and failures and demonstrate resilience. Leadership sustainability requires that leaders master the principles of learning: to experiment frequently, to reflect always, to become resilient, to face failure, to welcome success and not take it for granted, and to improvise continually. HR professionals further their learning by advocating and modeling these processes.

7. *Emotion.* Sustainability occurs when leaders not only know but feel what they should do to improve. This passion increases when leaders see their desired changes as part of their personal identity and purpose, when their changes will shape their relationships with others, and when their changes will shift the culture of their work setting. HR professionals can be architects of meaning in their organizations.

Action in the Change Champion Domain

HR professionals become change champions when their abilities to initiate and sustain change are applied at the individual, initiative, and institutional levels of change. In the process, they need to keep learning, master the informal rules within their organization, start where they can and find early successes, build coalitions of support, experiment and learn frequently, and stay optimistic about the change process.[12] The following sections offer specific tools for being a change champion at each level.

Target 1: Individual Change

Organizations don't think; people do. HR professionals help people in organizations change by personalizing HR practices around a tailored employee value proposition, by creating a work environment that encourages personal growth, and by coaching key leaders to build a personal leadership brand.

As knowledge employees increasingly become free agents, they have more and more choices of where to work. To attract, motivate, and retain talented employees, organizations need to create an employee value proposition that meets the unique needs of each employee. To do so, they can apply principles of mass customization of products and services to mass personalization with employees. This means segmenting the workforce based on common interests and abilities. It means offering cafeteria-style and modular choices to employees about work conditions. It means allowing employees to adapt their own rules given a common set of shared principles. This creates a workforce-of-one mentality that tailors an employee value proposition to each employee.[13]

HR professionals play a key role in shaping a positive work environment. They help leaders and individuals self-disclose, shape high-relationship teams, and inspire people to experiment with new behaviors. We have seen HR professionals sponsor mentoring, facilitate town hall meetings, invest in personal development plans, and help people learn and change. When HR professionals attend to and create a positive work environment, individual change that fosters growth is more likely to occur.

HR professionals can also coach leaders to create a personal brand that guides and enables their change. Throughout our careers, we have worked to help leaders develop a personal point of view about leadership. Now we believe we need to evolve this approach to helping leaders change and improve by building a personal leadership brand (see Table 6.4). A leadership point of view generally looks inward; it's about who I am as a leader. A personal leader brand looks outward and focuses on impacts on others. A leadership point of view offers insights and perspectives on what the leader needs to be, know, and do. A leadership brand offers a narrative and story that captures not only what to be, know, and do but also the emotion and feeling behind education and action. Leaders who focus on their brand more than just their point of view elicit greater productivity from employees, more confidence from customers, and increased security for investors. A leadership point of view too easily slips into being more rhetoric than resolve, more aspiration than action, and more hope than reality. Brand promises without subsequent results are not sustained. Leadership wish lists need to be replaced with leadership vows. When we ask leaders to prepare their personal brand, they are making commitments about what they have to do to sustain their personal brand in the eyes of those they serve. A brand focus builds leadership sustainability.

Table 6.4   Leadership Point of View and Personal Leadership Brand

Leadership Point of View	Personal Leadership Brand
Starts by looking at oneself: Who am I as a leader?	Starts by looking at key stakeholders: Who are the people I care about?
Focuses on "I" statements: I believe, aspire to, want, hope—statements focused on personal aspirations.	Focuses on impact of leadership on others ("so that"): How will my leadership affect those I care about?
Emphasizes what the leader should be, know, and do.	Offers a narrative story that brings emotion and feeling to leadership.
Increases sense of self-worth.	Increases value to others.
Comes through as aspirational and inspiring.	Comes through with value created for others.

As change champions, HR professionals help individuals change by creating a more customized work environment, a work environment open to change, and a personal leadership brand.

Target 2: Initiative Change

When facilitating in-company workshops, we like to have participants list all the initiatives their company has sponsored in recent times. This is usually a long list, reflecting the management ideas popular in recent years. These might include:

- 360-degree feedback
- Action learning
- Balanced scorecard
- Benchmarking
- Brand delayering
- Cloud computing
- Core competency
- CSR
- Customer-centricity

- Customer relationship management (CRM)
- Customer segmentation
- Development in place
- Distance learning
- Downsizing
- Empowerment
- Ergonomics
- ERP
- EVA
- Gainsharing
- High-performing teams
- Just-in-time (inventory, training)
- Knowledge management
- Lean
- Learning
- Management innovation
- Market timing
- Matrix management
- MBO
- Niche marketing
- Organizational diagnosis
- Outsourcing
- Portfolio planning
- Predictive analytics
- Process optimization
- Project management
- Quality circles
- Rapid prototyping
- Reengineering
- Rewards diagnostic
- Rightsizing
- Risk management
- Scenario planning

- Self-directed teams
- Self-managed teams
- Shared services
- Simplicity
- Six Sigma
- Social media
- Stretch assignments
- Supply chain management
- Strengths, weaknesses, opportunities, and threats (SWOT)
- Town hall meetings
- Total quality management (TQM)
- Triple bottom line
- Values
- Virtual organization
- Visions and missions
- Web 2.0

We favor management innovation, often specified because of a label that connects a set of management actions, and we have personally advocated or taught many of the ideas listed here as part of a management innovation initiative.

We see HR playing four roles to help transform these ideas from fads that peak and plunge to managerial innovations that stick. First, the disparate ideas need to be integrated through organizational capabilities (Chapter 5) or through integrated HR solutions (Chapter 8). Managers should not be seeking quick fixes; they need to find organization solutions that are sustainable. Second, the ideas need to be sequenced so that there is a logic that builds on the past. The evolution from quality circles to TQM to Six Sigma to lean offers additional insights on bringing principles into organizations. Third, the ideas need to be prioritized. Organizations cannot assimilate too many management innovations at once. Which of these innovations would have the most impact (on strategy, customers, finances, and other goals) with the least amount of resources? Fourth, once integrated, sequenced, and prioritized, how can HR actually help deliver the desired initiative?

Delivering desired initiatives is a primary role of a change champion. To do so, HR professionals should create a viable and credible change process and then build the discipline to apply this process to targeted initiatives. From the change processes outlined earlier, we have suggested seven key factors that help to ensure that initiatives happen by turning what people know they should do into what they actually do (Table 6.5). We can adapt these seven conditions for success to help make any initiative happen.

HR professionals can lead audits of these seven conditions for success, rating the current status of each on a 1–10 scale. The ratings can be profiled on Figure 6.1 to diagnose where to focus to make the most progress on any change initiative.

Target 3: Institutional Change

Sustained change has to become a pattern that extends beyond an isolated event. To become a pattern, the change needs to be institutionalized—that is,

Table 6.5   Conditions Needed for Successful Change

Conditions Needed for Successful Change	Implications for HR as Change Champion
1. **Leading:** Having leadership support for the change	Gain leadership support for the initiative.
2. **Creating a felt need:** Knowing why we are making the change	Build a case for why the initiative adds value.
3. **Envisioning:** Having a clear sense of the outcomes of the change	Develop a clear sense of the outcome of the initiative in aspirational and action terms.
4. **Engaging:** Mobilizing commitment from key individuals	Get buy-in from everyone required to deliver the initiative.
5. **Decision making:** Knowing the decisions that need to be made to move the change forward	Be clear about the decisions that need to be made to make progress on the project.
6. **Institutionalizing:** Making sure that the change is integrated with other business activities	Embed the initiative into technology (operations and IT), HR, and financial systems and processes in the company.
7. **Monitoring and learning:** Tracking the success of the change	Refine and adjust the blueprint, track progress, and learn from experience.

Figure 6.1   *Profile of change initiative—by integrating, sequencing, prioritizing, and delivering initiatives, HR makes change happen.*

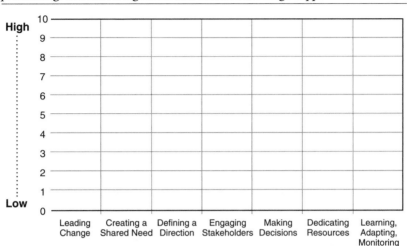

become part of the unspoken rules, rituals, norms, expectations, tacit assumptions, and behavioral expectations that every organization has. The patterns often determine of how employees behave. When these implicit expectations are not made explicit, employees tend to perpetuate the patterns they've been living with rather than change them.

HR professionals help create institutional change by exposing and confronting these hidden patterns. In our work, we have identified 36 common organizational viruses that can exist within a work group. These viruses keep the group from changing and improving. In medicine, once virus infections are detected, they can be treated. Likewise, when organizational viruses are identified, they can be eliminated. HR professionals can present the following list of the 36 identified viruses and ask members of a work unit to pick the 5 that they experience most often in their organization. Once these viruses are detected, labeled, and made transparent, they can be intentionally addressed:

1. *Overinform: Tell everyone—then have a meeting.* We make sure everyone gets the word, and then we have a meeting that slows things down.
2. *Have it my way.* We don't learn from each other; instead, we enjoy the not-invented-here syndrome.

3. *Saturday morning quarterback.* We criticize everything, even before something happens.

4. *False positive.* We say we agree when we don't.

5. *Concealed consensus.* We confuse participation with consensus. We think that everyone has to agree before we act.

6. *Forward to our past: Look for the future in the rearview mirror.* We are so afraid of losing our heritage that we don't change our culture; we are locked into our habits.

7. *Caste: Value by grade.* We judge people by their title and rank rather than by their performance or competence.

8. *Turfism: My business versus our business.* We defend our turf even to the detriment of the overall organization.

9. *Command and control.* We like to make sure that senior managers run the company, so we delegate responsibility upward; this keeps us from feeling a personal obligation to change.

10. *Activity mania.* We like to be busy; our badge of honor is a full calendar even if it excludes thinking and results. We hide behind our "busy-ness."

11. *Narcissistic competitiveness.* We like to win as individuals, not as teams.

12. *Show me the results: Results rule.* We like results—any way, any time, anyhow—and we pursue results according to our principles only if we have time or can afford it.

13. *Crisis jumping.* When in a crisis, we act decisively, and then we wait for the next crisis in order for us to act again.

14. *Customer antipathy.* We don't include customer criteria in our thinking; we are focused inward.

15. *Authority ambiguity: Not clear on accountability.* In our matrix, we are not sure who is responsible or accountable, so no one is.

16. *All things to all people.* We have too many priorities; each good idea gets energy and attention; we don't say no; we are not focused on the critical few.

17. *Flavor of the month.* We jump from program to program; we don't have integrated initiatives, and we're cynical about new programs; we end up with concept clutter.

18. *Overchanged.* We have a capacity problem with too many changes going on at once; we are burned out and stressed out on change; we cannot let things go.

19. *Misalignment: Disjointed actions.* We don't look at the big picture and see how our work fits in with strategy; we tend to get lost in the details.

20. *Compliant deflector: Overobedience is common.* We wait to do what we are told and follow directions and avoid responsibility for our actions.

21. *Process mania.* We are so consumed by process that we don't focus on results and outcomes.

22. *Kill the messenger.* We never hear bad news because it isn't safe.

23. *Glacial response: Whose decision is it?* We cannot get decisions made quickly.

24. *Perfectionism: Right way or no way.* We have to have the perfect answer before we do anything.

25. *What have you done for me yesterday?* After a successful change, we only want more.

26. *Overmeasure.* We measure everything, even to a fault. Our dashboards are way too complex.

27. *Undermeasure.* We don't have indicators that track the important stuff; we measure what is easy, regardless of whether it's what we need to know.

28. *Unsustainability.* We do not sustain the changes we start.

29. *Going for the big win.* We look for the mega change that will solve all our problems at once.

30. *Undeveloped skills or aptitude.* We don't have the skills required for the future.

31. *Event versus pattern.* Change is an event (do the checklist, attend the meeting)—not a sustained pattern.

32. *Fire hydrant syndrome.* Everyone has to mark every initiative or project before anyone can move on it.

33. *Guess what's in my mind.* When the leader has an idea of what to do, others have to guess it.

34. *The dog and pony show rules.* Style over substance; endless PowerPoint presentations but little action.

35. *This too shall pass.* Put your head down, ignore it, and it will go away.
36. *A culture of no.* We overevaluate and criticize everything.

We have found that newcomers to a work unit are more likely to recognize the unspoken patterns than long-term employees are. When you visit a friend's house for dinner, the family patterns are quickly evident to you—you will notice whether grace is said and by whom, where people sit, how quickly people eat, and what kinds of conversation occur, things that no one in the family thinks about. Likewise, in organizations, new employees with fresh eyes often see what has become routine to others. Once the viruses are exposed and overcome, then institutional change follows.

HR professionals also institutionalize change by finding ways to talk about and modify the culture of an institution. Culture represents the patterns of how people think and act. Using our outside-in metaphor, we believe that an organization's culture can best be defined as the identity of the organization in the minds of its target customers. Our definition of culture makes it a firm's brand. HR professionals can collaborate with customer-interfacing colleagues and business leaders to define an organization's desired culture. Once this customer-centric culture is defined, HR can play a significant role in making the external expectations real to employees through HR practices like staffing, training, succession planning, performance management, rewards, communication, and organization design.

Creating institutional change either by exposing and overcoming viruses or by turning a firm brand into an organization culture helps make institutional change happen.

Conclusion: Becoming a Change Champion

If we could wave a magic wand, HR professionals worldwide would become change champions like the ones featured at the beginning of this chapter. And we do have hope. It may not happen all at once, but we have laid out the axioms that change masters must accept, the skills they need to initiate and sustain change, and the tools to do so for individuals, initiatives, and institutions.

CHAPTER 7

HR INNOVATOR
AND INTEGRATOR

7

Creating capable culture requires a combination of both HR practice innovation and the integration of practices as a synergistic whole. The case following offers a useful example:

AXA Equitable

In mid-2011, AXA Equitable faced the challenge of implementing a reduction in staf while maintaining employee productivity and introducing more innovative and more profitable insurance products to the market. Rino Piazolla, CHRO of AXA Equitable, recognized the need to recommit the organization, and with us implemented a "work-out" initiative: engaging employees at all levels in identifying ways to take unnecessary work and cost out of the organization and enable employees to focus on the important activities—the ones that create value for customers.

Over the next three months, hundreds of ideas were generated, and a significant number were implemented—from eliminating reports that were marginally useful to identifying new and more effective ways of organizing work. An extensive review found that 80 percent of participants described work-out as having had a strong personal and organizational impact, and an equal percentage described work-out as personally meaningful and relevant to their work. Groups in finance, IT, and product development used work-out to kick off specific improvement efforts in their departments. In fact, more than 180 specific work-out initiatives were kicked off as part of the project. CEO Mark Pearson participated in a day-and-a-half session and wrote a note to all executives of the company reinforcing the importance of their participation and leadership of work-out. As a result of the success of work-out, line management identified leadership and engagement as critical organizational capabilities. HR is now addressing related needs for improvement in the development of leader coaching and performance management skills and is looking at other ways to reinforce a culture of employee engagement.[1]

In Chapter 6, we describe the competency domain of change champion and the importance of HR professional competence in initiating and sustaining change. In this chapter, the HR innovator and integrator competency domain picks up on and extends this theme. Effective HR practices have two important qualities. First, they are innovative, reflecting more robust ways of enabling and strengthening the capabilities on which the strategy is based. Effective HR practices are internally aligned and integrated. They are not strings of unconnected events or activities but instead are connected elements of a whole that is greater than its individual parts. Such practices create and maintain a culture that drives performance and adds value to the customers and other stakeholders of the business.

The AXA Equitable case is an example of innovation that has led to greater alignment and integration. By implementing work-out in concert with the staffing reduction, AXA senior management sent a strong message that the company was concerned with improving the experience of employees and committed to eliminating unproductive work. The progress made in work-out has led to improvement in other HR practices and increased integration with the demands of the business.

What We Mean by HR Innovator and Integrator

HR innovator and integrator makes up a more pointed competency domain than other domains. It is an extension and expansion of the talent management and organization design competency domain from the 2007 study. The focus is on ensuring that the organization has the right talent and leadership for the current and future success of the business. It emphasizes the need for innovation in designing HR practices that drive the talent agenda of the organization. That means ensuring good analytics on the current state of talent and competitive talent needs. Talented employees need to be attracted, recruited, on-boarded, and developed. Leaders need to be identified and placed in positions that utilize their skills and accelerate their competence. And teams and organizations need to be designed and staffed with competent employees who deliver the capabilities that make or break the strategy.

Consideration of HR innovation and integration frequently leads to a discussion of best practice. And over the past several years, best practice identification has become a popular offering for consulting firms and business school executive programs, as well as membership-based firms such as the Corporate Executive Board and Corporate Leadership Council. Just as investment firms make a point of saying that historical performance is not an indication of future gains, best practice should come with a warning label: what works for other companies may not be applicable or in the best interest of your organization.

It is all too easy to assume that best practice will work for any given organization simply because it has been identified and endorsed. In fact, best practice may be innovative, but it may be inconsistent with the needs of businesses. There are three drawbacks to a best practice approach:

1. *Appropriateness:* Goldman Sachs may exemplify best practice in executive compensation in its field, but investment banking logic would hardly be appropriate in most other industries.
2. *Relevance:* Best practice tends to be backward-looking, describing what has worked for other organizations in the past. Looking back is apt to distract from a focus on what's needed in the future.
3. *Synergy:* Specific practices for training, coaching, performance assessment, or other aspects of HR may be extremely helpful in one organization but not in another. Mixing practices from organizations that have different goals, strategies, industries, and brands can lead to confusion or to too frequent change.

We suggest the alternative logic of "best system" thinking. Best system invites HR professionals and leaders to start with whole cloth, not a patchwork. It encourages HR professionals to avoid starting with a solution in search of a problem to solve. Best system thinking leads to the best combination of activities that offer a combination of efficacy and alignment.

Culture isn't the most important thing. It's the only thing.

Jim Sinegal, former CEO of Costco

Core HR Systems

What are the elements of a best system? These are the core HR systems or practice areas that establish innovation and integration:

- *People*: People practices ensure that skills and abilities are in place in order to accomplish the goals of the organization. They create conditions that encourage people to be committed to and engaged in achieving the goals of the organization and to feel that membership in the organization contributes to their purpose and quality of work life.

- *Performance and reward*: Performance practices turn desired outcomes into measurable goals and incentives that motivate people to reach those goals. The basic criteria for performance management are *accountability* (tie individual and team behavior to clear goals), *transparency* (financial and nonfinancial rewards for contributions are understood and made public), *completeness* (performance management practices cover the full range of behaviors and goals required for overall business success), and *equity* (reward levels should track with contribution levels). When performance management practices are established and integrated according to these criteria, they help create value.

- *Information and communication*: Organizations must manage the flow of external information (customer, shareholder, economic and regulatory, technological, and demographic) to ensure that employees adapt to external realities. They must also manage the internal flow of information to coordinate actions within the organization. This includes outside-in (ensuring up-to-date knowledge of stakeholders), inside-out (keeping stakeholders informed of organization progress), up-and-down (from top management to employees at all levels and vice versa), and side-to-side (ongoing communication between organizational units and their leaders and employees).

- *Work and organization*: Organizations must manage the value chain from demand through fulfillment to make sure that obligations are met. To do so, they distribute goals to individuals and groups and set up job and organizational structures to integrate the varied output into a cooperative whole. They design processes for the work itself and for the physical environment that supports the work. HR professionals are ideally suited to assist in this process, but it requires them to be competent in several areas: relating organization design to strategy, assessing organizational effectiveness, implementing new organization structures, ensuring that rigorous work processes are in place, and building teams. In addition, aligning time and physical facilities is increasingly important—including where the job is performed (remote or on site) and when the job is performed (time flexibility).

- *Leadership*: Leadership practices ensure that the organization has established and implemented a clear and strong leadership brand. Leadership brand is the reputation of your organization's leaders: how they are viewed by customers and other stakeholders and by competitors. The processes for developing branded leaders incorporate the unique case for leadership (why investing in leadership is important), the description of what leadership is needed to drive outcomes, assessment of the strengths and weaknesses of current leaders, investments in leadership as a capability (assignment, training, feedback, external experiences), measurement (understanding the impact of investment and continuing needs for change or development), and building external awareness (communicating the brand to stakeholders).

Levels of Innovation and Integration

In a recent McKinsey & Company study of chief executives, 84 percent described innovation as "extremely or very important" to their company's growth and financial success. From the perspective of HR, we see three levels of innovation being driven by the HR function:

1. New to the world
2. New to the company
3. New to the division

"New to the world" innovation can drive significant business opportunity or performance. For example, GE found that potential industrial customers in emerging markets were eager to learn from GE how to accelerate the development and competence of local leaders. The opportunity for customers to participate in a leadership workshop at the Jack Welch Executive Development Center in Crotonville, New York, was a significant incentive to work with GE Capital or other divisions. This type of offering has been copied by a variety of other organizations.

"New to the company" innovation can be applied or adapted to the specific needs and culture of the organization. Building on the tradition of the Peace Corps, for example, in 2008 IBM created the Community Service Corps (CSC) as an opportunity for talented employees to work together in teams, across regions, to give back to the community and to develop as future leaders in the course of doing so.[2] IBM sends teams of high-potential employees to work with leaders in emerging markets to help them address high-priority issues.

Over 1,000 people from 50 countries have been part of the CSC, serving on more than 120 teams in more than 25 countries. Projects range from helping Tanzanian wildlife and tourism organizations improve their business processes to teaching leadership skills in Romania and the Philippines.[3] An evaluation by the Harvard Business School found that the program had increased participant leadership skills and cultural awareness, and it also enhanced the commitment of employees, who were less likely to leave IBM after participating. IBM has helped a half dozen other companies put together similar programs, including FedEx, John Deere, and Dow Corning.

IBM has recently launched its Executive Service Corps. Teams of five or six executives help municipal leaders solve problems related to issues such as traffic congestion, water conservation, public safety, and healthcare. As with the CSC, nobody is the boss, so everybody is forced to collaborate without the crutch of hierarchy. The on-site commitment is three weeks in recognition of the difficulty for executives to spend time away from their regular jobs.

"New to the division" innovation picks up initiatives developed by one part of an organization and applies or adapts them to other divisions. General Atlantic, a global growth equity firm, created a community of practice of HR leaders in its portfolio companies to share innovations. Pat Hedley, managing director of the firm, has led the effort to bring HR directors together to learn from one another and to build on one another's experience and initiatives. Similarly, Statoil, the Norwegian energy company, uses networks and communities of practice to communicate and share HR initiatives and innovations developed by one part of the organization with other parts.

A Framework for Innovation and Integration

Given the levels of innovation, a useful approach to exploring both innovation and integration is provided by the matrix in Figure 7.1.

Efficacy—the power to produce an effect—reminds us that innovation for its own sake is not a worthy goal. The test of an innovation is the value it cre-

Figure 7.1   Innovation matrix

	High Alignment	Low Alignment
High Efficacy	**Synergy:** Robust and aligned practices	**Piecemeal:** Increase alignment
Low Efficacy	**Low Impact:** Increase Efficacy	**Need to Fix**

ates for customers and other stakeholders. Consider American football. Only recently, the New Orleans Saints (a team in the National Football League) got into trouble with an innovative compensation scheme that backfired. It was paying bonuses of $1,000 to players who literally knocked out opponents, causing serious physical damage and their removal from the game.[4] The program really did reduce opposing teams' ability to compete with the Saints, but it generated a wave of bad publicity for both the team and its league when it was revealed. The offending officials were suspended. "We are all accountable and responsible for player health and safety and the integrity of the game. We will not tolerate conduct or a culture that undermines those priorities. No one is above the game or the rules that govern it. Respect for the game and the people who participate in it will not be compromised."[5]

By contrast, when efficacy meets alignment, value is created. The combination of the right practice and the right mix of practices to achieve the outcome—the capability—provides a winning combination. As the football example points out, the "bounty" for injuring players may have been an innovative HR practice, but it was certainly not in alignment.

The Factors of HR Innovator and Integrator

The HR innovator and integrator domain is closely associated with the competency of talent manager and organizational designer identified in the 2007 round of the HRCS. In that round, five factors contributed to the talent and organization domain:

1. Ensuring today's and tomorrow's talent
2. Developing talent
3. Shaping organization
4. Fostering communication
5. Designing reward systems

In the 2012 HRCS research, the emphasis on talent and leadership continues—but with a twist. It is not sufficient to create good systems of workforce planning, talent development, leadership, and organization design. The stakes are higher in 2012. Innovation becomes a more critical factor, driving a focus on more efficacious ways to deliver talent, leadership, and organization. And integration—the best system—is reinforced.

The factors of HR innovator and integrator are outlined in Table 7.1.

HR innovators and integrators define workforce requirements, develop employees, and shape organization and communication practices. However, in several areas we see a fairly significant and certainly interesting evolution of expectation. Workforce planning and analytics are a far more intense focus in the current formulation. Driving performance is a more significant factor in 2012. And a strong element of the competency domain in this round is building leadership brand: an organization's reputation for systematically developing strong leaders and leadership. This is new to the research in 2012. Although talent management has always included leader selection and succession as a key factor and leadership development as an essential aspect, the focus on leadership as a distinctive organizational capability (and the role of HR professionals in building this capability) is powerful and clear.

The impact of HR innovator and integrator on ratings of HR professional performance is, as noted in Chapter 2, significant. As with credible activism, high performers tend to be seen in positive terms when they score

Table 7.1   *HR Innovator and Integrator Competency Factors*

Factor	Mean	Individual Effectiveness	Business Impact
Optimizing human capital through workforce planning and analytics	3.95	22%	21%
Developing talent	3.83	16%	19%
Shaping organization and communication practices	3.94	23%	21%
Driving performance	3.87	19%	19%
Building leadership brand	3.87	20%	20%
Multiple regression R^2		.331	.078

well as HR innovators and integrators. However, the business impact of HR innovator and integrator is more significant; the role of HR innovator and integrator has the largest impact on business performance, explaining 19 percent of the variance.

Factor 1: Optimizing Human Capital Through Workforce Planning and Analytics

The International Labor Organization (ILO), a specialized agency within the United Nations system, does unique and important work; it advocates, recommends policy, and intervenes in support of decent work standards around the world. The problem is that a third of the members of the ILO professional staff will retire by 2020. Over the last two years, under HR director Telma Viale, ILO launched the "skills mapping" initiative, which combined workforce planning and analysis with an assessment of skill levels. Through this effort, which has challenged the culture of the organization, the HR function aims at helping ILO management and staff to align vision, skill, and action, by rigorously analyzing and addressing the ILO competency gap.

Other HR organizations are less proactive in identifying the challenges they face in identifying the skill base now in place; the key environmental and competitive conditions that will require more and different skills by unit and location; and how they will be attracted, oriented (or "onboarded"), developed, and retained. Dick Beatty of Rutgers University is the best-known researcher in this area. His work with Mark Huselid and Brian Becker is seminal.[7] In their view, the key challenge is to first understand where value is created. Good analytics start with understanding how and where the organization creates the capability that drives strategy, makes and loses money, and wins and loses key customers. This identifies the critical positions and the drivers of organizational performance—or what we call the "unit of competitive advantage." Beatty reminds us that there is not always a correlation between seniority and criticality. In the brewery industry, an obviously critical role is the brewmaster. In social networking, it is the application developer or programmer. In consumer product companies like PepsiCo, it is the marketer.

We recommend four principles in optimizing human capital through workforce planning and analytics:

1. *Define critical strategic roles.* Interviews and other data collection efforts, coupled with working together with the finance team, will help you develop a model of what functions and skills disproportionately deliver value to customers and investors. The purpose is to define which functions are truly strategic, which provide support but are not in themselves strategic, and which are essential but do not add strategic value or key support. Organizations and industries differ significantly. For example, in the chemical industry, manufacturing is a strategic function. In high-tech companies like Cisco and Apple, manufacturing is merely essential and therefore can be outsourced.

2. *Conduct a Strength, Weakness, Opportunity, and Threat (SWOT) assessment.* Assessing current strengths and weaknesses in delivering the strategy is critical, closely followed by developing the future state based on a consideration of opportunities and threats. For example, consulting firms such as McKinsey and BCG have identified the need to shift from strategic advisory services to solution support and implementation. This is a significant change in strategy and capability and will require considerable retraining for new skills in these firms.

3. *Buy, build, or both.* A shift in resourcing raises the question of how best to accomplish the result. Some organizations such as P&G or Exxon Mobil are committed employee developers, and they resist hiring senior experienced staff.[7] Other organizations such as Mars tend to buy experienced talent (that is, bring it in from outside). Still others such as Goldman Sachs and JP Morgan combine these strategies: they tend to be developers, but supplement with selective external hiring. Your plan should be both strategically prudent and culturally acceptable.

4. *Manage the change process.* This means initiating the process in a way that facilitates success It means involving the right individuals, providing effective information and homework, considering contingencies, monitoring and sustaining performance by reviewing the effectiveness of decisions made, and anticipating potential problems.

Optimizing human capital is an increasing challenge; Towers Watson recently reported that 65 percent of companies are worried about the retention of critical skills.[8] And the Aberdeen group has noted that two-thirds of companies are stepping up their efforts in workforce planning and analysis, and almost 30 percent of these companies hold the CEO and board directly accountable.[9]

Factor 2: Developing Talent

When it comes to developing employees, the focus is on both how and how well the organization is growing the technical and organizational or interpersonal skills needed for people to have productive and satisfying work lives. The actions that make up this factor are standard setting, assessment, investing in talent, and follow-up.

Setting a Standard

Competence begins by identifying the required competencies to deliver future work. Rather than focus on what has worked in the past by comparing low- and high-performing employees, more recent competence standards come from turning future customer expectations into present employee requirements. At any level in a company, an HR professional can facilitate a discussion of the following questions:

- What are the current social and technical competencies we have within our company?
- What are the environmental changes facing our business, and what are our strategic responses?
- Given our future environment and strategic choices, what technical and social competencies must employees demonstrate?

By facilitating these questions, HR professionals help general managers create a theory or point of view on competencies that leads to a set of employee standards. When general managers build competence models based on future customer expectations, they direct employees' attention to what they should be, know, and do. The simplest test of the competence standard is to ask target or key customers, "If our employees lived up to these standards, would they inspire confidence from you in our firm?"

Assessing Individuals and Organizations

With standards in place, employees may be assessed on how well the standards are met. We have long argued that performance is a function of both attributes (competencies) and results. Competent employees deliver results in the right way, and the right way is defined by the competence standards. Forward-thinking organizations are increasingly seeking outside perspectives on performance as well as internal collegial views. This 720-degree feedback includes external stakeholders such as customers, suppliers, investors, and community leaders. This helps individuals know what to do to improve, and it also provides valuable input to the organization about how to design and deliver HR practices in order to upgrade talent. In the words of a former Google employee:

> Google actually celebrates its hiring process, as if its ruthless ineffi-
> ciency and interminable duration were a sure proof of thoroughness, a
> badge of honor. Perhaps it is thorough. But I would be willing to wager
> that Microsoft's hiring process, which takes a fraction of the time, does
> not result in a lower-skilled workforce or result in a higher rate of attri-
> tion. And let me say this: If Larry Page is still reviewing résumés, share-
> holders should organize a rebellion. That is a scandalous waste of time
> for someone at that level, and the fact that it's "quirky" is no mitigation.

Investing in Talent Improvement

Individual and organizational gaps may be filled by investing in talent. In our work we have found six investments that can help upgrade talent:

1. *Buy:* Recruiting, sourcing, securing new talent into the organization
2. *Build:* Helping people grow through training or life experiences

3. *Borrow:* Bringing knowledge into the organization through external advisors or partners

4. *Boost:* Promoting the right people into key jobs

5. *Bounce:* Removing poor performers from their jobs—and from the organization if there are no jobs in which they will perform well

6. *Bind:* Retaining top talent through opportunity, reward, and nonfinancial recognition

When HR professionals create choices in these six areas, they help individuals and organizations invest in future talent.

Following Up on and Tracking Competence

President Ronald Reagan was fond of saying, "Trust but verify." Tracking performance and development is obviously important. How well are individuals developing their skills? Are we learning and performing faster than our competitors? Are we doing more of the right things—are we improving how well we deliver the capabilities that underpin our goals and strategies at the team, organization, and enterprise level? How well is the organization retaining and growing its talent? Are the right backups in place for key positions? Are leaders contributing to the longer-term development of the organization in its marketplace?

Factor 3: Shaping Organization and Communication Practices

In the 2007 research, shaping organization and communication were separate and distinct competency factors. In this round of research, we found that these two factors are combined, that shaping organization and communication practices fit together to form one effective whole.

Organization is not boxes on a chart. An effective organization is a set of operating protocols reinforced through relationships that necessarily involve communication combined into what we call capabilities. A process we find particularly helpful is described by our colleague Dave Hanna in the following questions[10]:

- What is the business result we are trying to achieve?
- What capabilities must be in place for the business result to be achieved and sustained over time?
- How do we activate these capabilities through HR systems and practices?
- How do we implement change in a way that reinforces this virtuous cycle?
- How do we measure and monitor effectiveness and efficiency?
- How do we ensure alignment over time?

For example, high-performing teams have a number of attributes in common, as shown in Figure 7.2 and in the list following.[11]

- *Purpose.* Any successful team needs a clear purpose or charter. This should capture not only the mind but the heart, and be clear about both what should be done and the meaning team members derive from their work together. Such a team purpose meets a number of criteria:
  - It is tangible or measurable.
  - Team members participate in defining it.

Figure 7.2   High-performing teams

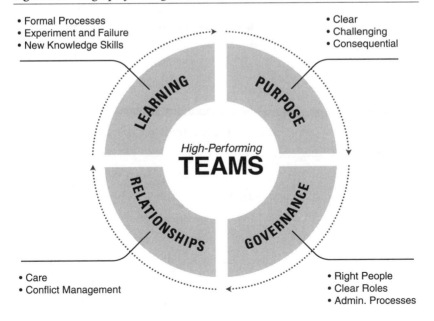

- It defines the outcomes or goals of the team and justifies the team's existence.

- It focuses on the future and on the outcomes of the team, not just the process, thus creating aspirational meaning.

  In addition, the team leader needs to reinforce the purpose through words, symbols, messages, and actions that make the purpose real to team members and users of team services and to track progress toward its purpose.

• *Governance.* Governance reflects how the team operates: roles and accountabilities, hierarchy, decision making, and support systems. These administrative routines shape meaning as members react to their team activity. Roles focus on who is on the team, which may include technical or functional specialists, customers who adapt knowledge to their requirements, and managers who coordinate work, set deadlines, and administer team activities. A team functions through the decisions it makes. Successful decision making increases with clarity, accountability, time lines, processes, and follow-up as follows:

  - *Clarity of decision:* Focus on the decision that needs to be made and the alternatives to consider in the course of making that decision.

  - *Assignment of accountability:* Who has the monkey? That is, who is accountable for this decision, and who must be involved?

  - *Practical details:* When must this decision be made? Who will ultimately make this decision, and how will it be made? What process will be used and on what criteria is it based?

  - *Affiliation.* A team begins with purpose but thrives on healthy relationships. Effective teams create caring relationships among their members: engaging, listening effectively, offering help, and building trust through results. They also manage conflict: accommodate different perspectives, disagree without being disagreeable, and debate without being demeaning. A colleague once described teamwork as "learning to fight without leaving scars." This requires that team members lean into problems rather than away from them, provide honest and direct feedback to each other, and sacrifice personal interests for team objectives. Effective teams avoid what psychologists call the "relationship killers": criticism, contempt, defensiveness, and stonewalling.

- *Learning*: Teams inevitably do some things well and other things badly, and so they need a commitment to learning. They should adopt the following practices:
  - Take time to reflect and assess. Katzenbach calls this "time together."[12]
  - Define what has worked well and what has not worked well and why.
  - Identify the pattern of common or repeated errors made by the team.
  - Have a spirit of learning, not blaming. Acknowledge that mistakes are made, apologize, and move forward without getting too consumed by them.
  - When a mistake is made, acknowledge it quickly, boldly, and publicly. Work to not make it again. Learning means that teams have a self-improvement process built into their regular work.

Conducting a Communications Audit

The quality of ongoing communication can provide a powerful measure of work and organizational effectiveness, but it needs to be looked at specifically. A communications audit will therefore repay the effort it requires. Table 7.2 outlines a number of different approaches to conducting a communications audit, along with the pros and cons of each one. Gear your audit to what will best provide the assessment you need given time, budget, and cultural considerations. For example, a survey may be the most efficient approach, but perhaps your organization has survey-fatigue. If so, focus groups may be a more prudent methodology despite the apparently greater cost.

Factor 4: Driving Performance

The 2007 findings did not explicitly address performance management as a key factor in the talent manager and organizational designer domains. In the 2012 research, the importance of performance management in innovative and integrated HR contribution turned out to be strongly reinforced.

Table 7.2   *Communication Audit Alternatives*[13]

Method	Pro	Con
Interviews	Qualitative in-depth information	Heavy time and resource investment
Surveys	Standardized and comparable responses to a limited number of questions	Do not provide in-depth commentary when used on their own
Critical incident review	Specific examples of what works and what doesn't work in practice	Useful in conjunction with interviews or surveys to explore in detail specific situations
Network analysis	Understanding of how process design and network structures help and hinder effective and efficient communication; strong information yield if done correctly	Heavy time and resource investment
Observation	Qualitative in-depth information	Heavy time and resource investment
Document review	Message clarification and evaluation: clarity, consistency	Useful as a follow-up step to address specific issues such as consistency of description of strategy
Focus groups	In-depth assessment of what is going well and what must be improved	Heavy time and resource investment

Effective HR professionals play a number of critical roles in driving performance:

• *Establishing clear performance standards.* Effective HR professionals ensure that a communications process is in place that establishes what performance is expected and why. In other words, the process creates a line of sight between the individual employee and the customer or other stakeholders. We encourage this outside-in focus, which makes the impact of performance real to employees at all levels and in all roles. Stories that describe the real impact of performance on customers are particularly powerful. For example, British Petroleum (BP) did an excellent job of making the impact of the Gulf cleanup meaningful to its employees by engaging them in cleanup efforts and drenching the organization in information about the real citizens of the Gulf region and the impact of the spill on their lives. GE Medical Systems similarly makes the impact of work on customers real by introducing its employees to cancer survivors.

- *Putting a clear process of performance assessment in place with well-defined performance metrics.* It is essential that the performance management process be effective, efficient, and transparent: who does what, when, how, and with what information or metrics in place.
- *Providing rich feedback on strengths and needs for improvement and development.* Relevant and meaningful feedback is the foundation for development. As we mention elsewhere, we see a shift from 360-degree feedback to approaches that directly involve customers, suppliers, and other external stakeholders.
- *Rewarding and recognizing good performance.* Driving performance depends on the combination of financial rewards and nonfinancial acknowledgment or recognition of achievement. We recommend the following principles in developing effective reward and recognition schemes:
  - *Equity.* The employees who contribute the greatest value to the organization should receive the greatest rewards.
  - *Transparency.* How rewards are determined should be clear to organization members. The perceived fairness of the system is undercut when people see significant variations in how rewards are determined from one type of employee to another.
  - *Meaningfulness.* Rewards should be meaningful to the individual. For example, some employees may be more interested in time off, others in financial reward, and still others in new opportunities or challenges. Understanding what individual employees find valuable is essential.
- *Teaching employees and line managers skills in providing and receiving feedback.* Effective performance management is based on skills in giving and receiving feedback. Top organizations don't take feedback skills for granted; rather, they reinforce these skills through regular education.

- *Adapting performance standards to changing strategic demands.* HR plays a critical role in ensuring that performance standards remain accurate and relevant. Standards should flow from strategic goals—and as goals change, standards must change along with them. For example, the window and sky-light company Velux Group puts a strong emphasis on implementing lean technologies in manufacturing. Performance standards are changing—led by HR—to reinforce the importance of this initiative. As competition has increased and particularly as less expensive alternatives are available to consumers, the company has focused more on reducing the cost of production without loss of quality.

- *Dealing with nonperformance in a fair and timely way.* Finally, how the organization deals with nonperformance has a significant impact on how the company is seen to value performance. Nonperformance must be dealt with respectfully and fairly—and above all promptly. The organization's response to high and low performance sends a message to all employees about the value of performance, the fairness and transparency of the system, and the importance that the company places on meeting its goals and serving its customers and other stakeholders.

Factor 5: Building Leadership Brand

The last of the key factors for HR innovator and integrator is what we like to refer to as "leadership brand."[14] Over the course of the last several years, RBL Group research on leadership effectiveness has identified a seminal shift in thinking about leadership and talent. We have made the case that a more strategic approach for leadership development should focus less on the social and technical skills of individual managers and more on leadership as an organizational capability: the ability of an organization to develop successive generations of leaders, at all levels, who reinforce external and internal confidence in the future and who are "branded" by the distinctiveness of their competence. For example, what are leaders at SONY or General Electric or Intel known for?

A leadership brand has two key elements. The first of these is leadership competence in the fundamentals of being in charge: what we called the "leadership code."[15] The second consists of the differentiators—the things that make a leader reflect and exemplify the character of a specific firm. Figure 7.3 provides a visual image of the model.

The Leadership Code

Leadership code reflects the common and consistent expectations of any leader in any organization, whether it be the Red Cross, PNB Paribas, or Heineken's. Effective leaders play these five roles wherever they lead:

1. *Strategist:* Positioning the organization for the future by having key objectives and goals focused on serving key customers
2. *Executor:* Installing the performance disciplines and execution protocols to achieve and measure the result
3. *Talent manager:* Coaching and communication with today's talent
4. *Human capital developer:* Identifying, recruiting, and developing the talent needed to address tomorrow's challenges

Figure 7.3   Leadership brand architecture

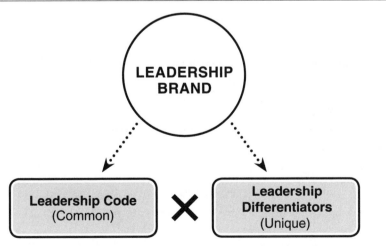

5. *Personal proficiency:* Earning the right to learn through personal attributes like emotional intelligence, learning agility, integrity, and social networking

Exercise 7.1 will help you assess your organization's strengths and opportunities for improvement in the leadership code elements. Give your organization a score for each element and then identify one element where you think the opportunity for increased impact is greatest:

Exercise 7.1   *Assessing the Leadership Code*

Leadership Code Element	Score (1–5)	Impact of Improvement on the Business (Be specific.)	Plan for Improvement
Strategist			
Executor			
Talent manager			
Human capital developer			
Personal proficiency			

Leadership Differentiators

The leadership code is one dimension of building a strong and distinctive leadership brand. The other is identifying the distinctive brand the organization needs to establish for its leaders. Apple leaders are known for innovation; Victoria's Secret's leaders are appreciated for customer-centricity; Tiffany's leaders have a reputation for demanding outstanding quality.

Developing a leadership brand architecture is a six-step process, as shown in Figure 7.4.

How well has your organization defined the distinctive brand it expects from its leaders? And how effective is your organization at developing leaders who exemplify that brand? Table 7.3 presents some possibilities for action that will improve the innovation and integration of branded leadership development, given a variety of immediate goals.

Figure 7.4   *Developing a leadership brand*

For example, Damco, the supply chain division of A.P. Moller-Maersk, has involved customers significantly and directly in leadership development. The Damco "Impact" program—a two-year developmental accelerator for young leaders that incorporates executive education, special project participation, and collaboration with peers across markets—invites customers to speak regularly to the organization's top young talent. The program pulls no punches in providing both positive and challenging feedback. The results have been interesting. Customers who have participated (Home Goods, Kellogg, Abercrombie & Fitch, HP) have expressed a good deal of appreciation for being involved, even though it required extensive preparation and travel.

Development of a leadership brand can be immensely revealing. HR leaders at Google were surprised to find that the key drivers of managerial success were not technical skills but good leadership code basics tied to innovat* strategy The findings led Google to rethink the role of a manager—an*

Table 7.3   Options for Building Leadership Brand

If Your Top Priority for Improvement Is:	Potential Actions for HR Professionals	Potential Actions for HR Leaders
Create a business case that leadership matters.	Identify the financial and operational benefits of stronger leaders and leadership in terms of growth, customer satisfaction, and risk mitigation.	Make leadership an explicit aspect of strategic discussions: Do we have the leadership cohort to implement the strategy? What is the value of stronger leadership?
Articulate the definition of an effective leader.	Use interviews to identify areas of agreement and disagreement re leadership differentiators.	Align leadership requirements with strategic requirements.
Assess leaders against a set of criteria.	Participate actively in assessing leaders and in auditing the assessment process.	Ensure a consistently demanding and rigorous assessment process.
Invest in future leaders.	Utilize databases such as the RBL/Hewitt "Top Companies for Leaders" to define how the best companies invest in future leaders.	Make global benchmarking a regular part of reviewing the effectiveness of investments in leadership development.
Measure or track leadership effectiveness.	Use focus groups to identify areas of integration and where better integration is needed.	Audit the leadership development process on an annual basis: How can we improve?
Integrate leadership development efforts.	Assess alignment and opportunities to improve the integration of HR practices that support leadership development.	Involve customers in assessing leaders: What skills must our leaders have 2–3 years from now for us to continue to meet your expectations?

its philosophy. Here are the eight principles of leadership that Google developed as a result of the study[16]:

1. Be a good coach.
2. Empower your team and don't micromanage.
3. Express interest in employees' success and well-being.
4. Be productive and results-oriented.
5. Be a good communicator and listen to your team.
6. Help your employees with career development
7. Have a clear vision and strategy for the team.
8. Have key technical skills, so you can help advise the team.

The Integration Challenge

Five core HR practice areas are the focus for innovation and integration:

1. People
2. Performance and reward
3. Information and communication
4. Work and organization
5. Leadership

How effective is industry at the integration of these HR practice areas? Its performance is not great. According to a recent study by the Human Capital Media Advisory Group, when asked if talent acquisition is fully integrated with other practices such as performance management and learning and development:

- 41 percent disagree or strongly disagree.
- 26 percent neither agree nor disagree.
- 33 percent agree or strongly agree.

There is no doubt that integration is essential in creating a shared mindset across an organization. But these data at least suggest that while integration is a good idea, it is not being done very well or consistently.

Conclusion: HR Professionals as Innovators and Integrators

The HR innovator and integrator domain offers us the opportunity to look into the expectations of HR and line management leaders. For both the message is clear: HR is expected to innovate in implementing HR practices, particularly in the talent space, that align with capability, have efficacy, and integrate to create capability and shared culture. Innovation may be original, adapted from outside the organization, or reflect the adoption or application of new ways of working from one division of an organization to another. But innovation is not enough. The job of HR is to enable culture through capability, and this requires alignment or integration across practices—particularly in areas where the impact of alignment is significant and the cost of nonalignment is confusion or disregard for HR.

CHAPTER 8

TECHNOLOGY
PROPONENT

8

(This chapter was contributed by M. S. Krishnan; Joseph Handleman, Professor of Information Systems and Innovation at the Ross School of Business at the University of Michigan; and Wayne Brockbank, one of this book's coauthors.)

Some time ago, the American Electronics Association held a two-day conference in Washington, D.C., to discuss the simmering relationship between the U.S. electronics industry and the U.S. government. Attendees were major players: CEOs on the industry side and senior officials representing the government, including several senators, representatives, and members of the administration. In the midst of one heated exchange, a U.S. senator went to the microphone and asked if Dave Packard was in the room. The cofounder of Hewlett-Packard was indeed in room—it was that sort of meeting—and he made his way to one of the audience microphones.

"Mr. Packard," the senator then said, "you are famous for creating a company that has been very successful because of its innovative and collaborative environment. You resolved issues between Silicon Valley companies and the local communities. You have played a central role in creating the American Electronics Association that brings us together today. Now we bring to you an even greater challenge. How do you suggest that we bring together the best interests of private companies in the country with the best interest of the U.S. government?" Packard stood thoughtfully at the microphone for a several seconds and responded, "I suggest that I convene a working group of CEOs from the electronics industry, from the senate and from the executive branch. We will propose an approach that will optimize the best interest for all. I have full confidence that we will be successful." Immediately following this meeting, Wayne Brockbank had an appointment to meet with Dave Packard to discuss business-government relations. The first question he asked was, "What is there about your thinking that leads you to build institutions that get people to share information and perspectives for their collective best interests?" Packard smiled as he said, "Every Friday morning HP's executive team meets. Sometimes the meetings last for a couple of hours; sometimes for a couple of days. And we spend at least 50 percent of our time trying to figure out how to get information from one part of the company to another part and to make sure that the information is used. The problem is that people who have important information frequently do not have the means or the desire to convey information, and those who need the information do not have means or the desire to receive and use the information. Addressing this issue makes us who we are."

What We Mean by Technology Proponent

Not all CEOs have Dave Packard's level of insight into what needs to be done to ensure that information is disseminated to where it is needed, and the urgency of the matter has only grown since his time. In the past two decades, while the cost of computing power and digital communication has plummeted, software applications have expanded to encompass every aspect of business. (See Figure 8.1.) From customer transactions to supplier management and from investor relations to employee engagement, technology is everywhere. Ubiquitous connectivity and pervasive digitization have transformed the face of IT in businesses large and small over the last two decades. Fortunately, HR can play an active role in addressing the issue of technology and information management, adding materially to its value to the business.

The technology supporting information architecture in firms started with applications that supported automation of functional transactions. Most of these systems were developed in-house, and they often used multiple data sources for the same entities, which led to redundancy of data definitions and integration challenges. Efficiency in executing transactions in various functions through these applications was difficult to attain in the face of conflicting information across silos.

Figure 8.1   *Reduction in computing costs*

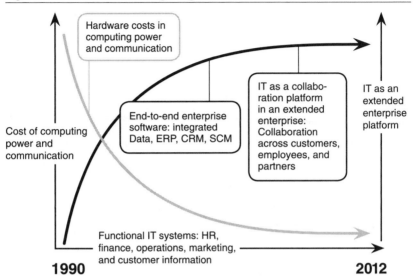

Hardware costs in computing power and communication

Cost of computing power and communication

End-to-end enterprise software: integrated Data, ERP, CRM, SCM

IT as a collaboration platform in an extended enterprise: Collaboration across customers, employees, and partners

IT as an extended enterprise platform

Functional IT systems: HR, finance, operations, marketing, and customer information

1990

2012

These challenges began to be addressed in the 1990s through integrated (and vendor-developed) enterprise resource planning (ERP) software that centralized the data and connected with other products such as customer relationship management (CRM) and supply chain management (SCM) software. Promising as these approaches were, however—and despite the millions of dollars organizations spent on them—the results were problematic at best. While the right implementation of these packages did lead to efficiency gains in transaction processing, even that level of success was by no means certain.

Worse, the data contained in these systems seldom turned into information that could be used to derive insights for decision making. The user interfaces made it difficult to extract answers to questions, in part because business functional leaders did not take an active role in designing the information architecture. Instead, this task was delegated to software vendors, information technology industry partners, and internal IT teams, all of whom lacked insight into the kinds of questions it would be useful to ask—and answer.

To a large extent, the same problems have continued into the twenty-first century. Technology is still not the zone of comfort for business functional managers. As a result business managers do not understand the information flow across the business processes that enable their functions—and the internal IT teams may be experts in technology, but they are not exposed to the business side of the organization. As C. K. Prahalad and M. S. Krishnan note in *New Age of Innovation*, while the procedural articulation of the business process and information flow are the core enablers of flexibility and innovation in organizations, this responsibility often falls through the cracks.[1]

The HR function is not an exception. Every aspect of the HR function—recruitment, compensation, training, employee learning, performance management, knowledge access, and even leadership development—is now enabled by information technology. Figure 8.2 illustrates the evolution of the role of IT in HR over the last two decades.

The first level in Figure 8.2 is the automation of HR transactions through IT systems. Almost every organization today is at or above this level. In the second level, HR integrates data across various activities, including other business functions. For example, recruitment may not be fully automated and integrated, but information technology still plays a role in getting the right people to the right places. It is also possible that some HR activities such as employee performance systems may be in a silo application and not integrated with other HR applications. However, most large organizations have evolved

Figure 8.2   *Evolution of technology in HR*

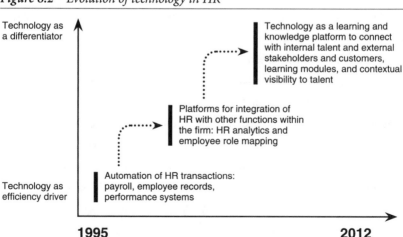

to the second level, where HR functions are encompassed in the HR module of ERP vendor systems. These systems improve the efficiency of HR through integration of data across various HR activities and minimizing data redundancy and dissonance. These systems also allow for specific employee roles to be mapped to the organization structure and enable transparency to assigned roles and performance. However, most of these systems are still transaction-oriented and provide HR analytics only in the context of these transactions.

While most organizations still use IT as an efficiency driver, technology can also be a differentiator in the application of talent and knowledge assets both inside and outside the organization. As depicted in Figure 8.2, firms at the third level use technology as a learning and knowledge platform to connect with internal talent assets and to collaborate with external stakeholders, including customers and other partners. These firms use their IT platform to deliver training and learning modules and track the usage of these modules. They create transparency for the expertise and performance of their employees and connect their employees across their global businesses via these platforms.

The Factors of Technology Proponent

Table 8.1 provides the statistical breakdown of the factors of the technology proponent domain, including the mean score of how well each is done and its relative impact on individual effectiveness and on business success. As noted previously in Table 2.8 in Chapter 2, the technology component is the weakest of the six competency domains when it comes to quality of execution (3.74 out of 5.00), but it has almost the highest impact of any domain on business success (18 percent of HR's total impact). Thus this domain represents a major opportunity for improvement and increased value.

Factor 1: Improving the Utility of HR Operations Through Technology

Although it's far more than a platitude to say that employees are among any business's most important assets, technology use in HR lags far behind technol-

Table 8.1   *Technology Proponent: Factors, Mean, Individual Effectiveness, and Business Success*

Factor	Mean (1–5)	Individual Effectiveness 100%	Business Impact 100%
Improving utility of HR operations	3.72	2.9	5.0
Leveraging social media tools	3.68	2.7	4.7
Connecting people through technology	3.77	4.6	6.3
R^2		12%	18%

ogy use in operations, finance, or marketing. The automation of HR functions such as payroll, performance appraisal, and employee benefits can deliver efficiency, and introducing employee self-service can increase it further. But this is only the starting point. The capacity for digitization of employee information, organizational roles, and workflow across functions opens up enormous opportunities for HR to improve its management of employee information and experience. For example, Cisco HR provides in-house medical checkups for employees and even manages employee health information, providing incentives for people to take steps to improve their health. In some companies, HR systems capture annual medical checkup records and even present incentives for maintaining a body mass index within appropriate levels. Such programs can both motivate employees to take care of themselves and address the healthcare costs issue.

American Express has empowered its customer care professionals by providing a flexible technology platform that enables these employees to trade work shifts with each other on their own, without having to go through the hierarchy of approvals from supervisors. This allows people to improve their work-life balance. For example, someone who wants to catch up on a school soccer game or attend to a sick child can trade shifts with another willing employee. The system records all the customer care shifts digitally, tracking them at the employee level. It thus allows management to keep employee empowerment from turning into license and damaging the customer experience. It is no surprise that this platform was recognized with the company's annual CEO innovation award.[2]

The BPS division is a multibillion-dollar global business solutions provider in the healthcare industry. It has built an integrated information platform to connect its employees and workflow activities in its operations, which are made up of a global network of on- and offshore technology centers and associates, providing a best-shore option to meet healthcare organizations' unique needs and goals. Its outsourcing model is designed to stabilize workforces, provide a single point for accountability, anddeliver measurable process savings. The BPS division serves more than 35 medical health specialties in multiple states in the United States. Additionally, it provides process improvement consulting and training to help businesses and government organizations improve performance, increase productivity, and achieve compliance with a variety of international standards and models, including ISO 9001 and Six Sigma.

The proprietary IT platform at BPS is designed to connect its employees to operations and external stakeholders such as customers and other knowledge partners. It includes team communication, talent information, past performance ratings, and full profiles of individual employees, and it can tailor its training and development offerings to the needs of individual employees. For example, if someone assigned to health insurance processing logs in, the platform provides relevant training modules for that role and also the best and average scores in those modules—allowing the individual to see both what's needed and what others have done with the opportunity. The same records allow management to see how training modules are working at an individual-acceptance and overall level.

The BPS platform automates and integrates almost every aspect of employee-related activities with core business operations. For example, from their first interviews at the time of recruitment, employees are asked to take specific electronic tests on this IT platform, and their performance in these tests is tracked. Employees are not allowed into classroom training unless they clear a few computer-generated self-tests well above cutoff scores. To make sure that employees stay up to date in the domain knowledge of the businesses and tasks they are serving, and also in operational process knowledge, they are scheduled to take weekly tests, and their scores over time are captured and made transparent. This platform enables BPS to manage the productivity and performance of its associates using real-time performance data and skills-based logic.

BPS also maintains a live skills database that captures the skill level of each employee on various tasks. Customers have access to this information so they can, for example, review the set of people assigned to their business processes, the skill levels of the employees, and their performance over the last six months in the tasks assigned to them. The system is akin to a manufacturing quality control process, maintaining live quality levels of employee performance on the job. Both employees and customers can see this information at any time, which does a great deal to keep quality at the forefront of everyone's attention.

The same employee portal records new ideas generated by each employee, and the monthly performance appraisal of each employee is conducted with a live screen indicating performance ratings. Similarly, supervisors and managers are assessed based on the collective performance of their group, once again captured live in the system. The benefits and compensation details for each employee are also available in the same platform. Hence performance appraisals are not based on perceptions but actual live data on performance. Employees are shown the different quartiles of performance levels in their roles across the organization and are informed where they stand. As a result, attrition at BPS is both well below the industry average and much less problematic than at other companies. As a senior executive at BPS says cheerfully, "While we also have attrition, we know exactly who is leaving, and we are OK with that." The performance assessment process is so transparent that employees performing below expectations leave on their own.

BPS workflow operations are also transparent to global customers, who can both collaborate and monitor the operations. The platform also includes a knowledge management tool and a knowledge acquisition process to capture both tacit and explicit learning about both customers and processes, allowing for immediate and fast learning of any changes in customer processes or healthcare industry regulations. Overall performance of quality at the process level and also at the individual employee level is made transparent to both the employee and the customer to whom the employee is assigned. The company has countered the usual outsourcing risk of global customers with this flexible and transparent information platform.

Factor 2: Leveraging Social Media Tools

According to the Gartner study in 2012, only 5 percent of organizations have taken advantage of social media as a platform to collaborate with customers to improve their processes.[3] In recent years social media and supporting technologies such as wikis and blogs have emerged as the platform for companies to engage with internal employees, customers, and partners. Almost every company has a page in Facebook and LinkedIn. HR departments use Twitter messages to attract prospective talent. Companies use videos and blogs on social media platforms to communicate about their work culture and present new opportunities to the external world. For example, Intel has a video on YouTube, and Deutsche Bank has developed a report called "Unofficial Guide to Banking" that simplifies content to demystify banking and attract new recruits.[4] GE presents its new innovation projects on social media to project its innovative culture.

Social media are also emerging as a way to connect employees with customers. Beyond simply addressing customer problems, these platforms are becoming a knowledge hub for collaboration among employees and customers to solve problems and generate new ideas to improve products and services. In essence, the traditional customer word of mouth is now spoken on social media platforms. And businesses cannot afford to ignore this new reality. A few years back, for example, some Dell laptops caught fire unexpectedly. The phenomenon was more intensely tracked on the social media sites than anywhere else, and Dell was able to use the same platform to grasp the source of these problems and address them rapidly.

The impact of social media is not limited to external engagement. We see companies creating platforms similar to social media within their organizations. These internal platforms connect employees and evolve as an internal collaboration space for new ideas, spotting talent, solving problems, and generating new ideas. Idea forums enabled through technology platforms are now common inside organizations (UBS, IBM, and Tata Consultancy Services, for example). These platforms create new channels of learning through sharing of best practices by employees across global business units in large firms. Some organizations, such as Pfizer, have even opened up strategy documents in the making and allow candid discussion of policies in these internal platforms to communicate the company's open culture and transparency.

Although social networks are rapidly evolving both inside and outside businesses, they also present some challenges. Returns from the use of these platforms are mixed. For example, employees immersed in these platforms could be either actively collaborating or wasting time. The legality around the governance of these platforms is also ambiguous. Sometimes it is less than clear who owns the content on these platforms. For example, it has been reported that there is a case about someone claiming that his or her Facebook member page contributed materially to the market value of Facebook ! In another instance, a large global company implemented a social platform inside the organization to encourage open communication. Soon the language used in these platforms, especially toward the senior management, was crossing the line of decorum maintained within the firm. Senior managers were not ready for that. They closed the platform down to rethink their strategy on how to get it right.

Overall, it is clear that this is still an evolving technology. Hence it should not be a surprise that this factor comes in low on business impact in our results.

Consider this case of leveraging social media. When IBM was on the verge of bankruptcy in the early 1990s, CEO Lou Gerstner championed a strategic shift from selling computer products to delivering business technology solutions tailored to customer needs—and brought the company back to health in the process. Since then the focus of IBM's business has been on knowledge. The company differentiates itself in the marketplace through unique and innovative custom solutions offered to capture a higher share of the customer wallet. Hence the knowledge and expertise of IBM employees is a critical asset. As early as 1997, when most organizations resisted the idea of employees accessing the Internet, IBM was encouraging employees to go online, both to access new information sources and also to collaborate with customers and partners.

More recently IBM has embarked upon what it calls a social business transformation. It has created platforms to help its employees understand social media and how to use them for their specific roles. IBM is deploying social media and similar networks inside the organization to capitalize on the expertise of its people. A companywide taxonomy of roles and expertise in the context of customer needs is available online to the more than 400,000 IBM employees across the globe.[5] And a social platform system called "The Greater IBM Connection" helps employees identify their strengths and further develop by connecting with people and partners both inside and outside IBM—IBM employees and potential customers or other partners alike—and it includes an internal search portal to "find an expert" within IBM on specific topics. For example, if a customer engagement specialist in Arizona needs a team of mixed expertise—perhaps a power systems expert in Europe, two software design experts in California, one systems integrator and two testing specialists from Bangalore and Mumbai, respectively—the group can be assembled in short order, collaborating across global time zones almost as smoothly as across the hall.[6]

Similar to the popular social networking platforms, IBM Connections allows employees to share status updates, collaborate on ideas, and share information. In addition, IBM employees manage more than 17,000 individual blogs on various topics. These platforms collectively become a terrific source of knowledge for IBM. IBM also uses social media for routine HR functions such as recruiting, employee education, sales training, and leadership development. For example, in leadership development IBM has created a special social network for new hires so that they can be in touch with one another no matter where in the world they are. This way they can pool their collective intelligence in learning about the organization and getting acclimatized.

IBM has succeeded in creating a unique internal social platform to build on the collective expertise of hundreds of thousands of employees across the globe to design and deliver unique solutions to their customers. The value of this is easily seen: in the last 10 years IBM's sales and profits have increased significantly, and return to shareholders has been four times that of the S&P and almost twice that of the Nasdaq.

Factor 3: Connecting People Through Technology

The "connecting people through technology" factor of the technology proponent domain is a dramatic and counterintuitive finding. The reasoning for this conclusion is reasonably straightforward. All technology proponent factors have the lowest personal effectiveness scores of any of the domains by noticeable margins. (See Table 2.9 and Figure 2.7.) While connecting people through technology scores highest of the three technology proponent factors, the differences among the three are small (see Table 8.1). The high drama occurs when we consider impact on business success. Connecting people through technology has the greatest impact on business success of any factor of any domain. It is simultaneously where HR professionals have the worst scores and where they can have the greatest impact. This is essentially the definition of potential competitive advantage. Something that is rarely done well but that boosts business success when it is done well is clearly the place to focus our energies.

The survey items that comprise this factor indicate a comprehensive communication strategy that can be expressed in the framework set out in Figure 8.3.

Taken together, the elements of Figure 8.3 constitute information strategy architecture. And we have observed that HR professionals in high-performing firms are becoming more involved in these activities. Some may ask if this focus takes HR too far from its core activities, and on the surface the answer might appear to be yes. But on further consideration, it makes sense for HR professionals to be involved in these activities. If we start from the premise that HR should be the architect of the human and organizational side of the business, certainly the information that companies expose their people to has a large impact on the way people think and behave together, the way they see their world together, their ability to coordinate actions over disconnected silos, and the development of key organizational capabilities: the organization's culture.

Figure 8.3   Communication strategy framework

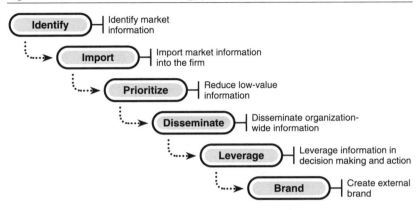

Over the past several months, we have visited with management teams in dozens of companies, and we have found an interesting trend. In general, each of these companies has a chief financial officer, a chief HR officer, a chief operating officer, a chief engineer, and a chief technology officer. Some have a chief information officer—but when we dig beneath the surface, we find that the title almost always belongs to the *chief information technology officer*—the one who is looking after the computer system, that is, minding the pipeline but not what goes through the pipeline. We did not find a single company where someone was responsible for thinking through the comprehensive end-to-end information flow architecture of the firm. Nonetheless, the logic of the business processes within a firm *is* the information flow architecture. In the midst of the information age, no one seems to be shouldering responsibility for that critical dimension of organizational success. As cited above, this is consistent with work of C. K. Prahalad and M .S. Krishnan.[7] We are not suggesting that HR be the chief information flow architect, but we are suggesting that HR professionals who actively attend to this issue may substantially enhance their impact on business success.

Identify Key Market Information

It may seem self-evident, but it's surprisingly difficult to realize what you don't know, and this is as true of organizations as of individuals. For example, when a major oil field service company experienced a substantial loss of market share, the cause was by no means obvious.[8] The new president, Buddy Parker, recognized that something had to happen quickly. He visited each department, including HR, and asked, "What do you think we need to do to solve this problem?" In most companies, the CHRO would probably respond, "We can help you cut your staff to keep up with the loss in revenues." Here, the reply was an emphatic, "Before we know what we should do in HR, we need to understand where we have gone wrong with our customers. We need a large-scale effort that gets us listening to our customers." Together with the marketing department, the HR department helped orchestrate a substantial effort in which large numbers of employees across functions and levels interviewed customers throughout the world. Based on the information they garnered, major realignments occurred in the kinds of people who were hired and promoted, what was measured and rewarded, and what was used as the focus of training and development. Within a year, the slide was halted; by the end of the second year, the company had experienced a substantial increase in market share.

Import Important Market Information into the Firm

In a few isolated but significant companies, HR departments are helping bring market information into the firm. For example, Disney has used its employees in its market research efforts, discovering that when employees make the research calls, it gets better information from its best customers. When customers learn that a frontline employee such as a receptionist from the Grand Floridian is on the line, they give more thoughtful information than if they were talking to an anonymous market research firm. As customers share their experiences with Disney employees, the conversation has direct impact on the employee involved, on the employee's colleagues, on the current customers, and on future customers. It is a great win-win situation.

Hindustan Unilever Limited (HUL), one of the most reputable companies in India, provides another good example. For decades it has been high on the list of employers of choice. As such HUL frequently has the option of hiring some of the best graduates from the best universities in the country. This means that HUL's management trainees frequently come from high-income families. The problem is that HUL is a firm believer in "wealth at the bottom of the pyramid." It seeks to mass market to individuals at the bottom of the socioeconomic ladder, so it has a potential disconnect between its future leaders and the customers they will serve. How does HUL bridge this gap? It sends management trainee recruits to live with poor families in remote villages—for up to six months. As they live with these families, the trainees experience their customers firsthand. The customer experience not only goes into their heads, but it also goes into their hearts.

Other practices by which customer information can be brought into the firm include the following (with examples of customers who have used them effectively):

- Traditional market research (P&G)
- Cocreation of new products and services (Mahindra and Mahindra)
- Employee visits to customer locations (Ford)
- Customer visits to company festive occasions (Medtronic)
- Video or audio tapes of customer experiences (GE)
- Rotation of employees through customer-facing experiences (Rubber-Maid)
- Customers present at key leadership meetings (Timken Company)

Eliminate Low Value-Added Information

In HRCS 2012 we found the identification, importation, sharing, and utilization of customer information was statistically related to the elimination of low value-added work. When we work with executives, we like to ask, "How many of you have gone home at the end of the day full of life and enthusiasm because you added great value?" Almost all hands go up. Then we ask, "How many of you had a stupid day at work that was filled with stupid work that added little or no value to anything?" Again, most of the hands go up. Then we ask, "What happened on the day of stupid work?" The responses almost always focus on irrelevant meetings, reports, approvals, redundant processes, and paperwork. Note that these are all different forms of internal information processing.

Companies have limited cogitative space, and they must take great care in determining how they use that scarce resource. Do they focus on internal bureaucratic information or on essential customer information? Our research indicates that you cannot focus on both. You must decide where the balance is, and if you want to increase the flow of customer information, you must reduce the flow of internal information. The problem is that throughout the history of the field, HR professionals have been much more skilled with the generation and use of internal information than with external information.

Many companies have consciously or intuitively recognized this dynamic and have worked to rebalance their information flow toward increased market information. We have seen this underlying assumption in GE's Work-Out, in GM's Go Fast, and in Unilever's CleanOut. While the processes for executing these programs can be fairly complex, the agendas are reasonably straightforward:

- What are our low value-added activities that inhibit productivity?
- What do we do to diminish the time and effort that we spend on these activities?

Disseminate Information

Information can flow within an organization in four ways: from the top down, from the bottom up, within departments, and across departments. Over the last two years we have asked more than a hundred company and university executive groups which of these is handled least well—and would have the greatest impact on business success if it were to be improved. The virtually unanimous response is the sharing of information across departments. Horizontal flows of information are apt to be blocked from both sides. As our colleague Steve Kerr has stated, "Other than the fact that those who have information do not want to give and those who need it do not want to receive, the sharing of information is not a problem."

Such sharing can be an important source of competitive advantage. In the pharmaceutical industry, for example, basic R&D is expensive and highly problematic. A major trend within this industry is for companies to find molecules that already exist in one part of the company and combine them with molecules that exist in other parts, thereby creating new molecules without building them from first principles. This is said to be one reason Pfizer purchased Wyeth, with its reputation and track record for creating value out of synergistic information sharing.

Despite the difficulty, information sharing in all directions remains an important mandate. Table 8.2 indicates the flow of information in the four directions and how each might be facilitated.

Table 8.2   Practices That Facilitate Communication

Direction	Practices
Across departments	• Measure and reward revenues that result from cross-unit collaboration • Best practices sharing meetings • Interunit staff rotation • Coordinating meetings • Matrix structure • Employee special interest groups • Linchpin roles • Traditional e-mail • Speeches by external dignitaries • Cross-department integration meetings • Cross-department training meetings • Jive, Socialize Me, and other internal communications software 360 feedback from other departments
Within departments	• Physical placement of people near those they have to work with • Efficient daily department briefings (of 15 minutes) before the work begins • Meeting rooms • 360-degree feedback
Top down	• Podcasts, websites, video conferencing, and teleconferences of quarterly results • Executive speeches • Policy statements • Management by walking around • Internal board meetings
Bottom up	• Town hall meetings • Executive lunches with employees • Employee surveys • Employee focus groups • Business partner roles

Leverage Information in Decision Making and Take Action

In today's information-rich environment, it is necessary that information be interpreted in a way that adds unique and important insights to decision making. Given that many firms in each industry have access to the same data at roughly the same time, bundling otherwise independent facts and observations in ways that provide unique insights is increasingly a source of competitive advantage.

This is certainly true in the cosmetics industry. Several years ago, a leading manufacturer began to recognize a combination of factors: young women were going to graduate schools that had been traditionally dominated by males, women's professional sports teams were coming into existence, and women were moving more aggressively into the national political arena. At the same time, young men were being allowed to show their more nurturing side as stay-at-home dads became acceptable in the United States and Europe; *Friends* became a dominant sitcom of the decade. The company bundled this information together, concluding that traditional gender role barriers were breaking down and that the world was ready for more gender-neutral fragrances. From this insight an entire generation of fragrances was born, and the new offerings continue as the top-selling fragrances in airports around the world.

Once information has been bundled, it must be accepted for utilization. In our hyperchange world, reluctance to accept frame-breaking information can be a major obstacle to accurate and timely decision making. Unfortunately, both people and firms tend to hear what they want to hear instead of what is actually being said. We all know the stories of Enron, Lehman Brothers, Polaroid, Kodak, and Bethlehem Steel. Each of these companies suffered from many maladies, but the common thread is that they saw what they wanted to see until it was too late to see what was really there.

We are not victims of the world we see; we are victims of the way we see the world.

—*William James*

Breaking through a firm's dominant paradigm usually requires much self-reflection and debate.[9] It requires allowing into decision-making forums many voices that would traditionally have been blocked in order to avoid unpleasant and unpopular debate. It requires facing short-term pain to salvage a successful long-term future. It requires accepting and understanding a new, unfamiliar, and potentially threatening world. It requires accepting the harsh reality that we are not victims of the world we see; we are victims of the way we see the world. In a very real sense, information flow within an organization is what determines the capacity of the organization to see reality and adapt while there is still time.

With accurate, timely, unique, and reality-based information in hand, answering the following questions in the affirmative will permit effective utilization of information in decision making:

- Are the right people in the room? That is, have we assembled those with information, those with insights about information, those having authority to act, and those who will eventually need to act?
- Are the decisions to be made properly framed for their implications for action?
- Are reality-based time frames for action commonly accepted?
- Is accountability for the final decisions and actions clearly defined?
- Is there clarity about the mission or vision that we are jointly trying to accomplish?

Create External Brand

Once messages are translated into internal decisions and actions, they may then be communicated to the outside in the form of brand identity. The first challenge of branding is to create the brand substance within the firm; it is disastrous to start communicating a brand promise to the outside too soon. Markets tend to be unforgiving when brand reality fails to live up to brand promise. Thus Intel's brand promises fast, reliable state-of-the-art technology, and the company focuses its entire organization capability agenda on delivering its brand promise. And it must do so. When a very minor flaw surfaced in the then-flagship Pentium chip in the mid-1990s, widespread condemnation led to a promise to replace the flawed processors—and a pretax charge of $475 million against earnings.

The second challenge is then to communicate the brand image. For many years, one of the world's most famous brand slogans has been GE's, "We bring good things to life." This is a statement of ongoing aspiration that GE continually strives to achieve through the creation and delivery of customer-focused products and services. To continually bring brands to life, companies must hire the right people, give them the right training, provide the right measurement and reward systems, communicate the right internal messages, and develop the right kinds of leaders.[10]

Conclusion: HR Professionals as Technology Proponents

The three factors of the technology proponent domain provide powerful agendas through which HR can create verifiable competitive advantage and high performance. This will be an important next-generation agenda item for HR professionals who wish to add greater value to their businesses.

CHAPTER 9

DEVELOPING YOURSELF AS AN HR PROFESSIONAL 9

The competencies defined by the 2012 HRCS call on HR professionals and departments to move beyond the performance that marked HR success in earlier years. As we describe earlier, HR has experienced four waves. This evolution has led HR from a historical grounding in administration to the development of functional expertise in areas such as compensation, performance management, and leadership development. In wave three, we see a shift from functional expertise to the role of strategic business partner.

What we call "wave four" or outside-in HR emphasizes the emerging responsibility of HR to be an informed observer and interpreter of the external trends and conditions that are likely to impact business success. Its focus builds on the prior phases, going beyond strategy to align its work with business contexts and stakeholders. HR professionals now build credibility on a base of technical and strategic excellence by looking outside their organizations. They need to learn how HR can help improve their business's customer share, investor confidence, community reputation, and financial performance.

The new HR competencies challenge HR professionals to contribute both more and differently. HR must continue to flawlessly deliver transaction and administrative services in most organizations, whether directly or by attending to the quality of outsourced work, and its practices must both adapt to and lead organizational capability.

The new wave is a change in context as well as competence. HR professionals must have the skills to interpret environmental events and trends, cocreate a strategic agenda that informs the human capital implications of business strategies and priorities, and play a leading role in ensuring the leadership, culture, and talent required for future success.

The stakes for HR leader and professional development have never been higher, as many companies are learning. A crisis of leadership almost destroyed Olympus of Japan in 2011. As the investigative panel wrote, "The core part of the management was rotten, and that contaminated other parts around it."[1] Around the same time, a talent drain threatened the performance of online gaming company Zynga, which fell sharply from the valuation set by its recent IPO.[2] And a decade ago, a culture of "performance at any cost" took down the energy giant Enron. Craig Donaldson interviewed Steven Cooper (HR head of Enron after the company's bankruptcy) early in 2004. He wrote:

> Cooper says the culture of Enron played a role in its downfall, with an "unbelievably aggressive" approach to doing business—particularly in its trading operations. "Senior management was adamant about sustaining a too-good-to-be-true performance, and there was a tremendous lack of focus, clarity and accountability. They were promoting that this was all a big mistake and convinced themselves that they couldn't lose money."[3]

Professional development has two aspects. The first is what individual HR professionals can and should do to develop their skills as business partners. But individuals working on their own can go only so far. They need leaders to encourage their efforts and reinforce growing competence, creating a robust developmental environment.

Individual Development

When you want to get somewhere, it's useful to map out your destination and the steps you need to take to get there. Based on the goal of developing competency in the six domains we have identified, these are the steps to take in an effective plan:

1. Own your career.
2. Learn about yourself. What turns you on? What gets in your way?

3. Define your brand. How do you want to be known in the organization?
4. Assess your strengths and weaknesses.
5. Create opportunities for growth—from the outside in.
6. Conduct projects and experiments.
7. Follow up to build and reinforce awareness.

Step 1: Own Your Career

Effective individuals own their own career. Tom Peters closed the case some years ago with his article "The Brand Called You."[4] As he observed, high performers do the Jedi mind trick of imagining themselves as entrepreneurs "renting" opportunity rather than seeing themselves as employees.

Owning one's career requires activism—credible activism. As outlined in Chapter 4, this domain is the combination of credibility and activism: building trust through results, establishing relationships of influence, growing through self-awareness, and contributing to the HR profession make it the cornerstone of perceived personal effectiveness. Make the decision to use all the sources of insight and support available to you—your manager, the mentors you can recruit inside and outside your organization, and your colleagues.

Don't wait for guidance. Seek it. Step up.

Step 2: Learn About Yourself

A key competency factor in the credible activist domain is, of course, improvement through self-awareness. Learning about yourself—and seeing yourself as others see you—is a critical step. And a useful starting point is applying the sources of individual abundance from *Why of Work*.[5] The seven questions presented there will help you focus:

1. *Identity: What am I known for?* How do you present yourself and who you are? How do you present your strengths and how do you apply your efforts on behalf of the organization?

2. *Purpose and direction: Where am I going?* What excites and engages you? What are your growth and development goals?

3. *Relationships and teamwork: Who is traveling with me?* What relationships must you identify, build, and maintain to support growth and contribution?

4. *Positive work environment*: How do you build a work environment that facilitates the best of what you and others bring to the organization?

5. *Engagement and challenge: What challenges most interest and excite me?* What opportunities are most engaging and emotionally resonant for you?

6. *Resilience and learning: How do I learn from setbacks?* How thoughtfully do you seek to learn from experience?

7. *Civility and delight*: What delights you, and how are you contributing to a respectful, appealing workplace?

These questions are the starting point for development. As you answer them, you will begin to develop a point of view on your focus of growth and challenge. Table 9.1 provides a version of where such a self-inquiry might lead.

This first cut will provide you with good initial ideas about changes you want to make in how you are seen and experienced by HR colleagues and business partners. The next step is to identify the best areas for you to seek concrete opportunities for growth that will drive value as well as development.

Step 3: Define Your Brand

Reviewing the seven key questions is a strong foundation for defining your personal brand. How do you want to be known in the organization? Whether you've consciously built it or not, like every employee, you already have a brand of some kind: how you are seen and experienced by those with whom you work. These are the factors that have created your brand:

- What you choose to work on
- The people and groups you choose to work with
- What you are good at and enjoy doing
- How you respond to difficult situations

Table 9.1 Developing Self-Development Focus

Question	Current Situation	Opportunity for Improvement	Game Plan
Identity	I'm seen as a technical expert with good skills in HR, but this is not all I want.	Build reputation for business knowledge.	Disciplined time and attention on the business: spend 30 minutes per day.
Purpose and direction	I'm starting to have a greater impact on the business.	Identify key priorities for increasing my contribution.	Talk with HR generalists about how my functional area can create more value.
Relationships and teamwork	I have a strong HR network, but I need broader line management relationships and a mentor.	Build my business network inside and outside the organization.	Get help from generalists in building my business network.
Positive work environment	I haven't really paid attention to this aspect.	Identify the factors that help me do my best work.	Not a priority for this period; will pick it up in the next quarter.
Engagement and challenge	Need to develop more of a global perspective.	Work in another country or on a project that has international impact.	Work with my boss on opportunities.
Resilience and learning	I tend to be defensive rather than openly learn from mistakes.	Seek feedback more actively and frequently.	Have quarterly meetings with HR generalists and my boss.
Civility and delight	I have good team skills.	Use my skills as a team builder to help grow the HR community.	Keep an eye out for opportunities to utilize and grow my team-building skills.

- How you deal with challenge
- How others have experienced you and your work

How do you build a brand? Exercise 9.1 will give you a good start.

Exercise 9.1   *Signature Strength Assessment*

Using the following list, identify three to five words that you see as representing your signature strengths that you have now or wish to acquire. Then identify how these will be incorporated into your work to begin to create the brand.

Signature Strength Adjectives

Accepting	Competent	Even-tempered
Accountable	Concerned	Fast
Action-oriented	Confident	Flexible
Adaptable	Confrontational	Friendly
Agile	Conscientious	Fun-loving
Agreeable	Considerate	Happy
Analytical	Consistent	Helpful
Approachable	Creative	Honest
Assertive	Curious	Hopeful
Attentive	Decisive	Humble
Benevolent	Dedicated	Independent
Bold	Deliberate	Innovative
Bright	Dependable	Insightful
Calm	Determined	Inspired
Carefree	Diplomatic	Integrative
Caring	Disciplined	Intelligent
Charismatic	Driven	Intimate
Clever	Easy going	Inventive
Collaborative	Efficient	Kind
Committed	Energetic	Knowledgeable
Compassionate	Enthusiastic	Listener

Lively	Polite	Self-confident
Logical	Positive	Selfless
Loving	Pragmatic	Sensitive
Loyal	Prepared	Service-oriented
Nurturing	Proactive	Sincere
Optimistic	Productive	Sociable
Organized	Quality-oriented	Straightforward
Outgoing	Reality-based	Thorough
Passionate	Religious	Thoughtful
Patient	Respectful	Tireless
Peaceful	Responsible	Tolerant
Persistent	Responsive	Trusting
Personal	Results-oriented	Trustworthy
Playful	Satisfied	Unyielding
Pleasant	Savvy	Values-driven

Example: Suppose your brand focuses on you being seen as account-able, collaborative, proactive, and enthusiastic. What actions follow? Here are some suggestions on how to begin to demonstrate those aspects of your brand in your behavior:

• Accountable
  – Take ownership for results.
  – Meet commitments and keep promises so people will see you that way.
  – Give candid observations based on knowledge and not opinion; be will-ing to take (reasonable) personal risk.
• Collaborative
  – Work well with others.
  – Get invitations to work on critical project teams.
  – Make sure you can be described consistently as a team player.
• Proactive
  – Show initiative.
  – Do the homework to identify the most important priorities, and avoid pur-suing details that interest you when they don't support those priorities.

– Volunteer to take on additional work that benefits the business or function.

• Enthusiastic

– Speak and act in ways that reflect an optimistic outlook.

– Think the best of colleagues without being naïve.

– Find ways to rally the team to take performance to the next level.

Step 4: Assess Your Strengths and Weaknesses

Once you've identified what excites you and your professional brand, the HRCS provides a framework for identifying strengths and weaknesses from a competency perspective. We invite you to answer three questions:

1. What competency mix does my current role require of me?
2. What mix will be increasingly important as I develop and advance in the organization?
3. Where do I stand? What are my priorities for improvement and development?

Table 9.2 provides a framework for individuals to assess the demands of their current job, future opportunity, and needs for improvement. The levels indicated in the cells ("Moderate" and so on) are examples of what a particular individual might come up with—not recommendations for HR professionals in general.

Imagine an HR generalist in a midsized pharmaceutical firm in India. Based on feedback and supervisory coaching, this HR professional has identified her strengths and given thought to areas where improvement would be valuable. The feedback she has received using 360 feedback reinforces her skills as a credible activist and a moderate level of competence as strategic positioner and change champion, both areas she must strengthen for future advancement.

There is, of course, no general answer. But we encourage each professional to develop a similar chart indicating current strengths, needs for improvement, and priorities for improvement. Note that priorities may not

Table 9.2   *Setting Priorities*

Competency Domain	Requirement in Current Role	Future Requirements	Priority for Improvement
Strategic positioner	Moderate	Moderate	Moderate
Credible activist	High	High	High
Capability builder	Moderate	Moderate	Moderate
Change champion	Moderate	High	High
HR innovator and integrator	Moderate	High	Moderate
Technology proponent	Low	Moderate	Low

focus only on remediating areas of weakness. It may also be an opportunity to build on strengths—particularly strengths that also strengthen colleagues and business partners.

Step 5: Create Opportunities for Growth—from the Outside In

Opportunities to both increase your impact and improve your development are best identified on an outside-in basis. Here are some examples of what others have done:

- GE HR professionals identified the opportunity to build the GE Capital business by providing support to customers in areas of HR excellence such as leadership development, engagement, and Six Sigma. Inviting customers to send people to the GE Welch leadership center at Crotonville has generated strong business opportunities and customer loyalty—both particularly critical in emerging markets.
- IBM HR professionals identified the opportunity to both build stronger ties to growth markets and improve the retention of high-potential millennials through the IBM Corporate Service Corps. The chance to participate in this

corps has become a significant contributor to business development, retention, and company reputation.

- After a 10 percent staff reduction, AXA Equitable HR professionals identified the opportunity to accelerate cost efficiency and employee engagement by using the work-out process. This produced significant cost efficiencies and a reduction of non-value-added work, reducing the pressure on the remaining staff and avoiding unwanted additional departures.
- Fresenius (India) HR professionals identified a deficit in business and customer knowledge and created "business knowledge week"—a week of enjoyable information-sharing activities—to close the gap. The session has contributed to team building as well as gains in customer and competitor knowledge and improvements in service.
- National City Bank HR professionals provided advice and guidance to midsized corporate clients in talent management and learning and development. This activity reinforced and solidified relationships with key clients, increased loan generation and other services, and reduced customer attrition.

These examples point out ways to improve the identification of developmental opportunity by focusing outside in. The power of the outside-in focus is the ability to identify areas of important change and development that may have been missed or overlooked by line managers. It is this perspective that enables the HR professional to serve as a true partner, rather than as a "pair of hands" executing the directives of others. To find development opportunities with customers, for example, ask questions such as these:

- Who are our target customers?
- Why do they buy from us?
- Who are our toughest competitors, and why do customers choose them?
- What is our customer attrition rate?
- Whom do customers leave us for? When? Why?

Visit customers or be a customer to get the answers. If you're in a retail business, try being a mystery shopper. Spend time listening to customer service calls and see what your product or service really means to people. If you are in B2B or commodity businesses, customers and partners may be identical; for example, many retail organizations such as Limited Brands work internationally through franchise partners. Partners would, in this case, be equivalent to customers.

Some questions to ask customers might be:

- How well are we partnering with you?
- Are the people who are working for us providing the quality of experience you expect as a partner?
- What new skills must our people develop to improve the quality of our work together?
- Are there areas where we are inconsistent in our service or quality and need to improve?

To find development opportunities with investors, ask questions like these:

- How do we make and lose money?
- Is our growth and profitability rate at, above, or below our peer group?
- Which of our competitors does the best job, why, and what can we learn from them?
- What are our critical opportunities? What are the risk factors in our business?
- How well are we managing our reputation and interest as an investment?

Read how the investment community views the organization. Learn the value chain and identify opportunities for HR to make a significant contribution from an investor's perspective. If the company is public, there will be ample sources of analysis by brokerage companies that cover the company for investors. If the company is private, investors such as public equity firms can provide perspective. And, in either case, there are likely to be press releases and news reports that respond to business updates and trends.

To find development opportunities with employees, ask questions such as these:

- What is facilitating employee productivity and engagement? What impedes these things?
- What is the value of increased productivity and engagement?
- In what specific ways would value be realized?

Review engagement survey data to get an overall impression. Then meet informally with employee opinion leaders. There are a variety of ways to do so. Hold informal coffee meetings with up-and-coming employees who have high potential, and put together focus groups with cohorts of employees at different levels or in different functions or locations. Pulse surveys targeting particular populations are often used in addition to larger companywide efforts. All these approaches have the potential to provide perspective on what employees are thinking and feeling about the opportunities for improvement. Link these to your development goals.

To find development opportunities with line managers, ask questions such as these:

- What are the strengths and weaknesses of our leaders and leadership?
- How are we seen externally?
- What is the gap between our intended and perceived leadership brand? How does that impact our ability to grow?

Map the strengths and weaknesses of managers based on performance feedback and engagement survey data and identify critical impacts and priorities for improvement. Assess and define what appear to be the top two or three opportunities for improving the effectiveness of leaders that are linked to your developmental ambitions.

To find development opportunities with partners and suppliers, ask questions such as these:

- How effectively does the organization work with suppliers?
- How are we experienced by our best suppliers?
- What is the value of building a better partnership?

Develop a survey to be completed by partners that identifies the strengths and weaknesses of the organization in dealing with partners and the benefit to the business of improvement.

To find development opportunities in your community, ask questions such as these:

- What is the reputation of the organization as a corporate citizen?
- What opportunities does it create?
- What challenges does it impose?
- How are our reputation and community brand likely to impact our ability to grow?

Figure out what you can do to build your business's reputation and improve its place in the community. The best way to understand the reputation of the organization is to review how it is described in the press. How does the profile of the organization vary from its intended brand? What HR contributions can help close the gap?

To find development opportunities with government agencies and other regulators, ask questions like these:

- How effective is the organization at anticipating and meeting regulatory requirements?
- How will regulations change over time?

Try to determine the likely and foreseeable areas of change in government interest and regulation, and what actions or skills will be required.

Use this analysis to consider the following:

- What are the most compelling opportunities to contribute to organizational performance and growth?
- Which provide the best opportunity for development—either doing new things or doing things in new ways that test and provoke professional development?
- What new skills and knowledge do I need to increase my readiness and competence?
- How do I get started? What help do I need and from whom?

Step 6: Conduct Projects and Experiments

The whole point of personal development—improving competence—is turning what you know into what you do. And unless you've already put in a great deal of work, there's almost certainly going to be a gap between the two.

Closing the know-do gap requires careful attention to your work assignment, backed up as needed by education and refined through project work, special assignments, and external experiences.

The foundation of competence is mastering the work itself. At least half of developmental opportunity is tied to day-to-day work, and good work design provides concrete and practical opportunities to build competence by focusing on measurable goals. As Hackman and Oldham pointed out in their landmark research on job design, good jobs combine significance (important goals), variety (opportunity to grow and develop), autonomy (accountability), impact (consequence), and feedback.[6]

Education provides the chance for people to learn new skills, and project work allows them to use those skills to deal with situations that require them. The reinforcement of new skill acquisition through practice and assignment is called *application*. Action learning and challenge projects provide the translation of theoretical knowledge into action—to close the know-do gap. Application works best when it is timely, practical, relevant to the current role and stage of development, and has a clear objective.

External experience provides an additional dimension of development. Through initiatives like the IBM Community Service Corps, individuals are put in new situations and challenged to grow and perform. Sitting on community boards provides an opportunity to play a strategic leadership role and develop your capability builder and change champion skills. Working as a team member implementing change in a customer organization helps reinforce credible activist skills. Consulting for a philanthropic or charitable organization provides experience in HR innovation and integration outside your own business, offering new insight into an environment separate from your own career.

Step 7: Follow Up to Build and Reinforce Awareness

It isn't enough to know or even to do; you also need to close the loop so you can extend your knowledge and refine your actions. This means being receptive to feedback and if possible acquiring a mentor.

Feedback increases what we know about ourselves by enabling us to see our behavior through the experience and perception of others. It's human nature to perceive your own behavior through the prism of your intentions, missing the impact on others. Feedback provides the view of what others experience—not what you intended—and therefore makes it possible to correct misimpressions.

The Johari window (Figure 9.1) is a helpful tool in collecting and assessing performance feedback. Working at the University of California in the 1950s, Joseph Luft and Harry Ingham observed that there are aspects of our personality that we're open about and other elements we keep to ourselves. At the same time, there are things that others see in us that we're not aware of, and there is a fourth area of which both we and others are unaware.

As you review 360-degree feedback you obtain using the HRCS survey or another similar tool—or even from simple discussions—try filling in the boxes in a Johari window. What do you see that you weren't aware of before? What can you deduce about that fourth box?

The most concentrated feedback you'll get is from a mentor. Mentors and coaches are a final educational support. Whatever your role, background, and experience level, find a mentor. A good mentor is a cultural translator,

Figure 9.1   *The Johari window*

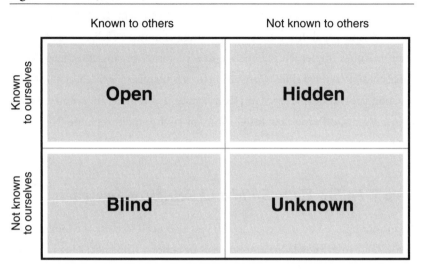

teacher, and early warning system who explains the nuances of how work is done, the values of the organization, and the unstated rules and expectations of the culture. A good mentor provides candid observations on organizational needs, how you are performing, and what you need to do more, less, or differently to be seen as a high performer. A mentor is a mirror that reflects the expectations of the organization and relates these to your contributions and development. Finally, a good mentor serves as a sounding board to help you anticipate organizational dynamics or responses to situations that need to be incorporated into your plans or priorities.

The HR Leader: Building Competent Teams

The HR leader's role is to create a culture in which performance improvement and developmental work are encouraged for everyone in the department. A thriving developmental environment incorporates the following practices:

- Performance standards are well developed and well known.
- Development is connected to performance.
- Feedback supports team development.

- HR supports professional developmentment through a combination of skill building and action learning practice that tests and challenges individuals and teams to grow.
- The HR department participates in learning partnerships.
- HR has its own brand, based on outside-in insights.

Performance Standards

HR professionals should know what their manager expects of them. The importance of clear objectives should be self-evident, but in an era of frequent and regular changes in roles, team membership, managers, and organizational structures, it is important to set out explicit expectations of good performance and sufficient developmental progress. This is an area where HR leaders generally do fairly well; less than half the participants in our HR business partner workshops say they have a difficult time responding to the statement, "I know what I need to do to be successful." To review your own standards, consider the following actions:

- Clearly define performance standards. Write them up and then test them to ensure that the standards are clear and well understood at all levels.
- Ask high performers and high potentials to describe the standards they follow. Don't assume that people who perform well invariably know what is expected of them.
- Articulate how performance expectations and measures have changed and how they are likely to continue to change over time.
- Use stories and anecdotes as well as facts to help your people understand performance requirements.

Development-Performance Connection

Most of the organizations with which we and others consult and teach are global and deal with differences in culture and economic maturity. To cope, many of their leaders are using HR strategy development and team building as an opportunity to define and develop the skills of their professionals. By connecting development to plans and priorities, leaders establish the importance of the skills they need to grow. They create a context and a logic that enables individuals to more fully own their own development.

Combining planning with an explicit discussion of strengths and weaknesses also creates the potential for professionals to hold one another accountable for individual and overall growth. Similar to the concept of spotting in acrobatics, team members become mentors and coaches for one another. Shane Dempsey, the head of the Novo Nordisk Europe's HR team, went a step further by engaging his HR team in collecting feedback on strengths and weaknesses. In advance of a three-day HR planning workshop, members of the executive team were asked to interview three to five business leaders. These conversations brought into sharp relief the business challenges that the organization faced from tough competition.

Feedback and Team Development

Aggregate feedback is a lens through which leaders identify team or organizational competency strengths and weaknesses. For example, the overall findings for individual competency show that the greatest gap in competence—the gap between impact on business success and personal effectiveness—is a technology proponent (mean = 3.74). A second area is HR innovator and integrator (mean = 3.90). These are also the areas where participants rated themselves lowest. This kind of feedback can become a source of organizational knowledge and a driver for team improvement in several ways:

- Bring the team together to identify "early win" opportunities for improvement.
- Direct individuals to identify actions that would benefit the overall team.
- Bring in a colleague from another area on a project or full-time basis to act as a guide or team leader in making change; for a technology proponent, a young IT high potential might provide useful perspective on how to improve HR technology proficiency and application.

- Use after-action reviews to assess the effectiveness of the organization's approach to technology changes and developments in the past.
- Consider acquiring a young mentor from inside the organization to help you gain insight into how to use technology to go beyond automating transactional HR work and to connect people and information in the new ways that have opened up.
- Adopt 720-degree feedback. Useful as 360-degree feedback is, we now encourage HR leaders to begin to look for feedback from the outside in. Many HR leaders are engaging customers, suppliers, and partner organizations in identifying needs for development and improvement in HR.

The Saudi energy company Saudi Aramco has gone a step further than most organizations in investing in HR development. It has begun to train line managers to be better partners with HR. The approach that Saudi Aramco has taken is, we believe, the future. If HR is first and foremost a business function with expertise in human capital and change management, it stands to reason that we should expect more movement between functions.

In the past, career movement has tended to be one-way: from line roles to HR. This sometimes reflects an intention to grow broader-based leaders and professionals, but more often HR is a place to move long-service employees who are well liked but not highly effective leaders. Alternatively, such transfers are an opportunity for the organization to attempt to fix a weak HR department by installing an effective leader. We hope for a time when there is an expectation that the development of senior executives requires experience in the HR function; in turn, we hope for a general belief that in order to be an effective HR leader, line experience is crucial.

HR Academy

Like other observers of the field, we are often confused and frustrated by what seems a lack of confidence and courage among many HR professionals. This weakness derives from lack of preparation as much as anything; understanding how the business works, its performance and challenges and positioning with customers and competitors, provides the knowledge needed to hold more informed and confident views. Having a process to convert this knowledge into a plan of action has led to creation of what might be called the *HR academy*. Over the course of one or more sessions, HR professionals learn how to operationalize competencies, to put them in practice through a combination of team and case work, develop an individual development plan based on feedback on strengths and weaknesses using the HRCS feedback, and participate in a challenge or action learning project of significance to the organization. The best HR academies have the following qualities:

- Participants work on problems that the business sees as important, not HR projects.
- Participants work in teams. Team members keep one another engaged, and when they are brought together across functional areas or business units, they see the bigger picture of the organization.
- Program administrators encourage line management participation. Executive participation provides a reinforcement of the importance of HR along with some perspective on what executives are thinking about and how they read the environment, assess the organization, and define goals.
- Program administrators also encourage customer and investor or analyst participation. There is power in asking key stakeholders to identify ways for the organization to improve the strength and competence of its human capital.

Action Learning to Learning Solutions

Action learning, sometimes called "challenge projects," starts with a set of principles and applies them to a project. Learning solutions start with a project or business challenge and then use training forums to make progress on those challenges. Learning solutions extend action learning by helping you do what you need to do better. Adults need to improve on what they do through learning since the half-life of nonapplied knowledge is brief. By bringing real business problems into education settings, it both reinforces skill development and gains measurable performance benefits for the organization. Here are some examples of learning solutions projects (typically led by high-potential individuals or teams):

- What type of HR organization do we need to support our future business?
- How do we increase speed and effectiveness of integrating new acquisitions?
- What impact should or will globalization have on our HR practices in the future? The goal here is to come up with a model for managing people from a truly global perspective.
- How do we better integrate how we assess, develop, and deploy talent?
- What HR practices are needed to deeply embed innovation in our company?
- What value proposition will drive our company to become an "employer of choice"?
- How well are we living our espoused culture and values?
- How do we best implement self-service HR on a global scale?
- How can we create a high-performing customer-focused culture?
- How can we provide strategic clarity for HR and our business leaders about our new HR shared services environment?
- How do we significantly improve workforce planning?

Learning Partnerships

The HR Learning Partnership is an innovative product of RBL partners, originally in collaboration with the University of Michigan. It is a version of an HR academy, but with an innovative twist; it engages teams of HR leaders from across companies and industries. Thus in a given year, GE HR leaders will learn in conjunction with colleagues from (for example) Pfizer, the BBC, Unilever, and Shell. This combined participation significantly advances the potential for accelerated development and transfer of innovation. In this example, BBC is a fabled creative organization, while GE is as effective as any organization in the world in Six Sigma. For both, access to colleagues in other industries, hearing their feedback and incorporating their suggestions, can prove invaluable. This type of consortium approach is extraordinarily powerful both for the education of participants and for ensuring that teams consider a wide range of options and alternatives in addressing their action learning projects. HRLP is the best-known example of the type, one that is breaking down walls between companies in addressing the strategic opportunity for contribution available to HR.

We are also big fans of what Mars calls "capability week." Mars's HR (or the "people and organization" department) annually brings people together on a regional basis from many areas, not just HR, to trade ideas, initiatives, and innovations, and to learn from both line executives and external experts. Novartis took a similar approach on a global scale. Over the past several years, it has used what it called "growing HR leaders" to build a stronger, more skillful, and more collaborative HR organization.

Capability week is a version of what we have called communities of practice. The psychologist Seymour Sarason defined a *community* as a network of mutually supportive, interdependent relationships.[7] Where cost and time constraints make face-to-face interaction prohibitive, more and more organizations are creating opportunities for networking and the use of technology in the process. Table 9.3 sketches the essential elements of a community of practice, as compared to a less focused informal network.

Rebranding HR

What can HR leaders do to create an outside-in mindset in their team or organization? Here are some useful actions:

- Arrange to visit customers.
- Be a "mystery shopper" in your business.
- Create "as if" situations that enable colleagues to experience what it is like to be a customer: for example, some years ago in a leadership workshop, we delivered 95 percent of the binders on time, the percentage equal to the group's proudly touted high performance. It was a revelation to these managers—when your package is late, it doesn't matter that the other 95 percent are on time.

Table 9.3 *Creating Communities of Practice*

	Community of Practice	Informal Network
Purpose	To develop members' competencies; to build and exchange knowledge	To collect and pass on information
Membership	Self-selection into the community	Friends and acquaintances
Connection	Passion for the topic, commitment to ongoing individual and community development, and identification with the group's expertise or interest	Affiliation and mutual interest
Operation	It typically has an agenda defined and communicated in advance, for which the members prepare	Informal
Programming	Frequently involves external speakers invited to provide new insight and new tool and process information	Sometimes involves external speakers, but more as entertainment than development

• Enlist customers for help. Ask customers: Are we hiring the kind of people that you want to work with? Do we understand your business as well as we need to in order to serve you well?

We have talked about the value of professionals branding themselves, but it raises the question of how the HR team or function is branded. By combining outside-in perceptions with an emphasis on performance standards and continuing development, HR leaders can begin to identify how they wish to be seen and the image they wish to create in the mind of the organization. Rebranding HR to fit current and developing requirements is crucial.

Conclusion: Developing HR

Unsurprisingly, HR professionals are too often the cobbler's barefoot children, last on the development investment list. HR staff members learn that their leaders are serious about the HR agenda when we invest in upgrading their skills to meet the challenge and connect what they are learning to the real issues facing the business. Once you develop a baseline benchmark of HR professional strengths and weaknesses, invest in your HR professionals through training, job assignments, and other learning avenues. Raising expectations for HR performance and contribution without giving HR professionals the tools to meet the challenge only raises false hopes.

CHAPTER 10

THE EFFECTIVE HR DEPARTMENT

10

Preceding chapters have addressed two of the three questions we promised to consider:

- What should HR professionals know, do, and be to be seen as personally effective?
- What should HR professionals know, do, and be to improve business performance?

We now turn to our third question for this research:

- What should HR departments focus on to improve business performance?

In this chapter, we share cases of upgrading the HR department, three research findings, and four techniques for creating an effective department.

Prudential PLC

Prudential PLC is an international financial services group with significant operations in Asia, the United States, and the United Kingdom. It serves more than 25 million customers with £349.5 billion of assets under management. Prudential follows a federated model; its business units operate with a high degree of autonomy, thus creating opportunities and challenges for collaboration between group functions and local ones, including HR. In a decentralized business organization such as Prudential's, clear definitions of authority and responsibility are required for group functions and business units to complement each other and not clash.

As the new head of HR, Peter Goerke believes in the role of HR as a source of competitive advantage. He sees it as a core element of business success, especially in the context of a global financial institution, so he makes sure that leaders throughout the business talk about business and HR as one and not as independent entities. Since HR is part of the business, the HR organization needs to match the business structure and have clear priorities.

Goerke wanted to redefine how HR could support business performance in each business unit and still have global leverage. He began by having all relevant stakeholders assess the state of the HR function, articulating HR's aspiration and creating a journey for HR improvement called "Good to Excellent."

Through this journey, the stakeholders agreed on priorities for each business unit, clarified the roles and responsibilities of the group and business unit HR functions, and created a shared mandate of the resource and development (called R&D) and reward functions. These changes moved Prudential away from its original one-size-fits-all group approach and toward a well-defined groupwide framework with business unit adaptation.

The Good to Excellent journey started with a thorough understanding of what each business unit required to gain and sustain a competitive advantage locally and for the group as a whole. Participants were able to draw a baseline on how HR was doing and what it needed to meet the defined aspiration going forward. They then adopted specific action plans to address the gaps and move forward with the Good to Excellent agenda.

Goerke learned that a key insight for a truly global and highly decentralized organization was that a one-size-fits-all approach falls short. With business unit autonomy, each business unit must satisfy higher standards of transparency and accountability while receiving leadership, guidance, and monitoring of progress from the HR group.

Accenture

Accenture, a global management consulting, technology services, and outsourcing company, has more than 244,000 people serving clients in well over a hundred countries. Today, as its clients become more global in their operations, Accenture's workforce must span countries and cultures—while at the same time becoming more specialized in specific industries, technologies, and functional areas.

The company's CHRO, Jill Smart, is a 30-year veteran of the business with deep experience serving clients. She runs Accenture HR like a business and believes that Accenture must be ahead of the curve in terms of anticipating and adapting to shifts in the marketplace and to client demands. She says, "As the rate of change accelerates, Accenture must adapt more quickly than our clients in order to provide them with the talent they need when they need it. And Accenture HR must be the most agile of all—the change agent driving the ongoing evolution of our workforce to meet the ever-changing needs of our business."

Smart reorganized Accenture HR using the same principles that the company as a whole applies to its client work. She divided her staff into business partners, centers of expertise, and service delivery, thereby transforming HR's organization and function to enhance its ability to both drive and adapt to change—and also to augment its efficiency and effectiveness.

HR business partners sit at the leadership tables of the business units. They use their deep understanding of the overall Accenture business and their respective business units to develop and deliver human capital strategies to meet business objectives and to work with other parts of HR to translate those business and human capital strategies into specific actions for HR.

Centers of expertise are virtual global teams specializing in particular HR functions such as resource forecasting, performance management, and rewards. They develop all dimensions of HR solutions that meet the business needs identified by the business partners, including principles, policies, processes, and tools.

HR service delivery is the implementation arm of HR. It includes on-the-ground resources who are the face of HR for employees, geographic specialists, global specialists, and shared service centers.

This nimble and scalable structure can adapt quickly whenever Accenture's business needs change. It also enables HR professionals to specialize in a particular HR process or function so that they are better positioned as experts to drive any changes necessary to their areas. Additionally, to better anticipate change, Smart aligned the target business outcomes of this transformation initiative with Accenture's long-term blueprint for talent, which is closely aligned to the company's business.

The results have been impressive. In fiscal year 2011, when Accenture expanded its headcount by 16 percent:

- HR reduced cycle times for performance management processes, improved management of global talent supply and demand, enhanced HR productivity resulting from process improvements, and clearly delineated more specialized job responsibilities.
- It spent more than $800 million, or 52 hours per person, on employee training and professional development in its last fiscal year to ensure that its people would have the necessary skills and capabilities to serve clients at the highest level and to advance in their own careers.
- It maintained the company's reputation as a great place to build a career in virtually every major country in which it operates—a point supported by the approximately 2 million résumés it received.
- It maintained global diversity, with more than 80,000 women on the Accenture staff.

As it continues to adapt to changing local and global cultural nuances, Accenture is meeting client needs by having the best people in the right jobs at the right time and in the right place.

HR Department Research

As summarized in Chapter 2, the 2012 HRCS had just over 20,000 respondents from about 650 companies. A major focus of our research was to define the competencies of HR professionals and how they impact personal effectiveness and business performance. But we also wanted to assess two aspects of the way HR departments operate and influence business performance:

1. Whom should the HR department deliver value to?
2. What should an HR department focus on?

Finding 1: Proper Recipient of HR Department Value

We asked the following question to determine where an HR department delivers value: *How well does your HR department design and deliver HR practices that add value to the following stakeholders of your business?* We referred to the stakeholder groups listed in Figure 10.1 (a repeat of Figure 1.1).[1] HR departments have traditionally delivered value more inside their company to employees (increasing productivity) and line managers (helping deliver strategy) than to external stakeholders (customers, investors, communities, and partners). As HR moves to an outside-in perspective, we wanted to find out how much the external stakeholders also shape the way HR works.

The mean scores in Table 10.1 show that, as expected, all respondents see HR delivering more value to employees and line managers inside the company than to customers, investors, and community stakeholders outside the company. It is interesting to note that the non-HR associates rate HR as delivering

Figure 10.1   *HR stakeholders*

less value to every stakeholder than the HR participants or the HR associates do. HR has not done a viable job of communicating to non-HR observers the value that HR creates.

Table 10.1 also shows that the value created for each of the stakeholder groups is about equal to the groups' ability to predict business performance. This is a remarkable finding. It shows that to design and deliver HR work, HR professionals need to be as aware of external stakeholders as they are of inside stakeholders. Yet, as Table 10.1 shows, HR professionals are dramatically less able to define and deliver value to customers, investors, and community stakeholders.

As we have proposed in the outside-in perspective, it is possible to have customers, investors, and communities help set the criteria for what constitutes effective HR. A CHRO might use these questions as a template:

- How aware are we of the targeted customer, investor, and community stakeholders—who they are and what they expect from us?
- In staff meetings, how much time do we spend on customer, investor, and community expectations?
- As we design HR practices regarding people, performance, information, and work, how much do we consider customer, investor, and community expectations?

Answering these questions will reinforce an emerging role of HR for recognizing and serving HR stakeholders both inside and outside the organization. At Prudential, for example, Goerke realizes that for his company to grow in Asia, he has to build a local talent pipeline of actuaries and agents. He spends a sizable portion of his time assessing conditions in Asian markets.

Finding 2: HR Department Focus

Every HR department has more demands for its services than resources to fulfill them. In our review of HR department leading practices, we identified 12 areas in which an HR department could its focus attention.[2] Via the mean

Table 10.1 Stakeholder Value

Question: To what extent does your HR department have the capability to design and deliver HR practices that add value to each of the following stakeholders of your business?

Stakeholder	Mean Scores for Different Participant Groups				Impact of Business Performance Weighted Score (0 to 100%)
	All Respondents	Participant	HR Associate	Non-HR Associate	
External customer	3.38	3.38	3.46	3.27	20%
Investors or owners	3.54	3.50	3.60	3.49	20%
Communities where you operate	3.53	3.50	3.58	3.49	18%
Line managers in your organization	3.77	3.81	3.87	3.64	21%
Employees	3.78	3.81	3.88	3.66	21%

233

scores and weighed regression scores, Table 10.2 reports the focus on and relative impact of these actions on business performance, with some fascinating results.

Table 10.2   Focus of HR Department

Question: To what extent are the following true of your HR department?

Department Characteristics	Mean	Relative Weighting
Interacts effectively with the board of directors	3.67	7.7%
Has clear roles and responsibilities for each of the groups within HR (service centers, centers of expertise, embedded HR)	3.65	7.6%
Matches the structure of the HR department with how the business is organized	3.64	7.8%
Ensures that HR initiatives enable the business to achieve strategic priorities	3.62	9.7%
Develops an HR strategy that clearly links HR practices to business strategy	3.61	9.2%
Ensures that the different groups within HR work effectively with each other to provide integrated HR solutions	3.50	8.2%
Effectively manages external vendors of outsourced HR activities	3.49	8.3%
Invests in training and development of HR professionals	3.46	7.3%
Ensures that HR is a cultural role model for the rest of the organization	3.42	8.4%
Holds line managers accountable for HR	3.38	8.2%
Connects HR activities to external stakeholder expectations (customers, investors, and so on)	3.25	8.9%
Tracks and measures the impact of HR	3.22	8.8%
Multiple regression R^2		**.32**

Figure 10.2 plots these findings on a grid of the mean score on the 12 practices (low to high effectiveness) and their impact on business performance. Figure 10.2 and Table 10.2 offer some fascinating insights about what an HR department should focus on.

First, the overall impact of these 12 practices on business performance is 32 percent (cumulative R^2 in Table 10.2). In Chapter 2, we noted that the R^2 of the HR competency domains on predicting business performance is about 8 percent. This finding suggests that the quality of the HR department is about four times as important as the quality of the HR professionals in predicting business performance. While line managers may like the HR professional they work with, their business is more affected by the overall quality of the HR department. This finding supports and drives our thinking in that organizations have more impact on business performance than individual talent does.

The same phenomenon shows up in other contexts. In sports, for example, the leading scorer in a sport such as soccer, basketball, or hockey is on the winning team about 20 percent of the time (about the same 1:4 ratio of 8 to 32 percent). And Boris Groysberg has found that individual stars are less impor-

Figure 10.2   *Prioritizing HR current performance and impact on business performance*

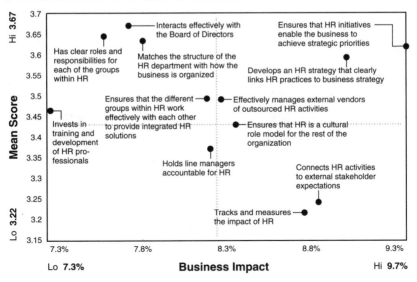

tant than organization in finance.[3] Since culture and organization capability are more important to business results than talent and individual ability, HR's job is clearly to build a workplace, not just a workforce. CHROs need to create and manage outstanding HR departments, ensuring that all the individuals in them meld their skills with the overall goals of the department and the firm.

Second, there is a range of effectiveness scores on the current delivery on the 12 items. We were surprised that the highest-rated HR leading practice was "interacts effectively with the board of directors" (3.67). Evidently, the 20,000 respondents perceive that HR work is being done at the senior levels of the company. We are less surprised at the lower scores on HR metrics (3.22) and HR connecting to external stakeholders (3.25).

Third, when we look at the interaction of how well the 12 practices are being done with their impact on business performance, we see some fascinating results (Figure 10.2). The items in the top-left quadrant (done well today but not impacting on business) suggest HR actions that may not deserve a lot of additional attention. Two of the three leading items in this quadrant involve the structure of the HR department (has clear roles and responsibilities for each of the groups within HR; matches the structure of the HR department with how the business is organized). The past 15 years have seen an ongoing and dramatic debate about how to organize the HR department with significant discussion about what's next and where to make improvements. Perhaps these data indicate that many HR departments are organized well enough, so continuing to seek and tweak new HR structures will bring diminishing returns. The greater challenge is to make existing HR structures work.

The top-right quadrant identified things that are working pretty well and need continual investment (ensures that HR initiatives enable the business to achieve strategic priorities; develops an HR strategy that clearly links HR practices to business strategy). CHROs need to continue to maintain the line of sight from HR investments to financial, strategic, and stakeholder results (see the discussion on strategic positioner in Chapter 3).

The bottom-right quadrant includes HR practices that are not done as well as others but have a strong impact on the business, making them candidates for priority treatment in HR departments with resource constraints. These are interesting areas of emphasis. HR can "connect HR activities to external stakeholder expectations" by following the outside-in logic that permeates this book. HR can also leverage its value by "tracking and measuring the impact of HR." This showed up in the workforce analytics factor for HR innovator and integrator and may be an important priority for HR investments. Perhaps it is not surprising that the data encourage line managers to be accountable for HR work. We have suggested that line managers are the owners of HR and that HR professionals are the architects. But it is also noteworthy that the HR department should be a role model for the rest of the organization. The data confirm the value of HR investing in itself—doing HR for HR—although we are not sure what to make of the low impact of investing in HR professional training on business performance.

These findings can offer some direction as to where CHROs and HR leadership teams might focus scarce resources. We are most intrigued by the finding that it may be time to stop the constant search for another HR restructuring and learn to make the existing HR structure work.

How to Build an Effective HR Department

Having reviewed these HRCS data and our experiences working on many HR transformations, we would suggest four priorities for creating an effective HR department:

1. Create an HR business plan.
2. Finalize your HR department organization.
3. Provide good HR analytics.
4. Do HR for HR—be a role model.

Create an HR Business Plan

To direct an HR department, a CHRO needs a clear HR business plan, one that lays out how the department will operate. We suggest seven steps for building an HR business plan, which are outlined in Table 10.3. Consistent with our outside-in logic, we start with the business context, establish an HR vision and HR deliverables, and follow this by investing in HR practices, governance, and competencies to accomplish the deliverables. Essentially, we suggest running an HR department as a business within the business.

Table 10.3　Human Resources Business Plan

Steps	Activities	Outcomes
1. Define business context.	• Define the business environment. • Recognize and define expectations of key stakeholders. • Master the business strategy.	Recognize the challenges facing the business, the stakeholder expectations, and appropriate business strategies.
2. Articulate HR vision.	• Who we are (partner, guide, director, leader, architect, etc.). • What we do (build individual and organizational capability, etc.). • Why we do it (competitiveness, etc.).	Articulate a vision of the HR function that can be shared inside the function (to excite HR professionals) and outside the function (to engage clients).
3. Specify deliverables or outcomes.	• Define the deliverables, outcomes, or guarantees from doing good HR work. These should be measurable and specific.	Define three to five deliverables of what the HR function can guarantee for the organization. These deliverables are often capabilities required for the organization to compete. They must specific and measurable.
4. Make human resource investments.	• Create a typology or menu of HR practices that can help reach outcomes. • Generate alternative HR practices. • Prioritize critical HR practices. • Make investment choices on critical practices (cost-benefit analysis).	Prioritize HR practices that must be implemented to accomplish the deliverables.
5. Create HR governance and structure.	• Identify who can do the work (HR, line managers, strategic vendors, staff managers). • Create a responsibility grid for who must do the work.	Define accountabilities and responsibilities for getting HR work done.

Table 10.3   Human Resources Business Plan (continued)

Steps	Activities	Outcomes
6. Prepare action plans.	• Prepare a specific action plan (who, what, when, where) for accomplishing HR priorities.	Prepare an action plan with detailed tasks, responsibilities, resources required, time frames, and so on.
7. Ensure HR competencies.	• Identify critical HR competencies needed to meet the HR plan. • Assess current state of competencies. • Prepare improvement plans.	Ensure that HR professionals are able to accomplish the business plan.

Here are some suggestions and actions for each step:

Step 1: Define Business Context

- Invite in, read books and articles by, or otherwise learn from industry or country futurists who can anticipate what might happen in the future.
- Prioritize environmental trends in terms of their probability of occurrence and potential impact.
- Recognize the expectations of your HR department that develop from corporate expectations, business customers, and business strategy.

Step 2: Articulate HR Vision

- Craft an HR vision that defines the aspirations of the department. The mission will likely include the following statements:
  - Who we are (partners, facilitators, advocates, players, contributors, etc.).
  - What we do (deliver or ensure individual ability, organization capability, talent, human capital, culture, leadership, etc.).
  - Why we do it (to ensure business success, financial results, customer share, market value, etc.).
- Share this HR vision with those inside and outside the department and ask them to identify behaviors consistent with the vision.

Step 3: Specify Deliverables or Outcomes of HR

- Do an organization audit to define the capabilities required for your organization to be successful. These capabilities become the outcomes and goals for the HR department.
- Create behavioral descriptors and measures for these top capabilities.

Step 4: Make HR Investments

- Design and implement HR practices within your department:
  - Staffing: Who comes into HR.
  - Training: How to develop HR professionals.
  - Performance management: How to build HR standards and rewards.
- Model the most innovative and integrated HR practices in the department's internal operations.

Step 5: Create HR Governance and Structure

- Align your HR organization with the business organization.
- If you are a diversified, allied, or matrix business, run your HR organization like a professional services firm.
- Create an engagement contract for how the separate roles in HR (centers of expertise, embedded HR, corporate) will work together.

Step 6: Prepare Action Plans

- Prepare an HR transformation plan with specific actions about moving the department forward. Assign clear accountabilities and time lines for the transformation plan.
- Create clear accountabilities with deadlines and consequences for the prioritized HR initiatives.

Step 7. Ensure HR Competencies

- Set clear standards for what is expected of HR professionals using the HR competency model we present here or another that suits your requirements.
- Assess HR professionals so they know what they need to do to improve performance.
- Invest in HR professionals so that they can improve.

Both Prudential and Accenture have HR business plans that lay out their priorities as they connect with business goals. As CHROs create an HR business plan, they set a clear agenda and action plan for the HR department.

Finalize Your HR Department Organization

An effective HR department needs to implement its strategy and business plan through its structure. As noted earlier, HR leaders have spent many years in a quest for the right HR organization with the clearest roles, responsibilities, and rules of operation. Consistent with the insights from Figure 10.1, we suggest that continually revising the present HR structure should not be a primary priority for HR leaders. However, the HR structure can be designed to deliver value by your taking the following actions:

- Define the basic organization design choices.
- Align the HR organization with the business organization.
- Organize to turn HR knowledge into client productivity.
- Clarify responsibilities for each HR role.
- Create an engagement contract for how the HR roles will work together.

Define the Basic Organization Design Choices

For the last 50 years, organizations of all types have been designed along two dimensions that go by a number of names (sketched in Table 10.4).

Table 10.4   *Two Primary Dimensions of Organization Design*

Centralized	Decentralized
Standardized	Customized
Efficient	Effective
Integrated	Differentiated
Tight	Loose

These two dimensions lead to four basic organization design choices:

1. *Centralized:* A strong corporate office with decisions made by a central body and shared throughout the organization
2. *Decentralized:* Independent business units (by product line or geography) that operate independently of each other
3. *Matrix:* Units that share resources but act independently
4. *Outsourced:* A corporate unit with a very small staff that primarily brokers and networks work

Figure 10.3 lays out these choices. All organization design choices for the overall enterprise or for any function can be defined as some variant of these four design options.

Following the same pattern, HR departments can be organized into one of four basic design models:

- *Centralized HR:* Organizations with centralized HR operations have a head of HR supported by specialists in staffing, training, benefits, compensation, organization design, and so on. These functional areas have responsibility for designing and implementing HR policies across the organization.
- *Decentralized HR:* With decentralized HR, each separate business unit has its own HR department staffed by a head and dedicated functional special-

Figure 10.3   Basic organization design choices

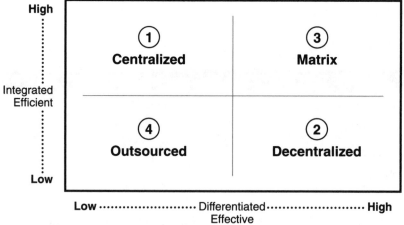

ists. Virgin in the United Kingdom, Tata in India, or Berkshire Hathaway in the United States are essentially holding companies in which each business has a dedicated HR staff with very little corporate oversight.

- *Matrix HR*: In matrix or shared services HR, the organization is trying to get the benefits of both centralization and decentralization. A matrix HR department is likely to have roles such as these:

  - *Service centers:* Using technology, HR service centers do routine, administrative, and standardized work. Service centers find ways to deliver staff work at low cost while maintaining quality and service parity. An example would be the development of common administrative systems or putting HR benefits online so employees can be self-sufficient.

  - *Centers of expertise:* Centers of expertise consist of specialists who have unique insights and great depth in HR practice areas around people (such as staffing or training), performance (rewards), communication, and organization (organization development, labor relations). Their detailed responsibilities differ from one organization to another, but they may create and control a menu of choices, provide specialist expertise on targeted problems, either reach out to help with corporatewide challenges or get pulled into the business to provide specialist expertise on targeted problems (or both), share learning from one business to another, and connect with external thought leaders.

  - *Embedded HR:* Embedded HR provides business partners who work on the business unit management team and participate in business discussions. They may perform talent and organization diagnoses to align with and drive strategy, act as strategic architects in shaping strategy, coach the business leader and other team members, help make strategy and change happen, and measure and track the quality of HR work in the business.

  - *Corporate HR:* Corporate HR oversees the overall HR function, providing advice to senior executives, managing HR careers, and shaping corporate direction.

  - *Outsourced HR*: In organizations that have outsourced most HR processes to external providers, the internal HR department is simply a broker and negotiator of contracts for talent and organization.

Align the HR Organization with the Business Organization

To choose one of the four design choices for an HR department to follow, start with the simple question, How is the business organized? HR department structure should match business structure. A holding company business structure would lead to a decentralized and dispersed HR organization. A single integrated company would have an HR department organized by functions (staffing, training, rewards, organization design, and so on). Since most large organizations diversify and operate with a multiple-business-unit structure, the vast majority of HR departments are governed by more complex organizational structures. See Figure 10.4 to capture the alignment between the business organization and the HR department. Accenture's HR organization, for example, reflects the business organization in that Smart has worked to match HR resources to business demands.

Organize to Turn HR Knowledge into Client Productivity

The vast majority of large organizations today (often multidivisional companies) are highly matrixed, so their HR departments should be organized around a shared services model. We estimate that 65–75 percent of large com-

Figure 10.4 *Aligning business and HR structures*

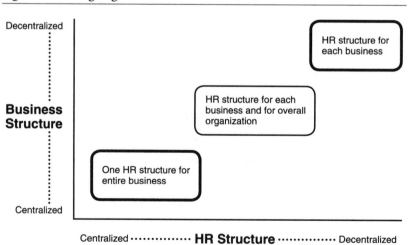

panies use a shared services matrix model. As discussed earlier, HR has four roles that it can play in a shared services model:

1. Service centers to do administrative work efficiently
2. Centers of expertise to ensure innovation and deep specialized knowledge in key HR areas
3. Embedded HR to diagnose client needs and build integrated HR solutions
4. Corporate HR to serve overall enterprisewide initiatives, presenting a common face to customers, investors, or the community and dealing with the corporate officers

Clarify Responsibilities for Each HR Role

The four HR roles can all innovate to make the shared services model more effective. Service centers focus on using technology either as a source of information (allowing employees to find out about their benefits program) or as a means of driving efficiency (replacing HR staff effort with self-service). Specialists in centers of expertise offer deep staff insights that can be adapted to solving problems. Embedded HR professionals have the challenge of diagnosing line manager and business issues and offering integrated and innovative solutions. Corporate HR professionals create a consistent firmwide cultural face and identity.

Create an Engagement Contract for
How the HR Roles Will Work Together

HR professionals in each of the four roles (service center, centers of expertise, embedded HR, and corporate HR) do not act independently. As our data show, when the HR department operates effectively as a unit, it has a dramatic impact on business performance. This means creating a shared mindset among the HR professionals based on a shared charter of how independ⌐ roles will work together, focusing on a common purpose. A⸀ ⌐ HR organization at Prudential, for example, he held a ings where HR leaders in the business and in the cent⸤ come to a common agreement on how to work together team-building sessions were important for the working relationships among the HR team.

Today, many CHROs are chasing new HR organizations. If they would follow these five design principles, they could ensure that their HR organization is fit for its real purpose.

What gets measured gets done.

Provide Good HR Analytics

There is no doubt that what gets measured gets done. Without HR metrics, decisions are made on impressions and instinct, not facts. In creating HR metrics, we suggest shifting from measuring HR activities (such as number of days of training) to measuring HR outcomes (the impact of training on building key organization capabilities), from a static HR scorecard or dashboard to predictive analytics that show how HR investments drive business results, and from focusing on data to emphasizing decision making.

To create predictive analytics, HR leaders start by being clear about the outcomes their organization requires. These outcomes are often capabilities essential for success, and they need to be defined and measured. Then HR leaders can identify decisions or choices that will help accomplish these outcomes. Linking HR decisions to outcomes becomes a key to success. Goerke at Prudential and Smart at Accenture focus less on static results and more on predictive indicators of how HR investments will lead to business outcomes.

Do HR for HR

The data in Figure 10.2 also suggest that HR needs to be a cultural role model for the rest of the organization. Too often, we have seen HR professionals as e cobbler's barefoot children, showing no signs of benefiting from the work ·tices they recommend and thus providing little incentive for other groups to try them. In seminars with HR professionals we often ask how many were placed in their present job through a thorough position-person assessment, how many have had a career conversation with their boss, how many have received a performance review, and how many could articulate the vision of the HR function. Few hands go up—it turns out that HR professionals rarely do what they ask of others. This HR hypocrisy creates cynicism not only among HR professionals but throughout their organization.

To be cultural role models, we invite HR professionals to apply the six competence domains to their own department by considering the following questions:

- Strategic positioner:
  - Do we bring customer, investor, and community insights into our HR conversations?
  - Do we partner with line managers and employees to shape our HR agenda?
  - Do we have an effective process for creating our HR business plan?
- Credible activist:
  - Do we build relationships of trust among the HR staff members?
  - Do our HR professionals in different roles respect and work well with each other?
  - Do our HR professionals appropriately challenge and learn from each other?
- Capability builder:
  - Does the capability within our HR department match the key corporate capability? (For example, if the business is working to be known for innovation, does this capability also reflect the identity of the HR department?)
  - Do our HR professionals have a line of sight between their daily work and the goals of their department?
  - Do we have a positive and meaningful work environment within the HR department?
- Change champion:
  - Do we initiate changes within our HR department?
  - Does our HR department have a reputation for implementing what we ask others to do?

- HR innovator and integrator:
  - Do we consistently seek to innovate within our HR department in each of the HR practice areas?
  - Are we early adopters of our innovative ideas in talent, performance, communication, and work?
  - Do the HR practices in our department reinforce each other?
- Technology proponent:
  - Do our HR professionals know how to use the latest technology?
  - Do we research and apply the right information to make decisions?
  - Do we use technology to improve how we do our HR work?

When HR professionals turn their competencies inward within the HR department, they become role models for others. When we train HR professionals, we often find that they are somewhat nervous about the increased expectations of facilitating strategy, building capabilities, championing change, and so forth. We sympathize with that anxiety and often tell them that the first few times they try out these new expectations, they're likely not to do all that well. So we point out that it's a good idea to practice within the HR department, where they will be relatively safe and be able to learn from their pilot tests before rolling the idea out to a broader audience. We envision the HR function as a beacon of great HR work. Goerke and Smart are exemplary HR leaders because they attend to those on the HR team as much as they attend to business leaders. They are proud of their professionalism and have modeled in HR what they intend for the rest of their organizations.

Conclusion: A Worthwhile HR Department

Many line managers have told us, "I like my HR person, but I don't like HR." This is a problem because the HR department has more potential for business impact than any individual HR professional. When CHROs are as thoughtful and rigorous about building their HR department as they are about developing HR professionals, they will create more sustainable success.

CHAPTER 11

WHAT'S SO? SO WHAT? NOW WHAT?

11

In this book, we have reported on the 2012 HR Competency Study data to lay a foundation for framing what's next for the HR profession. As we have reported, this 25-year study represents a partnership of leading HR professional associations, offers a global perspective on competencies for HR professionals, reports findings and suggests implications for six HR competency domains, recommends how to develop HR professionals, and proposes how to better lead an HR department. All these findings and recommendations developed from HR evolving to an outside-in perspective, where external business conditions shape organization actions and influence individual behaviors.

We also know that these findings are complex. To conclude and simplify them, we wrap up by addressing three questions:

1. What's so? Our top insights from this research.
2. So what? Implications for HR professionals and HR departments.
3. Now what? What these insights offer for the future of HR.

What's So? The Most Interesting Findings of This Research

We began this round of research as soon as we finished the 2007 study. As we interacted with HR professionals in conferences, workshops, seminars, and consulting engagements, we were constantly thinking about the competencies for HR professionals and requirements for HR departments. We also stayed current on the latest thinking and research on HR roles, departments, and trends. We formally began this sixth round of HR research in January 2011 by asking global partners to identify the business and HR challenges in their regions. The partners held interviews and focus groups among their constituents to determine what HR professionals should be, know, and do to be effective. We worked with partners and other advisors both in person and virtually to tailor a survey to current business requirements. We were surprised at receiving more than 20,000 responses to analyze. Over the last year we have lived with and worked through the data and have attempted to synthesize what we have learned into a series of 10 insights or key findings that merit attention:

1. *Recognize HR's evolving demographics.* The profession continues to be staffed and increasingly led by highly educated women (from 23 percent in 1987 to 62 percent in 2012), and by individuals who are specialists in talent and related areas rather than generalists (generalists declined from 61 percent in 1987 to 40 percent in 2012). The change in the HR demographic profile has interesting implications for the state of the profession and may also be consistent with demographic and role changes in other strategic support functions such as marketing, IT, and finance. The feminization of the profession may lead to stereotypes that need to be faced and overcome. The gender divide (line managers in our sample are primarily male) presents a challenge to work for gender diversity for both HR and line managers. In addition, increased specialization may provide more rigorous and scientific insights but may also splinter the field unless specialists can integrate their unique insights into common solutions.

2. *Accept common global patterns and standards.* We are struck by the global and functional similarities in how the 20,000 participants and respondents in this research have described and rated HR competence (the impact of HR competencies on personal effectiveness and business success is much the same in each region of the world). These data suggest that HR has truly become a global profession. Although some differences exist between HR professionals and non-HR associates (line managers), between those in

smaller and bigger organizations, and between those in different regions, the similarities significantly outweigh the differences. The message to HR professionals, leaders, and associations should be clear: global standards for HR competencies exist. Efforts by HR associations to develop uniquely national solutions, rather than work together in a common cause, are likely to be ineffective and misguided. We believe we have identified the HR code—the core requirements of effective HR professionals no matter where they are in the world. Of course, personal backgrounds, company differences, geographic cultures, and role expectations may require different competencies of HR professionals, but the data show a clear global standard.

3. *Think and behave from the outside in.* HR professionals must go beyond understanding the business from the inside out. To be effective business partners and strategic HR advisors, they need to go beyond finance, beyond strategy, and beyond specific stakeholders (customers and investors) to external trends and conditions—as we have described, our recommendation focused on key drivers of industry change and development: social, technology, economic, political, environmental, and demographic, or *STEPED.* The strategic contribution of HR starts with thinking and acting from the outside in, based on these drivers, performing the role of strategic positioner: interpreting external conditions, recognizing potential opportunities and threats, and cocreating a strategic response that builds the capabilities that underpin strategy. Knowing the language and flow of business, how the organization makes and loses money, and even what customers expect and how they experience the organization is no longer sufficient.

4. *Attend to the HR department as well as to individual development of HR staff members.* While HR professional competence explains 8 percent of business performance, HR department effectiveness explains *four times* that (32 percent). The data suggest that HR professionals are important to business results but that the HR department is more important. HR departments impact business success when they attend equally to stakeholders both

inside the organization (employees, line managers) and outside (customers, investors, communities). At a more general level, these data confirm that HR should not limit itself to a narrow focus on talent, or human capital, but should pay attention to both talent and organization. Business success is not all about talent; it is about the combination of talent and culture delivered by an effective HR organization.

5. *Move forward beyond the diminishing returns of reorganizing HR departments.* HR transformation in the last 15 years has tended to focus on HR roles, structure, and automation of transactional HR functions. These data reinforce the need for a greater focus on how HR links its priorities and investments to customer experience, HR analytics, modeling the culture, and including line managers in HR planning and assessment. It is critical to organize an HR department to meet strategic needs, to have clear roles and responsibilities, and to govern HR decision making with clarity. But once an HR department is aligned with the business organization, it is time to move beyond HR structure to other activities.

6. *Leverage the benefits and acknowledge the limits of being a credible activist.* Strong competency as a credible activist is fundamental to the personal effectiveness of HR professionals but also to HR's impact on the business or business success. HR professionals have, in the past, mistaken the positive regard of line managers for productive performance. The HR profession has worked for decades to get a "seat at the table." The data from HRCS 2012 suggest that we have won that battle and have both access and the expectations of leaders. Now HR must focus on innovating and integrating in the areas that drive business success. Trust is very important as a point of entry, but now that we are at the table, we must contribute something significant to the discussion there.

7. *Pay attention to sustaining change.* Change and capability were linked in the 2007 research (culture and change steward) but are differentiated in the current research as separate and highly important competence domains. It is not surprising that change championship has returned as a unique and critical competency. Organizations are dealing with the lingering impacts of the great recession of 2008, globalization, accelerating technology,

increased competition for talent, a greater regulatory burden, and other factors. HR professionals are slightly better at initiating than sustaining change, but sustaining change has a greater impact on business success. HR has sometimes been accused of fads, and we are familiar with derisive descriptions such as "sheep dip" and "flavor of the month." These comments point out the need for HR to do a more effective job of sustaining change. We cannot slow the pace of change, but we can be more skillful at how we work to make change stick. It is probably better to do fewer initiatives that are sustained than to start many that are not.

8. *Become current on technology and information.* The technology proponent competencies are among the more intriguing and potentially powerful findings of this study. Effectiveness in this domain may not have the same impact on personal effectiveness as in the credible activist domain, but it has considerably greater impact on business performance—as much impact as any other area of HR involvement, in fact. However, technology is changing how work is done in dramatic and unexpected ways, and it is essential that HR have both knowledge and expertise in understanding the effects of new analytical and social media technology. The new HRCS suggests that automating administrative and transactional work is the tip of the HR iceberg. HR needs to go beyond using technology to do HR work more efficiently and use technology to drive knowledge and relationships inside and outside the company. For example, HR professionals need to be more adept at connecting people and work through technology. Today's work is not only defined by geographic or functional boundaries, but it is also defined by common interests.

9. *Capitalize on capabilities.* Integrated HR comes when isolated practices meld into a definitive set of organization capabilities. HR professionals should perform organization audits to determine the right capabilities for the future. The ability to create meaning is an underlying capability that stands out because as we create any capability (innovation, service, collaboration, or whatever), we need to see that the personal needs of people are addressed and that work is not just about task accomplishment but about the meaning behind the tasks.

10. *Build organization.* Organization-focused HR competencies (capability builder, change champion, HR innovator and integrator, technology proponent) should get significant HR development attention. These competence domains connect the individual to external environmental conditions. They sustain isolated events. It is very easy for HR to turn to talent solutions when sustained success comes from organization solutions.

Of course, others may draw different insights from these data. But these are our top insights that we think have enormous implications for HR professionals.

So What? The Implications for HR

In previous work, we have suggested that HR professionals need to deliver required competencies by mastering the actions of being a coach, architect, designer-deliverer, and facilitator. Coaches work one-to-one with business leaders (and others) to help them improve their personal behavior. Architects build organization blueprints for how to turn strategy into results. Designer-deliverers create and implement aligned, innovated, and integrated HR practices. Facilitators help organizations manage processes and change to ensure that desired goals are achieved. We believe these four actions continue to be viable for HR professionals.

But, based on the work behind this book, we suggest some additional actions that HR professionals should master:

• *Observer:* As observers, HR professionals should learn how to interpret external business conditions, to connect with key stakeholders, to clarify strategy, and to help the business make money. As observers, they become informed about trends and translate them into actions.

• *Diagnostician:* HR professionals should become adept at diagnosing individual, leadership, and organizational behaviors. Diagnosis can come through observations, interviews, focus groups, and surveys. Through diagnosis, HR professionals can anticipate the effects of causes, set priorities, and track results.

- *Thought leader:* HR professionals should do more than react to conditions; they should create them. As thought leaders, they not only know relevant theory and research, but they bring unique insights into their work. These insights bridge the paradoxes we outlined in Chapter 1.

- *Doer:* Ultimately, HR professionals act on what they see, diagnose, and learn. As doers, they make the right things happen and ensure that their organizations respond as quickly as the environment requires.

As HR professionals master these new actions, they deliver on the competencies identified in this research. These four actions may apply to each of the six competence domains as HR professionals adapt and apply the ideas we present in each of the preceding chapters.

Now What? Where HR Is Headed

Our insights and the proposed actions provide the most up-to-date, global, and empirical insight on where HR stands from a competency perspective. But where is HR headed? We cannot provide the same level of detailed insight on HR's future as its present, but there are some signs of where HR is headed:

1. *A larger role for HR.* It's not surprising that HR is expected to play a bigger role in most organizations, particularly large, complex, and global organizations. There is hardly a consulting or academic report that doesn't reinforce the degree to which talent, culture, and leadership are among the top items on the agenda of the CEO. McKinsey reports that, among CEOs in a recent study, 52 percent said that labor productivity and talent management would have a significant impact on their performance,[1] and The Hay Group identifies achieving success through people and placing a high value on talent and leadership as critical indicators of high-performing organizations.[2] And PricewaterhouseCoopers reports that CEOs plan to increase

their investment in talent and leadership.[3] Some of the specific areas where organizations and their leaders are paying greater attention include:

- Developing local talent in emerging markets
- Increasing the participation of women in senior roles and on boards
- Implementing more demanding performance management systems
- Dealing with the challenges of executive compensation
- Managing and engaging Millennials
- Forming, disbanding, and re-forming highly productive teams across geography and time zones
- Creating more effective and efficient organizations

2. *Greater integration with other functions.* The importance of the strategic positioner competency reveals a trend in HR's interaction and partnership with other strategic support functions, notably finance and IT, but also lean manufacturing, the supply chain, and other areas of functional specialization. Mars already describes its HR generalists as "copilots" jointly supporting a business general manager with the unit CFO. More and more HR organizations are describing their generalists as "HR business partners," which reflects an effort to reinforce the quality of integration with the business. And reports of stronger partnership between HR and the finance function are significantly on the rise in organizations as varied as Dow Chemical, the U.S. Government Accountability Office, and First Tennessee Bank.[4]

3. *Shift in administrative responsibility.* Responsibilities are shifting throughout the business world. Divides are opening between sales and marketing, between traditional accounting and strategic finance, and between IT help services and architecture. Each of these functional areas has recognized the difference between its administrative activities and the more strategic work it performs, and each has divided the function accordingly. We see strong signs that this is occurring in HR as well. It would not be surprising to see that some of the traditional administrative work of HR no longer regards HR as a functional home. There is no compelling case for HR to lead payroll or benefits administration, pensions or mobility (transfer administration), particularly as managed on a contractual outsourcing basis.

On the other hand, we see an increasing number of HR departments incorporating employee (and sometimes stakeholder) communication in recognition of the important role HR plays in shaping the message to the employee population and to key stakeholders. And we are seeing more HR involvement in strategy work, in lean consulting, and in other areas that are not traditionally HR but that make sense in the context of a more strategic, externally attentive HR function. For example, the integrated contribution of communication and HR has been cited as supporting more effective mergers and acquisitions work.[5]

4. *Global innovation.* The center of HR innovation has shifted from North America and Western Europe. It is already distributed broadly, and this trend will only continue. Global companies like Kraft, IBM, GE, P&G, and others are "HR leader feeders" bringing HR innovations to the BRIC (Brazil, Russia, India, China) countries and to N11 (the "next eleven" nations: Bangladesh, Egypt, Indonesia, Iran, South Korea, Mexico, Nigeria, Pakistan, the Philippines, Turkey, and Vietnam). Communication technology and HR association conferences have made contemporary HR more accessible. Asian and Latin American companies have created their own innovations in HR based on the culture and business challenges unique to their marketplaces.

   Similarly, Singapore, devoid of rich natural resources, aspires to make itself a center of commercial leadership and innovation for the new Asia; it has funded a potentially powerful and creative organization to lead this effort called the Human Capital Leadership Institute. Norway and Singapore are collaborating on HR transformation of the public sector. Denmark's local government department has brought considerable leadership development education and talent management practices to Danish municipalities. The competency data points out the degree of similarity across regions in how HR competencies are perceived, a nice base for continued global innovation in HR practices.

5. *More impact of technology.* As Chapter 8 points out, HR will become a far more wired function over time, sophisticated in its use of technology in several areas:

- The effective and efficient management of transactional services
- Big data analysis
- Playing a much more significant role as the architect and implementer of information and communications strategy
- Engaging social networking technology and the new media as a means of connecting individuals and teams, and connecting the organization with customers and other stakeholders.

Data analysis is a particularly interesting point. It will expand beyond singular data sets such as engagement surveys and databases that can be correlated for insights into specific relationships, like that between customer loyalty and employee behavior or, on a more specific level, between customer purchases and employee engagement.[6] Technology and analytics have advanced significantly. For example, predictive analytics have made it possible for Comcast to identify a strong, positive relationship between employee satisfaction, employee retention, and customer satisfaction.[7]

6. *A different organizational mix and demographic.* The data point to a different landscape in many, perhaps most, HR organizations. We've learned from our 20,000 participants that the demographics and roles played in HR have changed and are continuing to change. For example:

- *More women in senior roles.* Almost two-thirds of HR professionals were women, a continuity of the gender shift we have seen over time. Expect that the mix will continue to have a majority presence of women at all levels.
- *Managing the diversity gap will be a challenging journey.* The shift to more women in the department and in senior roles is in contrast with the profile of HR heads today, in general, and with the line managers who are HR's business partners. According to a recent PwC report:

> The average head of human resources in the Fortune 100 is a 53 year old man with Bachelor's degree who spent 15 years with their current employer and about half their work life in HR roles. SVP is their title, had been VP immediately before. The most common HR experience to have had is time in the workforce development

function. One in five had an overseas assignment, and almost a third had jobs that could be described as directly involved in international operations. Just under a third were hired into the top job from another company.[8]

- *Greater appreciation for the business within HR and in the business for HR.* In our data, a shrinking number of participants over time have 10 or more years of experience in HR. Respondents are both younger as a population and have had less experience in industry or have come from functions other than HR. More HR professionals are seeking experience and opportunities in other functions, which increases HR understanding of the business, and the business's appreciation of HR's contribution.

7. *Higher expectations and rewards.* As a result of the increased priority and challenge of managing talent, culture, and leadership, performance expectations for HR will continue to climb. It will not be acceptable for HR to make operating errors or to manage capital projects badly. HR will be seen as a business within the business. For that reason it will also be held accountable to perform as efficiently as any other business department. As a result, top-performing HR leaders will be amply rewarded. HR currently stands just behind the general manager and CFO roles in compensation averages by functional area, and we are confident that as long as HR leaders and professionals deliver the high standard of competence identified in our research, they will be amply rewarded.

8. *Roles and structures will continue to evolve.* In our data, an increasing proportion of respondents over time are individual contributors. HR departments, like other functions, are delayering. There are fewer true managerial roles and more working managers with smaller staffs; efforts are being made to consolidate where possible. The impact of outsourcing and technology has been a reduction in staffing; we have seen some leading global organizations essentially cutting their full-time HR staffing levels in half. Project contractors and consultants play an increasingly large role in t' full-time equivalent staffing of HR. And we are seeing a new mix of f' tions. Over the period of the HRCS, we have seen an evolution of em

toward compensation, strategy, organization development, recruiting, and training, and away from benefits, labor relations, and HR generalist work.

These data provide a window into the emerging composition of HR departments. The new structure features a shift away from traditional administrative and employee relations work and away from a focus on union relations and contracts. It is a shift toward business success drivers of capability and culture building, leadership development, talent, and initiating and sustaining change.

These trends have exciting implications for HR.

Conclusion: Continuing to Build HR

We have chronicled the development of HR for the past 25 years. The HRCS has provided a unique frontline view of the evolution of the HR function. Over that period, we have seen a great deal of change in HR, but also wonderful signs of its maturation as a critical business and organizational function. As the findings for each round of the HRCS indicate, our view of HR has become more nuanced and granular. As HR plays a larger role and deals with more challenging issues, we see the work of HR in greater detail and relief.

The feedback from this round of the HRCS is unmistakable and exciting; HR is expected to operate from the outside in. Just as Wayne Gretzky in hockey or Magic Johnson in basketball were able to anticipate where the action was headed on the court, HR needs the same sort of anticipation of where action is headed in its field. As HR professionals, we must provide an interpretive ability to see the connection between what is happening outside and the oppor-

ⁱⁱes or threats it portends for our organizations. And that insight must

managers at every level to convert vision into action—and action

benefit the customers and stakeholders of our organizations.

sitioner, joined by the relationship and influence skills

les HR to build capability through HR practices

e in creating a system of HR that attracts talent,

ds well-aligned, high-performing teams and organizations that are connected by communications technology that reinforces teamwork and collaboration.

We are incredibly optimistic about the future of HR. By our count, there are almost one million HR professionals around the world. A growing number of graduate programs focus on HR, HR is an increasingly attractive concentration in MBA programs, and we see Google, Zappo, Baidu, and other organizations redefining and reinventing how HR is done in exciting ways. And in our programs at RBL—with clients in more than 50 countries—and in our work with HR executives at the Ross School of Business, University of Michigan, we are inclined to believe that the golden age of HR is still climbing toward its zenith.

IDEAS FOR HOW HR PROFESSIONALS CAN DEVELOP THEIR COMPETENCE

HRCS Development Guide

The following (Figures A.1 through A.20) are samples of development ideas for each of the 20 factors within the six competency domains (see the "HRCS Development Guide" for a complete list).

Strategic Positioner

Figure A.1   Interpreting global business context

Know and Do:

- Identify the global business requirements and implications for your organization.
- Grasp the external political environment.
- Be able to clarify social issues that may impact your industry and company.

Development Ideas:

- Prepare a three-page memo on the context of the industry and culture in which your business primarily operates. Take into account all stakeholders: investors, customers, communities, regulators, partners, employees, and line managers.
- Prepare a presentation on the demographic trends that will affect how your department crafts HR practices within your business.
- Interview an investment analyst who is a specialist in your company's industry about the factors that constitute wealth creation in your industry.

Figure A.2   *Decoding customer expectations*

Know and Do:

O   Segment customers into target groups.

O   Know the requirements and expectations of key customers.

O   Facilitate dissemination of customer information.

Development Ideas:

O   Conduct a study that includes a value chain analysis of your major customers. Include a definition of who the customers are. What are their buying criteria? Who do they currently buy from? Where are you strongest and weakest versus key competitors?

O   Serve on a cross-functional team whose task is to identify customers' buying habits and recommend steps to improve market share.

O   Spend time with customers and customers' customers. If this is not possible, spend time with sales and marketing staff, review customer feedback, and sit in regularly on call center calls to develop an informed view of what customers are thinking and concerned about.

Figure A.3   *Cocrafting a strategic agenda*

Know and Do:

O   Know how your company creates wealth.

O   Define the key wealth-creating positions within the company.

O   Help establish the business strategy.

Development Ideas:

O   Lead a discussion with a diagonal cross-section of informed people in your company on the topic wealth creation activities. Determine what percentage of your employees creates 90% of the wealth and what they do.

O   Conduct an industry analysis that includes a detailed plan for increasing the performance of your company relative to the competition.

O   Work on a future scenario-building team whose task it is to develop a vision for the future of your company and the industry within which you compete.

Credible Activist

Figure A.4 Earning trust through results

Know and Do:

O Set clear goals and expectations.
O Focus on meeting pre-negotiated or pre-stated commitments.
O Strive to be error free.

Development Ideas:

O Carefully manage your commitments. Your desire to be helpful can lead to the inability to say "no," which results in taking on more than you can deliver, which in turn creates the perception that you don't follow through on commitments.
O Admit mistakes and take personal responsibility.
O Create HR measures that track both the output of HR and the means of generating the output. Create predictive measures that show cause-and-effect relationships.

Figure A.5 Influencing and relating to others

Know and Do:

O Take appropriate risks, both personally and for the organization.
O Provide candid observations, particularly with data.
O Practice "HR with an attitude" by taking positions, anticipating problems, and offering solutions.

Development Ideas:

O Honestly evaluate your willingness to express opinions and ideas in staff meetings or in other forums. If you have a tendency to be quiet or hesitant in these meetings, make a goal to remedy the situation. Commit to making at least one business-related comment in each meeting.
O Find something that is within your power to fix and fix it. Don't let your actions or inactions be subject to co-worker approval.
O Build personal and professional relationships with those outside the HR function.

Figure A.6   Improving through self-awareness

Know and Do:

O   Be aware of your personal strengths and weaknesses.

O   Know your predispositions and be willing to experiment with new behavior.

O   Use your strengths to strengthen others.

Development Ideas:

O   Elicit feedback from colleagues on your interpersonal skills. Act on the feedback. Don't be defensive. Translate the feedback into simple and focused action.

O   Avoid using the word "I" for an entire day.

O   Practice nonjudgmental empathizing with family members or close friends.

Figure A.7   Shaping the HR profession

Know and Do:

O   Participate in local, regional, and/or national HR associations.

O   Know the standards for certification in your field.

O   Become technically competent in your area of expertise.

Development Ideas:

O   Be willing to question the standard way of doing things in HR. Think of ways in which you can create positive change in your organization. Watch these TED talks on creativity for inspiration: http://www.ted.com/talks/ken_robinson_says_schools_ kill_creativity.html.

O   Volunteer to co-host a best practice or community HR forum.

O   Prepare a presentation for an HR professional audience.

Capability Builder

Figure A.8   Capitalizing organization capability

Know and Do:

O Define your organization's capabilities.

O Audit your organization or department's capabilities through interviews and/or surveys.

O Prioritize and measure targeted capabilities.

Development Ideas:

O Prepare a report on the organizational capabilities of different competitors in your industry.

O Do a content analysis of your leaders' talks to identify how they talk about organizational capabilities.

O Work with those who prepare the annual report to weave organizational capabilities into the texts.

Figure A.9   Aligning strategy, capability, and employee behavior

Know and Do:

O Define culture from the outside in (the identity of the firm in the mind of the key stakeholders).

O Audit your organization's culture and make sure it aligns with your strategy and stakeholders.

O Audit and align management practices to drive and sustain your organization's culture.

Development Ideas:

O Collect stories of behavior that models the desired culture. Share these stories in conversations, presentations, newsletters, etc.

O Audit key management practices (budgeting, performance management, communication, meetings, etc.) for alignment with the culture. Are certain practices unintentionally sending the wrong symbolic messages about what you value as a company?

O Conduct a cultural audit alone or with an HR or management team. Identify the cultural characteristics that your business must have to meet the needs of stakeholders and advance your business strategy. Identify the gaps between what is and what should be.

Figure A.10   Creating a meaningful work environment

Know and Do:

O   Help identify what gives employees meaning and purpose in your organization.

O   Go beyond commitment or engagement surveys to probe for meaning and purpose.

O   Help shape an employee value proposition that highlights how employees can be motivated by what matters to them.

Development Ideas:

O   Coach leaders to become meaning makers by helping them see the impact of meaning on employee productivity.

O   Identify the negative elements of your work environment and talk about them in a staff meeting.

O   In one-on-one interactions with co-workers, help them see the purpose and meaning in their work.

Change Champion

Figure A.11   Initiating change

Know and Do:

O Help individuals define and build a process for change.

O Build a disciplined process for turning what we know into what we do.

O Understand how to make things happen.

Development Ideas:

O Design a change process that will lead to an important shift in your organization's culture and will better align with the expectations of external customers.

O Evaluate your work processes and HR practices and consider the signals they send about the experience you are trying to create for key customers.

O Gather information from internal and/or external sources regarding the future of your business. Does your current culture support future success? If not, what needs to change? How will you change it?

Figure A.12   Sustaining change

Know and Do:

O Learn how to engage others in the process of change.

O Break larger changes into simple first steps.

O Make sure that desired changes show up in behaviors, HR processes, and metrics.

Development Ideas:

O Look at change initiatives in your company that did not last. Figure out why they did not. Prepare a summary report for HR and leadership teams.

O Interview former employees about the barriers they see to sustained change.

O Do a "virus detector" on your organization or work unit.

HR Innovator and Integrator

Figure A.13 *Optimizing human capital through workforce planning and analytics*

Know and Do:

- ○ Define the technical and social competencies required for our workforce of the future.
- ○ Create an employee value proposition that engages and commits employees.
- ○ Build a sense of contribution for employees.

Development Ideas:

- ○ Practice translating general cultural attributes into specific behaviors. For instance, if someone were flexible, cost conscious, team-focused, creative, or disciplined, what specific and observable behaviors would he or she exhibit?
- ○ Be involved in college recruitment with a team of experienced recruiters. Start with a statement of what technical and cultural skills you expect.
- ○ Work in a volunteer position within an association that requires you to evaluate members for promotions.

Figure A.14 *Developing talent*

Know and Do:

- ○ Identify future skills required for employees to succeed.
- ○ Build individual development plans to help employees learn which include training, work experience, coaching, and life experience.
- ○ Create an employee development system that links performance review, development, and career planning.

Development Ideas:

- ○ Create inventories of key developmental jobs and experiences. Identify what the incumbents learn from these experiences, and how the learning prepares them for greater contribution and leadership.
- ○ Work with managers to create realistic lists of potential successors to key jobs and roles.
- ○ Pay attention to the development of technical people, not just future executives.

Figure A.15   Shaping organization and communication practices

Know and Do:

- Help define and clarify the roles, responsibilities, and rules of the successful organization.
- Identify and improve on work processes.
- Create workforce policies that help sustain the organization.

Development Ideas:

- Work with a department to create a more effective work process design.
- Coach a manager on the design and delivery of a key presentation. Teach basic techniques, critique, and offer feedback. Volunteer to take the lead in designing the communication strategy for an upcoming organizational change, such as the implementation of a new policy, system, or process.
- Engage your work team in identifying and reducing low-value work.

Figure A.16   Driving performance

Know and Do:

- Articulate strategy in clear terms that can be measured.
- Design a measurement system that includes individual and organization-level measures and is focused on both behaviors and outcomes.
- Align measures to desired strategies.

Development Ideas:

- Work with a management team to identify behaviors that are critical to your unit's performance. Formulate these behaviors into an evaluation process.
- Identify what percentage of employees creates 90 percent of the wealth. Interview them concerning what they desire in terms of financial and nonfinancial rewards. Design customized rewards for those individuals.
- Determine what might be done to tie your reward system more closely to performance.

Figure A.17 Building leadership brand

Know and Do:

O Build a case for why leadership matters in your organization that is tied to clear business results.

O Clarify your organization's theory of leadership with explicit standards and expectations.

O Assess leaders against the standards.

Development Ideas:

O Observe leaders in your company and in your community who are successful. Figure out what things they all do and figure out what things each of them do that are unique.

O Look at five leadership competency models in the literature, in other companies, or from your company. Synthesize the basic, shared requirements of a good leader.

O Examine your organization's media campaign in print, television, radio, or on the Internet. What are the messages you are sharing with customers? Are these messages showing up in your competency model?

Technology Proponent

Figure A.18   Improving utility of HR operations

Know and Do:

O Figure out the key information your company needs to share to make better decisions.

O Identify where there are opportunities to increase cost efficiency through technology in HR without affecting the HR service relationship.

O Understand the latest technology trends in HR.

Development Ideas:

O Draw a graphic representation of the flow of major information in your HR department and identify the points at which HR technology might be more effectively utilized.

O Identify how to leverage 360-degree feedback more effectively through online follow-up.

O Determine which critical competencies within HR can be best taught through online technology, which are taught best on the job, and which are best taught in a classroom setting.

Figure A.19   Leveraging social media tools

Know and Do:

O Access social media tools (e.g., LinkedIn, Facebook) to source and connect employees.

O Examine your organization's brand in the social media space.

O Assign people to track your organization's social media footprint.

Development Ideas:

O Understand and manage the organization's employee brand through monitoring discussions of what it's like to work at your organization on Facebook, employment websites, etc.

O Explore the use of video games or online worlds (Second Life, etc.) for training.

O Audit your organization's use of social media—who in the organization is using which sites and for what purposes—and identify ways to coordinate and improve the organization's social media footprint.

Figure A.20   *Connecting people through technology*

Know and Do:

O Find ways to create learning communities both inside and outside your company.
O Build web-based information systems that enable employees to connect with each other.
O Form bottom-up information-sharing processes so leaders can quickly learn how they are doing.

Development Ideas:

O Form a social community through the Internet of people in similar positions outside of your company.
O Audit existing internal information systems and identify current usage, user needs, and opportunities for improvement.
O Identify ways to create a mini online community within the organization (blogs for training cohorts, listservs for technical areas, etc.).

HRCS COMPETENCY SELF-ASSESSMENT

B

Instructions: The following items (Figures B.1 through B.6) provide a brief self-assessment version of the feedback survey that the authors have created, based on the results of the 2012 HR competency research. A full version of the HRCS feedback survey is available through the RBL Group as either a self-assessment, a 180-degree feedback survey (manager and self), or a 360-degree feedback survey (manager, self, HR colleagues or reports, line management colleagues, or other stakeholders).

There are two ratings you are asked to provide. The first is your assessment of your current competency in this factor. The second is the importance of your improvement of this competency. Remember to answer as candidly as possible. Both ratings are 1–5, where 1 = low and 5 = high.

Figure B.1   *Credible activist*

	My current competence	Value of improved competence to business
Earning trust through results	⬇	⬇
Has track record of results	① ② ③ ④ ⑤	① ② ③ ④ ⑤
Demonstrates personal integrity and ethics	① ② ③ ④ ⑤	① ② ③ ④ ⑤
Influencing and relating to others		
Works well with his or her management team	① ② ③ ④ ⑤	① ② ③ ④ ⑤
Communicates effectively	① ② ③ ④ ⑤	① ② ③ ④ ⑤
Improves through self-awareness		
Takes appropriate risks	① ② ③ ④ ⑤	① ② ③ ④ ⑤
Seeks to learn from both successes and failures	① ② ③ ④ ⑤	① ② ③ ④ ⑤
Shaping your profession		
Plays an active role in professional bodies	① ② ③ ④ ⑤	① ② ③ ④ ⑤
Invests in developing the HR function	① ② ③ ④ ⑤	① ② ③ ④ ⑤

Figure B.2   Capability builder

	My current competence	Importance of improving my competence

Auditing organizational capability

Ensures the organization clarifies organizational capabilities required for business success	① ② ③ ④ ⑤	① ② ③ ④ ⑤
Audits capability effectiveness	① ② ③ ④ ⑤	① ② ③ ④ ⑤

Aligning strategy, capability, and employee behavior

Measure the impact of culture on achieving sustained business performance	① ② ③ ④ ⑤	① ② ③ ④ ⑤
Design and deliver integrated HR practices (e.g., staffing, training, rewards and recognition, performance management, etc.) that create and sustain the desired culture	① ② ③ ④ ⑤	① ② ③ ④ ⑤

Creating a positive, meaningful work environment

Craft a culture that encourages work/ life balance	① ② ③ ④ ⑤	① ② ③ ④ ⑤
Craft a culture that helps employees find meaning and purpose in their work	① ② ③ ④ ⑤	① ② ③ ④ ⑤

Shaping your profession

Play an active role in professional bodies	① ② ③ ④ ⑤	① ② ③ ④ ⑤
Invest in developing the HR function	① ② ③ ④ ⑤	① ② ③ ④ ⑤

Figure B.3   Technology proponent

	My current competence	Importance of improving my competence
Improving efficiency of HR systems through technology	⬇	⬇
Leverage technology for HR processes (HRIS)	① ② ③ ④ ⑤	① ② ③ ④ ⑤
Remove low value-added or bureaucratic work	① ② ③ ④ ⑤	① ② ③ ④ ⑤
Connecting each other through technology		
Formulate a comprehensive communication strategy	① ② ③ ④ ⑤	① ② ③ ④ ⑤
Provide alternative/flexible policies to motivate different generations of employees	① ② ③ ④ ⑤	① ② ③ ④ ⑤
Leveraging social media for business		
Leverage social media for business purposes	① ② ③ ④ ⑤	① ② ③ ④ ⑤
Use technology to facilitate remote and mobile workforce	① ② ③ ④ ⑤	① ② ③ ④ ⑤
Shaping your profession		
Play an active role in professional bodies	① ② ③ ④ ⑤	① ② ③ ④ ⑤
Invest in developing the HR function	① ② ③ ④ ⑤	① ② ③ ④ ⑤

Figure B.4   *Strategic positioned*

	My current competence ⬇	Importance of improving my competence ⬇
Interpreting business context		
Understand industry dynamics and competitive forces	①②③④⑤	①②③④⑤
Understand expectations of investors (e.g., valuation, intangibles)	①②③④⑤	①②③④⑤
Decoding customer expectations		
Understand expectations of external customers	①②③④⑤	①②③④⑤
Help articulate a customer-value proposition that guides internal organization actions	①②③④⑤	①②③④⑤
Cocrafting a strategic response		
Spot potential opportunities and obstacles to business success	①②③④⑤	①②③④⑤
Translate business strategy into a talent (workforce) and culture (workplace) set of initiatives	①②③④⑤	①②③④⑤
Shaping your profession		
Play an active role in professional bodies	①②③④⑤	①②③④⑤
Invest in developing the HR function	①②③④⑤	①②③④⑤

Figure B.5   *HR innovator and integrator*

Ensuring today and tomorrow's talent	My current competence ↓	Importance of improving my competence ↓
Establish standards or competencies for required talent	① ② ③ ④ ⑤	① ② ③ ④ ⑤
Assess key talent	① ② ③ ④ ⑤	① ② ③ ④ ⑤

Developing talent		
Design meaningful developmental experiences	① ② ③ ④ ⑤	① ② ③ ④ ⑤
Develop local talent for local markets	① ② ③ ④ ⑤	① ② ③ ④ ⑤

Shaping work and organization		
Know how to form and leverage teams	① ② ③ ④ ⑤	① ② ③ ④ ⑤
Perform organizational diagnoses and audits	① ② ③ ④ ⑤	① ② ③ ④ ⑤

Delivering performance management		
Ensure that performance standards adapt to changing strategic demands	① ② ③ ④ ⑤	① ② ③ ④ ⑤
Deal with nonperformance in a fair and timely way	① ② ③ ④ ⑤	① ② ③ ④ ⑤

Building leadership brand		
Invest in future leaders	① ② ③ ④ ⑤	① ② ③ ④ ⑤
Measure or track leadership effectiveness	① ② ③ ④ ⑤	① ② ③ ④ ⑤

Figure B.6   *Change champion*

	My current competence ⬇	Importance of improving my competence ⬇
Initiating change		
Help people understand why change is important (i.e., create a sense of urgency)	① ② ③ ④ ⑤	① ② ③ ④ ⑤
Identify and overcome sources of resistance to change	① ② ③ ④ ⑤	① ② ③ ④ ⑤
Articulate the key decisions and actions that must happen for change to make progress	① ② ③ ④ ⑤	① ② ③ ④ ⑤
Sustaining change		
Ensure the availability of resources to stick with the change (e.g., money, information, technology, people)	① ② ③ ④ ⑤	① ② ③ ④ ⑤
Monitor and communicate progress of change processes	① ② ③ ④ ⑤	① ② ③ ④ ⑤

1. Review the competency factors/items where you have identified a high benefit to improvement.
2. Pick 1–2 to work on. As you decide, consider both the performance impact of improvement and your energy or interest in working on this competency.
3. Be as specific as possible about your goal—e.g., "I will ... so that ..."
4. What help do you need? From whom?
5. What will you accomplish in the next 30 days to get started?
6. How will you measure improvement within these competencies?

SUPPORTING DEVELOPMENT: HR ACADEMY OPTIONS

C

Following is a range of options that we have found helpful in building skill, performance, and self-awareness in HR competence (Table C.1). Workshops described below include those best for all members of the organization and those options that are most appropriate for senior HR leaders and professionals. The alternatives range from least to most demanding in both time and budget, but, as might be expected, they also range from least to greatest impact.

Table C.1

Investment in Development: Options	Requirement	Considerations
HRCS overview	Half day or full day. Typical full-day agenda is given below: **AM:** • Welcome, overview • Value of stronger, more strategic HR • Key business challenges and priorities: implications for HR competence **PM:** • Review of HRCS competency research: how HR expectations have changed • The new HRCS competencies • Our HR department strengths and developmental priorities • Game plan for improvement	• Should be facilitated by an individual with a strong knowledge of the HRCS competency research; the RBL Group will facilitate, train internal staff, or advise • Important to design the workshop to be highly participative and engaging • Group size is discretionary; groups are as small as a team or as large as 100 people
HRCS research overview and feedback	Half day or full day with similar agenda but includes HRCS feedback (either self-assessment or 180/360 feedback) and provides time for participants to review their feedback, see the overview of group ratings, and create specific individual development plans.	• Highly participative and engaging • Requires pre-planning for HRCS self-assessment or 180/360 feedback (manage feedback requests to avoid feedback fatigue; allow 3–4 weeks for collection of feedback using the RBL survey feedback system) • Can be part of a customized executive HR strategy-setting session • Delivered by RBL Group faculty or faculty trained by the RBL Group • Delivered on site in the organization

Table C.1   (continued)

Investment in Development: Options	Requirement	Considerations
Impact: Building HR consulting skills	2–3 day workshop that builds the skills of credible activist and change champion, and includes: • IMPACT survey feedback • Skill building in the change champion and credible activist domains • Casework and simulation • Team work • Action learning: planning for back home application on a project that delivers measurable business value	• Focus on feedback, skill building, and practical application back on the job • Geared to independent contributors with 5–10 years of experience • Appropriate for generalists and functional specialists or individuals who have recently entered the HR field from another function • Delivered by the RBL Group faculty or internal faculty trained by the RBL Group • Delivered on site in the organization
HR competency focus: Strategic positioner, etc.	1–2 day skill-building workshops focused on each of the 6 HRCS competencies. • Use a variety of learning methods including; assessments, cases, videos, simulations, etc. • Teaches theory but focuses on application through tools and practice	• Can be customized to the specific needs of the organization • Appropriate for generalists and functional specialists, or individuals who have recently entered the HR field from another function • Delivered by the RBL Group faculty or internal faculty trained by the RBL Group • Delivered on site in the organization

(continued on next page)

Table C.1   (continued)

Investment in Development: Options	Requirement	Considerations
HR business partner workshop	A 3–5 day workshop that addresses the key actions and behaviors that grow HR professional and leader competence. Incorporates: • HRCS feedback • Skill building in all competency domains • Casework and simulation • Coaching • Additional content in key competency areas based on the feedback or HR leadership • Action learning: planning for back home application on a project that delivers measurable business value • Follow-up	• Provides a broad overview of the HRCS competencies • Versions available that are appropriate for multiple audience levels: independent contributors, HR generalists and functional specialists, individuals who have recently entered the HR field from another function, and HR leaders or managers • Action learning has the potential to deliver significant measurable results • Delivered by the RBL Group faculty • Delivered on site in the organization

Table C.1   (continued)

Investment in Development: Options	Requirement	Considerations
HR academy	Multiple (2 or 3) 3-day workshops delivered over 6–9 months that provide in-depth skill building, lasting behavioral changes, and HR community building based on the new HR competencies. Incorporates: • HR and line management participation: why HR needs to continue to improve effectiveness • Interviews in advance: how HR needs to create value in the future • HRCS assessment feedback and development planning • Skill building across competency domains • Casework and simulation • Coaching and development support • Additional content in key competency areas based on the feedback or HR leadership • Action learning: a project that delivers measurable business value • Follow up and measurement	• Provides a broad overview of the HRCS competencies and in-depth skill building and development support • Versions available that are appropriate for multiple audience levels: independent contributors, HR generalists and functional specialists, individuals who have recently entered the HR field from another function, and HR leaders or managers • Action learning has the potential to deliver significant measurable results • Most impactful when it includes the active participation of both senior HR and line leaders • Includes team-based action learning projects • Delivered by the RBL Group faculty • Delivered on site in the organization

(continued on next page)

Table C.1   (continued)

Investment in Development: Options	Requirement	Considerations
HR executive program (HREP) and advanced HR executive program (AHREP)	• Two-week public program designed for HR executives. The workshop incorporates: • Knowledge and skills in turning business strategy into HR priorities. • Latest thinking in strategy, HR value creation, strategic HR, and HR analytics • Knowledge and skill in targeted HR areas of talent, workforce planning, organization design, leadership, change, rewards, performance management, and communication • Insights on building the right HR department and increasing HR competencies for HR professionals • Building the agenda for your organization's strategic realignment and HR practice redesign	• Sponsored by the Ross School of Business, University of Michigan • Designed for HR executives who are either generalists or specialists • Two-week public program with participants from around the world • Delivered by the RBL Group and University of Michigan faculty along with experts in targeted areas • Delivered at the Ross School of Business, University of Michigan

Table C.1   (continued)

Investment in Development: Options	Requirement	Considerations
HR learning partnership	The HRLP is a two-week consortium that brings together HR leadership teams. The workshop is organized around playbook of insights in: • Strategy • HR value proposition • Organization capabilities of collaboration, customer service, innovation, and change • HR analytics • Leadership • Talent • HR for HR • Executive rewards • Coaching	• Designed for teams of 5 HR executives from the same company from a range of different organizations and industries • 10-day program at the RBL Group facilities • Skill building organized around teams investing time in a significant project to adapt and apply learning • Each participant receives personal coaching from faculty, self assessment support in guiding development decisions to guide career choices • Delivered by the RBL Group faculty and selected other thought leaders • Delivered on site at an RBL venue

For more information please email us at rblmail@rbl.net or visit us at www.rbl.net.

NOTES

Chapter 1

1. http://www.guardian.co.uk/world/interactive/2011/mar/22/middle-east-protest-interactive-timeline.
2. See Treacy, M., and F. Wiersema (1997), *Discipline of Market Leaders*, New York: Basic Books; and Porter, M. (1998), *Competitive Advantage*, New York: Free Press.
3. The standard typology for risk management has been prepared by the Committee on Supervising Organizations (commonly known as COSO) of the Treadway Commission.
4. Chappuis, B., A. Kim, and P. Roche (2008), "Starting Up as CFO," *McKinsey Quarterly*.
5. Keeling, D., and U. Schrader (2012), "Operations for the Executive Suite," *McKinsey Report*.
6. Mark, D., and E. Monnoyer (2004), "Next Generation CIOs," *McKinsey Quarterly*.
7. Court, D. (2007), "The Evolving Role of the CMO," *McKinsey Quarterly*.
8. "HR Transformation in EMEA" (2010), Mercer Report.

Chapter 2

1. McClelland, D. (1973), "Testing for Competence Rather Than Intelligence," *American Psychologist* 28 (1), pp. 1–14.
2. Ibid.
3. McClelland, D. (1976), *A Guide to Job Competency Assessment*, Boston: McBer.
4. Spencer, L., and S. Spencer (1993), *Competence at Work*, New York: Wiley.
5. Kolb, D. (1984), *Experiential Learning*, Englewood Cliffs, NJ: Prentice-Hall.
6. Intagliata, J., D. Ulrich, and N. Smallwood (2000), "Leveraging Leadership Competencies to Produce Leadership Brand," *Human Resource Planning*, pp. 12–22; Christensen, R. (2005), *Roadmap to Strategic HR*, New York: Amacom.
7. Ibid.

8. Kochanski, J., and D. Ruse (1996), "Designing a Competency-Based Human Resources Organization," *Human Resource Management* 35 (1), pp. 19–33.

9. Ibid.

10. Ulrich, D. (1987), "Organizational Capability as a Competitive Advantage: Human Resource Professionals as Strategic Partners," *Human Resource Planning* 10 (4), 169–184; Nadler, L., and Z. Nadler (1989), *Developing Human Resources*, San Francisco: Jossey-Bass; Schuler, R. (1990), "Repositioning the Human Resource Function: Transformation or Demise?" *Academy of Management Executives* 4 (3), pp. 49–59; Morris, D. (1996), "Using Competency Development Tools as a Strategy for Change in the Human Resources Function," *Human Resource Management* 35 (1), pp. 35–51; Ulrich, D. (1997), *Human Resource Champions*, Boston: Harvard Business School Press; Losey, M. (1999), "Mastering the Competencies of HR Management," *Human Resource Management* 38 (2), pp. 99–102; Mehan, N. (1999), "HR Competencies in Malaysia," *The New Straits Times*, p. 2; Schoonover, S., and D. Nemerov (1999), "Competency-Based HR: Early Results of the 1999 HR Applications Survey" (2002), available at www.andersen.com.

11. Hogan, M. (2007), *Four Skills of Cultural Diversity Competence*, Pacific Grove, CA: Belmont Brooks/Cole.

12. Kierstead, J. (1998), "Competencies and KSAOs," Public Service Commission of Canada. Reprinted in 2002. Available at http://www.psc .cfp.gc.ca/research/personnelcomp_ksao_e.htm.

13. Taylor, F. (1911), *The Principles of Scientific Management*, New York: Harper.

14. Christie, M., and R. Young (1995), *Critical Incidents in Vocational Teaching*, Darwin, Australia: Northern Territory University Press.

15. McClelland, D. (1973), "Testing for Competence Rather Than Intelligence."

16. Townley, B. (1999), "Nietzsche, Competencies, and Übermensch: Reflections on Human and Inhuman Resource Management," *Organization* 6 (2), pp. 285–305; Kierstead, J. (1998). "Competencies and KSAOs" (2002). Available online.

17. Kamoche, K. (1999), "Strategic Human Resource Management within a Resource-Capability View of the Firm," in Schuler, R., and S. Jackson, *Strategic Human Resource Management*, London: Blackwell; Catano, V. (2001), "Empirically Supported Interventions and HR Practice," *HRM Research Quarterly* 5 (1).

18. Boyatzis, R. (1982), *The Competent Manager*, New York: Wiley.

19. Greatrex, J. (1989), "Oiling the Wheels of Competence," *Personnel Management*, pp. 36–39; Jackson, L. (October 1989), "Turning Airport Managers into High Fliers," *Personnel Management*, pp. 80–85; Glaze, T. (1989), "Cadbury's Dictionary of Competency," *Personnel Management*, pp. 44–48; Morgan, G. (1988), *Riding the Waves of Change*, San Francisco: Jossey-Bass.

20. Kenny, J. (1982). "Competency Analysis for Trainers: A Model for Professionalization," *Training and Development Journal* 36 (5), pp. 142–148.

21. Lippitt, G. and L. Nadler (1967), "Emerging Roles of the Training Director," *Training and Development Journal* 21 (8), pp. 2–10; McCullough, M., and P. McLagan (1983), "Keeping the Competency Study Alive," *Training and Development Journal* 37 (6), pp. 24–28.

22. McLagan, P., and D. Bedrick (1983), "Models for Excellence: The Results of the ASTD Training and Development Study," *Training and Development Journal* 37 (6), pp. 10–20.

23. McLagan, P., and D. Suhadolnik (1989), *Models for HRD Practice: The Research Report*, Alexandria: ASTD.

24. Ulrich, D. (1987), "Organizational Capability as a Competitive Advantage: Human Resource Professionals as Strategic Partners," *Human Resource Planning* 10 (4), pp. 169–184.

25. Brockbank, W., D. Ulrich, and R. Beatty (1999), "HR Professional Development: Creating the Future Creators at the University of Michigan Business School," *Human Resource Management* 38 (2), pp. 111–118.

26. Yeung, A., P. Woolcock, and J. Sullivan (1996), "Identifying and Developing HR Competencies for the Future," *Human Resource Planning* 19 (4), pp. 48–58.

27. Wright, P., M. Stewart, and M. Ozias (2011), *The 2011 CHRO Challenge: Building Organizational, Functional, and Personal Talent*, Ithaca, NY: Cornell Center for Advanced Human Resource Studies (CAHRS).

28. *Creating People Advantage 2009 and 2011*. Boston Consulting Group report.

29. See the Center for Effective Organizations (CEO) website. Also, Lawler, E., and J. Boudreau (2009), *Achieving Excellence in Human Resources Management: An Assessment of Human Resource Functions*, Stanford, CA: Stanford University Press.

30. Lawler, E. (2012), *Effective Human Resource Management: A Global Analysis*, Stanford, CA: Stanford University Press.

31. Boudreau, J., and I. Ziskin (2012), "The Future of HR and Effective Organizations," *Organization Dynamics*, in press.

32. Deloitte (2011), *Business Driven HR: Unlock the Value of HR Business Partners*. Available at http://www.deloitte.com/assets/DcomCanada/ Local%20Assets/Documents/Consulting/ca_en_con_Unlockingthe ValueofHRBusinessPartners_030812.pdf.

33. Hewitt (2009),. *Managing HR on a Global Scale*. Available at http:// www.aon.com/attachments/thought-leadership/Global_HR_Survey_ Highlights_2009.pdf.

34. Griffin, E, and L. Finney (2009), *Maximizing the Value of HR Business Partnering*, London: Roffey Park.

35. Lawson, T. (1990), *The Competency Initiative: Standards of Excellence for Human Resource Executives*, Alexandria: SHRM.

36. Wooten, K., and M. Elden (2001), "Cogenerating a Competency-Based HRM Degree: A Model and Some Lessons from Experience," *Journal of Management Education* 25 (2), pp. 231–257.

37. The CIPD professional map can be found on their website: http://www .cipd.co.uk/cipd-hr-profession/hr-profession-map/professional-areas/.

Chapter 3

1. Information on MOL comes from Varjasi Gábor, head of human resources for MOL.

2. M. Wong (2011), "Estimating the Impact of the Ethnic Housing Quotas in Singapore," University of Pennsylvania working paper.

3. Interview with Vikramaditya Bajpai, head HR, Group Emerging Markets.

4. Ulrich D., and W. Brockbank (2005), *HR Value Proposition*, Boston: Harvard Business Press.

5. Ulrich, D., N. Smallwood, and M. Ulrich (2012), "The Leadership Gap," *CFA Magazine*, 23 (1), pp. 3–6.

6. Lev, B. (2001), *Intangibles*, Washington, D.C.: Brookings Institution; Ulrich, D., and N. Smallwood (2003), *Why the Bottom Line Isn't*, New York: Wiley.

7. Ulrich et al. (2012).

8. We call this "architecture for intangibles" and offer a disciplined process for defining intangible value (see www.rbl.net).

9. See work on the future of work in Gratton, L. (2011), *Shift: The Future of Work Is Already Here,* London: Collins.; Malone, T. (2004), *The Future of Work,* Boston: Harvard Business Press; Meister, J., and K. Willyerd (2010), *The 2020 Workplace: How Innovative Companies Attract, Develop, and Keep Tomorrow's Employees Today,* New York: Harper; website: http://thefutureofwork.net/.

10. Bourne, V. (2011), "The Link Between Strategic Alignment and Staff Productivity: A Survey of Decision-Makers in Enterprise Organisations"; http://www.successfactors.co.uk/resources/resource-item/the-link -between-strategic-alignment-and-staff-productivity/.

11. See a discussion of stories by B. Hall (2012), *Once Upon a Time, Chief Learning Officer,* p. 16.

Chapter 4

1. Maister, D., C. Green, and R. Galford (2001), *The Trusted Advisor,* Boston: Touchstone.

2. "Blame It on the Brain: The Latest Neuroscience Research Suggests Spreading Resolutions Out over Time Is the Best Approach," *Wall Street Journal,* December 26, 2009. Available at http://online.wsj.com/article/ SB10001424052748703478704574612052322122442.htm.

3. Shepard, H, "Rules of Thumb for Change Agents." Undated and unpublished document. See http://www.uthscsa.edu/gme/documents/chiefres/ Change%20Leadership/Rules%20of%20Thumb%20for%20Change% 20Agents.pdf.

4. "Top Companies for Leaders Survey," *Fortune,* November 10, 2009; see also http://money.cnn.com/2009/11/19/news/companies/top_leadership _companies.fortune/.

5. Groysberg, B. (2009), *Chasing Stars,* Boston: Harvard Business Press.

6. Milgram, S, "The Small World Effect," Cited in http://en.wikipedia.org/ wiki/Small_world_experiment.

Chapter 5

1. Chandler, A. (1977), *The Visible Hand,* Boston: Harvard University Press.

2. The study of organization culture has been synthesized in Schein, E. (1992), *Organizational Culture and Leadership: A Dynamic View*, San Francisco: Jossey-Bass; Deal, T., and A. Kennedy (1982), *Corporate Cultures*, Harmondsworth: Penguin Books; Kotter, J. (1992), *Corporate Culture and Performance*, New York: Free Press; Cameron, K., and R. Quinn (2005), *Diagnosing and Changing Organizational Culture*, San Francisco: Jossey-Bass; Corporate Leadership Council (2003), *Defining Corporate Culture*, Washington D.C. Corporate Executive Board.

3. The process approach may be seen in the balanced scorecard work: Norton, D. (1992), "The Balanced Scorecard: Measures That Drive Performance," *Harvard Business Review*, Jan–Feb.

4. Kaplan, G., and D. Norton (2000), *The Strategy-Focused Organization: How Balanced Scorecard Companies Thrive in the New Business Environment*, Boston: Harvard Business School Press.

5. Kaplan, G., and D. Norton (2004), *Strategy Maps: Converting Intangible Assets into Tangible Outcomes*, Boston: Harvard Business School Press; Smith, H., and P. Fingar, *Business Process Management: The Third Wave*, available at http://www.fairdene.com/; Kohlbacher, M. (2010), "The Effects of Process Orientation: A Literature Review," *Business Process Management Journal* 16 (1): 135–152.

6. Prahalad, C. K., and G. Hamel (1996), *Competing for the Future*, Boston: Harvard Business School Press.

7. The resource-based view of organizations is discussed in: Barney, J. (1991), "Firm Resources and Sustained Competitive Advantage," *Journal of Management* 17 (1), pp. 99–120; Makadok, R. (2001), "Toward a Synthesis of the Resource-Based View and Dynamic-Capability Views of Rent Creation," *Strategic Management Journal* 22 (5), pp. 387–401; Sirmon, D., M. Hitt, and R. Ireland (2007), "Managing Firm Resources in Dynamic Environments to Create Value: Looking Inside the Black Box," *The Academy of Management Review* 32 (1), 273–292; Barney, J. (2001), "Is the Resource-Based Theory a Useful Perspective for Strategic Management Research? Yes," *Academy of Management Review* 26 (1), pp. 41–56; Wernerfelt, B. (1984), "The Resource-Based View of the Firm," *Strategic Management Journal* 5 (2), pp. 171–180.

8. The concept of organization as capabilities was briefly introduced by Igor Ansoff, then advanced in 1990 in work by Dave Ulrich and Dale Lake, followed by many who worked to identify the key capabilities of an

organization: Ulrich, D., and D. Lake (1990), *Organizational Capability: Competing from the Inside/Out*, New York: Wiley; Stalk, G., and T. Hout (1990), *Competing Against Time*, New York: Free Press; Collins, J. (1994), "Research Note: How Valuable Are Organizational Capabilities?" *Strategic Management Journal*, Winter 1994, pp. 143–152; Ruyle, K., R. Eichinger, and D. Ulrich (2007), *FYI for Strategic Effectiveness*, New York: Korn Ferry.

9. "Learning and Development, 2011: A Focus on the Future." Duke Client Study, Duke Corporate Education reports.

10. This focus on capabilities represented a key change in the role of L&D in organizations. Many L&D organizations (and their colleagues in human resources) have traditionally focused on developing individuals by building the competencies required by each individual's current role and expected for advancement in the company. A focus on capabilities implies something different. Over the past eight years or so, our client work has profited from our paying attention to capability building rather than focusing exclusively on the matter of competencies.

11. Stalk, G., P. Evans, and M. Shulman (1992), "Competing on Capabilities," *Harvard Business Review*, March–April.

12. Ruyle, K., R. Eichinger, and D. Ulrich (2007), *FYI for Strategic Effectiveness*, New York: Korn Ferry.

13. Ulrich, D., "Integrating Practice and Theory: Towards a More Unified View of HR." In Wright, P., L. Dyer, J. Boudreau, and G. Milkovich (1998), *Research in Personnel and Human Resources Management*, Greenwich, CT: JAI Press; Ulrich, D., and N. Smallwood (2004), "Capitalizing on Capabilities," *Harvard Business Review*, June–July; Ulrich, D., and N. Smallwood, "Organization Is Not Structure," in Hesselbein, F., and M. Goldsmith (2009), *Organization of the Future*, New York: Wiley.

Chapter 6

1. We are very grateful for Dale Lake's unique input on the ideas in this chapter.

2. We have had the privilege of personally learning from and working with some of the thought leaders in the change profession. We take the liberty of culling and synthesizing their insights into our "top 10" list. It is difficult to give credit to one person since we have tried to integrate their unique contributions. Our personal thought partners include: Chris Argyris, Ron

Ashkenas, Dick Beatty, Mike Beer, Warren Bennis, Bill Bridges, Warner Burke, Kim Cameron, Ram Charan, Clayton Christensen, Bill Dyer, Bob Eichinger, Malcolm Gladwell, Marshall Goldsmith, Lynda Gratton, Gary Hamel, Dave Hanna, Gareth Jones, Todd Jick, Bill Joyce, Steve Kerr, Jon Katzenbach, John Kotter, Dale Lake, Ed Lawler, Joe Miraglia, Bill Ouchi, Richard Pascale, C. K. Prahalad, Jeff Pfeffer, Bob Quinn, Bonner Ritchie, Ed Schein, Len Schlesinger, Herb Shepard, Norm Smallwood, Bob Sutton, Paul Thompson, Noel Tichy, and Terry Warner.

3. Vicki Swisher, *Becoming an Agile Leader,* Los Angeles: Korn Ferry, 2012.
4. O'Reilly, C., D. Caldwell, J. Chatman, M. Lapiz, and W. Self. (2010), "How Leadership Matters," *Leadership Quarterly* 21, pp. 104–113.
5. Foster, R. N., and S. Kaplan. (2001), *Creative Destruction: Why Companies That Are Built to Last Outperform the Market—and How to Successfully Transform Them,* New York: Prentice-Hall.
6. Joyce, W., N. Nohria, and B. Roberson (2003), *What Really Works: The 4+2 Formula for Sustained Business Success,* New York: HarperCollins.
7. Sutton, R., and J. Pfeffer (2001), *The Knowing-Doing Gap: How Smart Companies Turn Knowledge into Action,* Boston: Harvard Business Press.
8. Correspondence with Dale Lake, who is one of our change thought leaders.
9. Many were involved with the GE Change Acceleration Process. Dave Ulrich was one of the team members in creating this process.
10. Personal correspondence with Bob Eichinger and part of a presentation he has prepared called "10 Essential Principles of Change Management for Executive Dummies" copyrighted by Bob Eichinger.
11. Ulrich, D., and N. Smallwood, *Leadership Sustainability,* Unpublished manuscript.
12. Shepard, ibid.
13. Cantrell, S. and D. Smith (2010), *Workforce of One: Revolutionizing Talent Management Through Customization,* Boston: Harvard Business Press, 2010.

Chapter 7

1. AXA Equitable internal evaluation of the Work-Out initiative, 2011; personal correspondence, EVP Rino Piazolla.
2. IBM's Corporate Service Corps. Internal IBM document, 2011.
3. http://www.ibm.com/ibm/responsibility/corporateservicecorps/press/2009_05.html.

4. "The NFL Bounty System: Mama Said Knock You Out," *Workforce Magazine*, March 5, 2012.

5. http://www.nola.com/saints/index.ssf/2012/03/new_orleans_saints_were_out_of.html.

6. Becker, B., M. Huselid, and R. Beatty (2009), *The Differentiated Workforce*, Boston: Harvard Business School Press.

7. Younger, J., N. Smallwood, and D. Ulrich (2008), "Developing a Brand as a Talent Developer," *HR Planning Journal* 30 (2), pp. 21–29.

8. http://www.towerswatson.com/services/Talent-Management-and -Organization-Alignment?gclid=CM-gscup_a4CFYuK4Aod4hwD4Q.

9. Aberdeen Group (2010), *Strategic Workforce Planning: Winning Scenarios for Uncertain Times*, Boston: Aberdeen Group.

10. Personal correspondence with Dave Hanna.

11. Ulrich, D., and W. Ulrich (2010), *The Why of Work*, New York: McGraw-Hill.

12. Katzenbach, J., and D. Smith (2003), *Wisdom of Teams*, New York: HarperCollins.

13. See Hargie, O., and D. Tourish (2000), *Handbook of Communication Audits for Organizations*, London: Routledge.

14. Ulrich, D., and N. Smallwood (2006), *Leadership Brand*, Boston: Harvard Business Press.

15. Ulrich, D., N. Smallwood, and K. Sweetman (2007), *The Leadership Code*, Boston: Harvard Business Press.

16. Bryant, A. "Google's Quest to Build a Better Boss, *New York Times*, March 12, 2011.

Chapter 8

1. Prahalad, C., and M. Krishnan (2008), *New Age of Innovation*, New York: McGraw-Hill.

2. Krishnan, M., and C. Prahalad (Undated), "Customer Service at American Express: A Relationship, Not a Transaction." Case study. Ross School of Business, University of Michigan.

3. Plummer, D., and P. Middleton (2012), "Predicts 2012: Four Forces Combine to Transform the IT Landscape." In Gartner Research, http://www.gartner.com/technology/research/predicts.

4. Grochowski, J., and K. Lawrence (2012), "Social Media and HR Implications." RBL Miniforum white paper. Available at RBL.net.

5. Boudreau, J., "IBM's Global Talent Management Strategy: The Vision of the Globally Integrated Enterprise" (2010), SHRM Case Study Part-B, SHRM.

6. Carr, D., "IBM: From Networked Business to Social Media," *InformationWeek*, June 6, 2011.

7. Prahalad, C., and M. Krishnan (2008), *New Age of Innovation*, New York: McGraw-Hill.

8. Ulrich, D., and W. Brockbank (1990), "Avoiding SPOTS: Implementing Strategy through Organizational Unity. In Glass, H. (ed.), *Handbook of Business Strategy*, New York: Gorham and Lambert.

9. Prahalad, C. K., and R. Bettis. (1986), "The Dominant Logic: A New Linkage Between Diversity and Performance," *Strategic Management Journal*, 7, 485–501.

10. Smith, S. (2004), "Brand Experience." In Clifton, R., and J. Simmons (ed), *Brands and Branding*, Princeton: Bloomberg Press.

Chapter 9

1. "Panel Slams Olympus in Accounting Scandal," *Wall Street Journal*, December 6, 2011.

2. "Zygna's Tough Culture Risks a Talent Drain," *New York Times*, November 27, 2011.

3. Donaldson, C., HR Crisis Management: An Enron Case Study," *HC Online*, May 2, 2004; available at www.hcamag.com/news/profiles/hr-crisis-management-an-enron-case-study/110573/.

4. Peters, T., "The Brand Called You," *Fast Company*, August 31, 1997. See also http://www.fastcompany.com/magazine/10/brandyou.html.

5. Ulrich, D., and W. Ulrich (2011), *The Why of Work*, New York: McGraw-Hill.

6. Hackman, J., and G. Oldham (1976), "Motivation Through the Design of Work: Test of a Theory," *Organizational Behavior and Human Performance*, 16, 250–279.

7. Sarason, S. (1982), *Culture of the School and the Problem of Change*, New York: Allyn & Bacon.

Chapter 10

1. In our research we examined five of these six stakeholders. Based on our recent experience, we have added "partners" as a sixth stakeholder, although this is not included in this survey.

2. We determined these 12 leading practices from thoughtful colleagues and from personal experience in companies. We rely on work by:
- John Boudreau

Boudreau, J. (2010). *Retooling HR: Using Proven Business Tools to Make Better Decisions about Talent.* Boston: Harvard Business Review Press.

Boudreau, J., and W. Cascio (2008). *Investing in People: Financial Impact of Human Resource Initiatives.* New Jersey: FT Press, 2008.

Boudreau, J., and P. Ranstad (2007). *Beyond HR: The New Science of Human Capital.* Boston: Harvard Business School Press.

- Chris Brewster

Brewster, C., et al (2008). "Similarity, Isomorphism or Duality? Recent Survey Evidence on the Human Resource Management Policies of Multinational Corporations." *British Journal of Management,* 19 (4), 320–342.

Makela, K., and C. Brewster. (2009). "Interunit Interaction Contexts, Interpersonal Social Capital and the Differing Levels of Knowledge Sharing." *Human Resource Management,* 48 (4), 591–613.

Mayrhofer, W., et al. (2011). "Hearing a Different Drummer? Convergence of Human Resource Management in Europe: A Longitudinal Analysis." *Human Resource Management Review,* 21 (1), 50–67. Haslberger, A. and C. Brewster, (2009). "Capital Gains: Expatriate Adjustment and the Psychological Contract in International Careers." *Human Resource Management,* 48 (3), 379–397.

- Peter Capelli

Capelli, Peter, ed. (2008). *Employment Relationships: New Models of White Collar Work.* Cambridge: Cambridge University Press.

Capelli, Peter (2008). *Talent on Demand: Managing Talent in an Age of Uncertainty.* Boston: Harvard Business School Press.

- Tamara J. Erickson

Erickson, T. (2008). *Retire Retirement: Career Strategies for the Boomer Generation.* Boston: Harvard Business School Press.

Erickson, T. (2009). *What's Next, Gen-X?: Keeping Up, Moving Ahead, and Getting the Career You Want.* Boston: Harvard Business Review Press.

Dychtwald, K., T. Erickson, and R. Morison (2006). *Workforce Crisis: How to Beat the Coming Shortage of Skills and Talent.* Boston: Harvard Business Review Press.

- Jac Fitz-enz

 Fitz-enz, J. (2010). *The New HR Analytics: Predicting the Economic Value of Your Company's Human Capital Investments*. New York: AMACOM.

 Fitz-enz, J. (2009). *The ROI of Human Capital: Measuring the Economic Value of Employee Performance*. New York: AMACOM.

- Lynda Gratton

 Gratton, L. (2009). *Glow: How You Can Radiate Energy, Innovation, and Success*. San Francisco: Berrett-Koehler Publishers.

 Gratton, L. (2007). *Hot Spots: Why Some Teams, Workplaces, and Organizations Buzz with Energy—and Others Don't*. San Francisco: Berrett-Koehler Publishers.

 Gratton, L. (2000). *Living Strategy: Putting People at the Heart of Corporate Purpose*. London, U.K.: Financial Times/Prentice Hall, 2000.

- Charles Handy

 Handy, Charles (1995). *The Age of Paradox*. Boston: Harvard Business Review Press.

 Handy, Charles (1991). *The Age of Unreason*. Boston: Harvard Business Review Press.

- Mark Huselid

 Huselid, M., B. Becker, and R. Beatty (2009). *The Differentiated Workforce: Transforming Talent into Strategic Impact*. Boston: Harvard Business Press.

 Ulrich, D., M. Huselid, and B. Becker (2001). *The HR Scorecard: Linking People, Strategy, and Performance*. Boston: Harvard Business Review Press.

- Steve Kerr

 Kerr, S., and Rifkin, G. (2008). *Reward Systems: Does Yours Measure Up?* Boston: Harvard Business School Press.

- Edward Lawler

 Lawler, E. (2003) *Treat People Right!: How Organizations and Employees Can Create a Win/Win Relationship to Achieve High Performance at All Levels*. New Jersey: Jossey-Bass.

 Lawler, E., and J. Boudreau (2009). *Achieving Excellence in Human Resources Management: An Assessment of Human Resource Functions*. Stanford, Calif.: Stanford Business Books.

Lawler, E., and S. Mohrman (2003). *Creating a Strategic Human Resources Organization: An Assessment of Trends and New Directions.* Stanford, Calif.: Stanford Business Books.

- Jeffrey Pfeffer

Pfeffer, J. (1998). *The Human Equation: Building Profits by Putting People First.* Boston: Harvard Business Review Press, 1998.

Pfeffer, J., and Sutton, R. (2000). *The Knowing-Doing Gap: How Smart Companies Turn Knowledge into Action.* Boston: Harvard Business School Press.

- Libby Sartain

Sartain, L., and M. Schumann (2006). *Brand from the Inside: Eight Essentials to Emotionally Connect Your Employees to Your Business.* New Jersey: Jossey-Bass.

Schumann, M., and Sartain, L. (2009). *Brand for Talent: Eight Essentials to Make Your Talent as Famous as Your Brand.* New Jersey: Jossey-Bass.

- Patrick Wright

(ed.) "Strategic Human Resource Management in the 21st Century." Special issue of *Research in Personnel and Human Resources Management*

(ed.) "Research in Strategic HRM for the 21st Century." Special issue of *Human Resource Management Review.*

Wright, P., M. Stewart, and O. Moore. (2011). *The 2011 CHRO Challenge: Building Organizational, Functional, and Personal Talent.* Ithaca, NY: Cornell University Press.

3. Groysberg, B. (2011). *Chasing Stars: The Myth of Talent and the Portability of Performance.* Boston: Havard Business Press.

Chapter 11

1. Dye, R., and E. Stephenson (2010), "Five Forces Reshaping the Global Economy," *McKinsey Quarterly*, May 2010.
2. See www//haygroup.com.
3. "13th Annual Global CEO Survey" (2010). Price Waterhouse Coopers.
4. Bates, S. (2012), "Business Partners: HR and Finance Are Learning to Team Up Effectively to Develop Strategy and Resolve Operational Problems," *HR Magazine*, March 22, 2012.
5. http://www.ileraonline.org/15thworldcongress/files/papers/Track_1/Poster/CS1W_13_BHASKAR.pdf.

6. Rucci, Anthony J., Kirn, Steven P., and Quinn, Richard T., "The Customer-Service-Profit Chain at Sears," *Harvard Business School Working Knowledge for Business Leaders*, October 12, 1999. Available at http://hbswk.hbs.edu/archive/801.html.

7. Carrig, K., "Leveraging Human Capital Analytics." Conference board presentation, October 2010.

8. Capelli, P., and Y. Yang (2010). "Who Gets the Top HR Job?" Price Waterhouse Coopers. See also: http://www.pwc.com/en_US/us/people -management/assets/hr-leader-attributes.pdf.

INDEX

Note: Boldface numbers indicate tables and illustrations